SPSS Explained

R Routledge

Taylor & Francis Group

LONDON AND NEW YORK

SPSS

Explained

Perry R. Hinton, Charlotte Brownlow, Isabella McMurray & Bob Cozens

 **Routledge**
Taylor & Francis Group

LONDON AND NEW YORK

First published 2004 by Routledge
27 Church Road, Hove, East Sussex, BN3 2FA

Simultaneously published in the USA and Canada
by Routledge Inc,
270 Madison Avenue, New York, NY 10016

Routledge is an imprint of the Taylor & Francis Group

Copyright © 2004 Perry R. Hinton, Charlotte Brownlow, Isabella McMurray & Bob Cozens

Typeset in 11/13.5pt Times by Graphicraft Limited, Hong Kong
Printed and bound in Great Britain by TJ International Ltd, Padstow, Cornwall
Cover design by Anú Design

This book is not sponsored or approved by SPSS, and errors are in no way the
responsibility of SPSS. SPSS is a registered trademark and the other product
names are trademarks of SPSS Inc. SPSS Screen Images © SPSS Inc. For further
information, contact: SPSS UK Ltd, First Floor St Andrew's House, West Street,
Woking, Surrey GU21 6EB, UK

Windows is a registered trademark of Microsoft Corporation. For further information,
contact: Microsoft Corporation, One Microsoft Way, Redmond, WA 98052-6399, USA

This publication has been produced with paper manufactured to strict environmental
standards and with pulp derived from sustainable forests.

British Library Cataloguing in Publication Data
A catalogue record for this book is available from the British Library

Library of Congress Cataloging in Publication Data
SPSS explained / by Perry R. Hinton . . . [*et al.*].
        p.   cm.
   Includes bibliographical references.
     ISBN 0-415-27409-5 (hbk) − ISBN 0-415-27410-9 (pbk.)
   1. SPSS (Computer file)   2. Psychology−Statistical methods−Computer
programs.   I. Hinton, Perry R. (Perry Roy), 1954−
BF39.S68 2004
300′.285′536−dc22
                                                    2003026286

ISBN 0-415-27409-5 (hbk)
ISBN 0-415-27410-9 (pbk)

To our families

Contents

CONTENTS

4 Illustrative statistics   39

5 Working with your dataset   73

6 Introduction to statistical tests   93

CONTENTS

Figures

Preface

SPSS is a wonderful statistical analysis package. The advances in computer technology now mean that anyone can have SPSS on their desktop computer. We can perform complex statistical analysis on research data in a matter of minutes, or even seconds, that would have been impossible to undertake just a matter of years ago without expert help and an enormous amount of time.

SPSS allows us to undertake a wide range of statistical analyses relatively easily. While this is extremely useful it does mean that we do need to know what analysis is appropriate to the data we have. So a certain amount of basic statistical knowledge is required before using SPSS. This book will assume that the readers are students from the social sciences and other interested new users of SPSS with a little background knowledge of data analysis.

In our experience as teachers and advisors to students, many students experience some confusion when they first encounter the computer output from statistical programs. They often ask questions such as: Why so many tables? What do they mean? Which is my result? Is it significant? This is because the statistical programs print out a range of useful information with each analysis. Not all of this information is readily understandable to a new user. Furthermore, some students are taught statistical analysis in one class and SPSS in another so they do not always see the link between the computer output and the statistical tests, and they do not know what each aspect of their output means. We have seen students on a daily basis who simply want a clear explanation of the SPSS output they have produced on the computer at a level they can understand. Therefore, the aim of this book is not to explain every SPSS option but to focus on the key undergraduate statistical tests, describe how to undertake them and explain the output produced by SPSS for these tests.

There are two types of explanations: ones for the novice and ones for the expert. Often we hear a technical explanation and cannot understand it. We may even be tempted to ask: Can you say that again in English? This is one of the difficulties of learning statistics and understanding output from statistical packages. The terminology may not be readily understandable. In psychology, for example, we have a technical definition for a term like 'attitude' but most people have an everyday understanding of the word 'attitude' that is not so different from its technical meaning. However, with statistical terms such as 'general linear model', 'homogeneity of variance' or 'univariate analysis' the technical terms are not readily understandable without explanation. We have found in our experience that students seek advice from us when the statistical explanations they are given (from textbooks and lecturers) don't really make sense as explanations for them (as they are still students without the technical knowledge at that time). What we have tried to do, in this book, is to give the explanations for the different parts of the SPSS output in terms that can be understood by students without a sophisticated understanding of statistics.

For the more advanced reader the complex aspects of the output are also explained. The reader is able to choose the level of explanation they feel comfortable with.

Acknowledgements

We would like to thank our colleagues Pat Roberts and Ian Robertson for their helpful comments on the book, Dave Stott and Steve Brindle, two former colleagues and fellow SPSSers, for their sound advice. Finally, we would like to thank the many students who have sought our SPSS advice over many years, without whom this book would not have been written.

Chapter 1

Introduction

1

T HIS IS VERY MUCH a 'how to' book, in that we provide the reader with the information on how to perform a number of statistical tests with SPSS. We provide screen shots of SPSS at each stage of the procedure from inputting data to performing the test. The reader can use the book alongside the computer and follow the analysis on the screen and by referring to the information in the book. The screen shots used are from version 11 of SPSS, although the book is compatible for use with version 12 for the procedures detailed. Where version 12 is significantly different from the screen shots displayed, a note of this has been made and, if applicable, an additional section added to the chapter specifically for use with version 12. Please note that some drop-down menus and options within statistical procedures may include additional functions. As the primary features of the procedures are the same for both versions of SPSS these are the ones described within this book.

If we were to write a book that explained every single test that can be performed using SPSS with all the possible variations then it would be an extremely large book. SPSS is a large and flexible statistics program and requires more than is possible in this book to explain everything it can do. However, that is not our purpose. We, as teachers and academic advisors of undergraduates, have found that there is a core set of statistical tests common to many undergraduate programmes, particularly in the social sciences, and we shall focus on these. Furthermore, there are some extremely complex tests that can be performed on SPSS, and to be performed properly they do require a good knowledge of statistics, often beyond that of an undergraduate student. So our explanations will be pitched at the level of the undergraduate student learning to use SPSS at the same time as learning about statistical analysis.

Some basic understanding of statistics must be assumed in a book like this, as there is not the scope to explain concepts such as the mean and standard deviation as well as explaining the SPSS procedures. However, we attempt to make as few assumptions as possible so that someone new to statistical analysis can still follow the book. But readers are advised to consult a basic statistics textbook to pick up an understanding of statistical tests. A book which complements this text is *Statistics Explained* by Perry Hinton. (See Hinton, P.R. (2004) *Statistics Explained*, 2nd Edition, Hove: Routledge.)

SPSS prints out a lot of tables, not all of which are easy for a new user to understand, and it also uses terminology which is not always familiar. Where these situations arise we try to make clear the importance of each table, and to explain the different terminology used.

The book outline

The chapters are set out so that the reader can work through the book from the beginning, where we discuss basic SPSS skills, to more advanced statistical procedures. However, each chapter can be dipped into in order to undertake a specific test.

Initially Chapter 2 introduces the reader to thinking about the data they have collected and how they will actually enter it into SPSS. The book naturally progresses on to basic procedures in SPSS (Chapters 3 and 4) such as producing descriptive statistics and creating graphs, before moving on to explain how to make changes to the data you have entered (Chapter 5). Chapter 6 gives a brief introduction to statistical tests describing the logic of significance testing and some useful terminology, which will be encountered when generating inferential statistics in SPSS. We then examine two sample tests in SPSS such as the independent and related *t* tests and two commonly used nonparametric tests: the Mann–Whitney and Wilcoxon (Chapters 7 and 8). Chapter 9 discusses some background information regarding the general linear model, the model underlying most of the tests examined in the book. We then go on to describe the procedure and explain the output for a variety of ANOVAs (Chapters 10 and 11), multivariate analysis of variance (Chapter 12), and also nonparametric ANOVA (Chapter 13). Chapters 14 to 16 examine tests of association, including crosstabulations and chi-square, linear correlation and regression, and multiple correlation and regression. The final two chapters introduce the reader to factor analysis (Chapter 17) and reliability analysis (Chapter 18).

The chapter outline

Each chapter begins with a brief introduction to the test and the assumptions required to perform it. Following this we show how to perform the test using SPSS, selecting commonly used options, with each stage of the procedure clearly described. Finally, the output from SPSS is given and each table is explained.

Output tables

In order to help the reader to understand the output, each output table has either a grey box containing useful information, or in larger tables has the numerical values in a grey box with a clearer explanation detailed below.

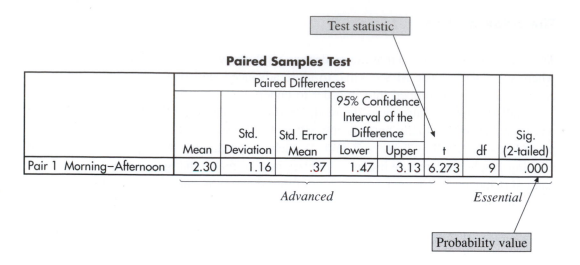

Paired Samples Test

| | Paired Differences | | | | | | | |
| | | | | 95% Confidence Interval of the Difference | | | | |
	Mean	Std. Deviation	Std. Error Mean	Lower	Upper	t	df	Sig. (2-tailed)
Pair 1 Morning–Afternoon	2.30	1.16	.37	1.47	3.13	6.273	9	.000

Advanced   *Essential*

Explanation sections

We have also divided our explanations below the output tables into two aspects: essential and advanced.

SPSS essential

- The essential output is what we believe is required in order to understand that the test has been carried out correctly and also to present the results of the test in a report.
- Someone new to SPSS might find it more manageable to work their way through the output understanding the essential information first.

SPSS advanced

- Often SPSS appears to produce more tables and complex information that initially you may be told just to ignore. As users get more confident with working with SPSS they might wish to examine what this part of the output means.
- We have labelled these aspects of the output as *Advanced* in that they are very useful to understand but do require a little more advanced understanding of statistics to fully appreciate.

Advice boxes

Within each chapter you will find a number of boxes with ticks in them.

> ✓ It is a good idea to read the advice boxes as they offer you reminders of information previously discussed or general useful advice.

Frequently asked questions

Finally, at the end of each chapter we have included a frequently asked questions section entitled *FAQ*.

FAQ

What does the FAQ section of the chapter contain, and why is it there?

This section includes many of the questions we have been asked in our teaching and 'advisory drop-in' sessions for our own students. Indeed, the experience of listening to students' concerns about their statistical analysis has been a major motivation for writing the book. We have found that students' questions are not always addressed in textbooks. Sometimes students feel embarrassed to ask their lecturers to explain these problems, thinking themselves to be at fault ('I knew statistics would be hard!'). For example, if you have made a mistake while entering data, SPSS informs you that you have made an error but sometimes you don't know what you have done wrong, and don't know how to make it right. The FAQ section of each chapter aims to address some of the questions that students often ask us.

Chapter 2

Data entry

Things to think about before entering data

Before you enter any data into SPSS, you need to think about what type of data you have and what you want to do with it. For example, you may have the details of a person's gender (male or female) and their preference for a certain product, or you may have collected a set of reaction times. Are you trying to find differences within your data or any relationships? Or do you just want to summarise and describe it?

What is the level of data? Is it *nominal* (where the data is labelled by the category it belongs to, such as car colour), *ordinal* (where the data defines an order, such as rating a group of vegetables on how much you like them), *interval* or *ratio* (where the data is measured on a scale of equal intervals, like a clock or a tape measure)? This needs to be considered before entering any data. If you have nominal data then you may need to use this as a 'grouping variable' when entering the data in SPSS. We can explain the use of a grouping variable by the following example. If you were going to calculate statistics by hand you would probably write the scores of males and females on a mathematics test in the following fashion:

Person number	Male	Person number	Female
1	84	6	49
2	79	7	86
3	64	8	85
4	73	9	74
5	75	10	81

Notice here that the variable 'gender' is measured on a nominal scale and the variable maths score is measured on an interval scale. Gender is our grouping variable because it defines our two groups. Later on we may wish to compare the maths scores between these two groups. We need to give the values of the grouping variable a label, so we will allocate the males an arbitrary number 1 and the females the number 2. When we do enter our data into SPSS it will look similar to the data shown below, which, as you can see, is a lot different from how you intuitively think about entering the data.

Person	Gender	Maths score
1	1	84
2	1	79
3	1	64
4	1	73
5	1	75
6	2	49
7	2	86
8	2	85
9	2	74
10	2	81

> ✓ Details on how to assign values to categories in SPSS are discussed later in this chapter.

A grouping variable is related to the research design. With an independent measures design (where the data in different samples come from different participants), you will have at least one grouping variable. The example above is an independent measures or unrelated design. However, if you have a repeated measures or related design (where the scores in each sample come from the same or matched participants) your data will be set up without any grouping variables and looks very much how you would set it out by hand. This is because the key rule for putting data into SPSS is that each row is a different case, so each row has all the data from a single participant. For example, two similar maths tests are undertaken, one in week one and the other in week two by each participant. The data would be entered as below.

Person	Maths score (week 1)	Maths score (week 2)
1	84	89
2	79	83
3	64	69
4	73	74
5	75	80
6	49	59
7	86	87
8	85	87
9	74	78
10	81	84

Notice that we do not use 'week' as a grouping variable here. This is because we have a repeated measures design and so want both scores from person 1 in row 1, person 2 in row 2 and so on. This is an important feature of inputting data into SPSS and we need to understand the link between grouping variables and research designs. Independent measures variables (such as gender in the first example) are used as grouping variables but repeated measures variables (such as week in the second example) are not.

Using SPSS for the first time

If you are using SPSS for the first time, you will be presented with the **What would you like to do?** window before being able to use the data editor screen. This window gives you the opportunity to run a self-help tutorial, type in data, run an existing query, create a new query using Database Wizard, open an existing data source or open an alternative type of file (an example of this could be some data that had been prepared in Microsoft Excel).

- Select **Type in Data**.
- Click on the **OK** button.

✓ You can tell SPSS not to show this dialogue box in the future by clicking in the box at the bottom of the window. Users of SPSS in public areas such as universities or users who share a computer may not see this window as a previous user may have already clicked in the box. If this is the case then the first active window you are presented with will be the SPSS **Data Editor**.

Data Editor

The SPSS **Data Editor** is where the data is entered in order to carry out the statistical analysis. On first view, the Data Editor looks very much like other spreadsheets. However, there are a number of differences. In SPSS the row numbers down the side of the data entry sheet refer to participants or cases. The columns are not lettered, as they would be in a spreadsheet but carry the label 'var'. This is the case until the variables have been defined.

If you look at the bottom left-hand corner of the screen you will notice two tabs, **Data View** and **Variable View**. The **Data View** tab is the current active sheet and this is where raw data is entered. However, it is advisable to define your variables first. To make the **Variable View** sheet active click on the **Variable View** tab as shown below.

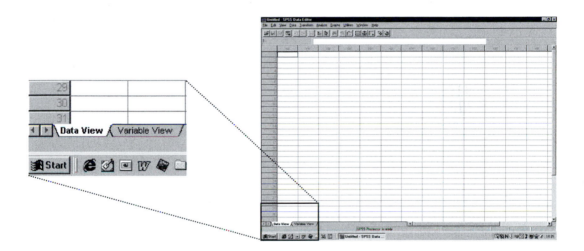

In the **Variable View** sheet the column headings have now changed from 'var' to the ones shown in the screen overleaf. The sheet is no longer a data entry sheet but the location where your variables are defined. You can switch between the **Data View** and **Variable View** sheets by clicking on the appropriate tab. An alternative way of accessing the **Variable View** sheet is to double click on 'var' in one of the columns within the **Data View** sheet. The latter way is useful if your variables are already defined and you wish to edit the one you have double clicked on as this method takes you directly to chosen variable.

✓ Many new users of SPSS get confused when switching between the **Data View** and **Variable View** sheets. This is because when in **Data View** the variables are in columns so the data should be entered and read moving down the sheet. When in **Variable View** the variables are in rows. Therefore, the variable information should be entered and read moving across the sheet.

Data View

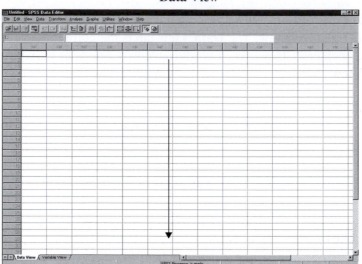

Variable View

Now we are going to look at a scenario and consider how each variable should be set up.

Scenario

A teacher wanted to see whether there was a difference in the amount of time boys and girls spent on their homework. He asked ten boys and ten girls aged 9 years to make a note of the number of minutes they spent studying over a 2-week period.

Setting up variables

31		
32		
◄ ► \ Data View \ **Variable View** /		

- Click on the **Variable View** tab in the data editor window.
- Click in the **Name** column on row **1**.
- Enter the name 'gender' and press the return key on your keyboard.

Untitled - SPSS Data Editor

File Edit View Data Transform Analyze Graphs Utilities Window Help

	Name	Type	Width	Decimals	Label	Values	Missing	Columns	Align	Measure
1	gender	Numeric	8	2		None	None	8	Right	Scale
2										

✔ You will now notice that SPSS has automatically filled in information in the cells for the remaining columns. This information will not necessarily be correct so you need to check each cell and add information or correct it if needed, as discussed below.

SPSS has a few rules about the name of your variable. For example, it cannot exceed eight characters. Therefore, sometimes it might be more appropriate to call your variable an acronym of the name you really wanted. Some other rules for variable names are that you cannot use blank spaces or special characters; the name must begin with a letter and cannot end with a full stop. Each variable name must be unique to that variable and you should try to avoid ending the name with an underscore.

Now we will briefly describe the remaining columns within the **Variable View**.

Within the **Type** column you need to identify what type of variable you have. If you click inside the **Type** cell in row 1 for gender, you will see that the default is **Numeric**. To change the variable type:

- Click on the grey box that will appear next to the word **Numeric**. You will notice a variety of options.
- If you have a variable that is a currency or a date then it is advisable to use one of these options. **String** should only be used if you want to identify a participant or case by name. When you have selected this option, you can change the number of characters to more than the default of eight if you wish.

✓   The **String** option will limit the type of numerical data analysis that can be carried out with that variable, so use it with caution. If you are in doubt, leaving the default option of **Numeric** will generally suffice for most types of data analysis. In the case of our scenario, we would leave the variable type as **Numeric**.

The **Width** column allows us to specify the total number of characters required for the column. The default setting is for eight characters to be displayed and input into each cell. There is no need to change this option unless you will be using more than eight characters.

The **Decimals** option allows you to specify the number of decimal places for your variable. For example, if you are using whole numbers then you may wish to change the decimals to 0. SPSS always defaults to two decimal places.

Many users of SPSS underestimate the importance of the **Label** cell. You may already have expressed frustration at only being able to use eight characters for the variable name. This is where you can give your variable a longer label with spaces, as this label will appear on output tables instead of the shortened variable name.

Also, if you have used acronyms or short titles when naming your variables, SPSS will show the full label assigned to that variable when the mouse pointer is held over the variable name in **Data View**.

As stated earlier, if we have a grouping variable we need to assign each category of that variable to a number because SPSS will only recognise numerical data.

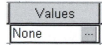

- Click within the **Values** column along the row of gender and a grey box will become apparent.
- Click on the grey box, the **Value Labels** window appears.

In our scenario we have the grouping variable 'gender'. We have decided to call 'males' number 1 and 'females' number 2.

- Enter '1' into the **Value** box and then either press the tab key or click the mouse to arrive at the **Value Label** box. Type in 'male'.
- Click on the **Add** button and you will see **1.00 = "male"** appear in the box below. Then follow the same procedure, entering '2' in the **Value** box, for females.

Value Labels	? X
Value Labels	OK
Value: 2	Cancel
Value Label: female	Help
Add 1.00 = "male"	
Change	
Remove	

✓ When you come to enter your raw data you will need to enter the numeric values assigned to your two groups. It is therefore important to remember which way round you assigned these labels.

As default, SPSS considers that you have no missing values. However, within your data there may be various reasons why you have missing values. The **Missing** column enables you, under the **Discrete Missing Values** radio button, to assign up to three values to be counted as missing data. SPSS will then ignore that participant or case during the analysis. A good example of this might be that a participant did not want to answer a question rather than could not as this may be useful information for your research. It is also possible to identify a range of missing numbers using the **Range plus one optional discrete missing value** radio button.

✓ When assigning missing values always ensure that you choose a value outside your data range.

- If the 'gender' variable above did have missing values, the range is only between 1 and 2 so assigning the value of 99 as shown here would be fine.
- Once missing values have been assigned, click on **OK** to continue.

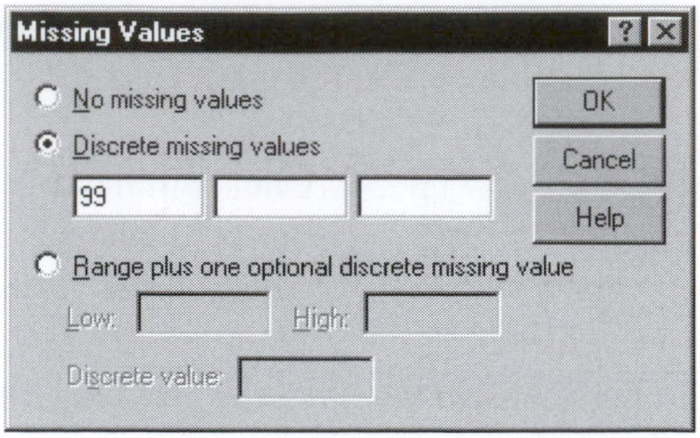

The **Columns** feature need only be used if you have more than eight characters in a column. For example, if you were using very large numbers or string variables with large names, the width of the column which is shown in the **Data View** sheet can be adjusted. Alternatively, you may wish to reduce the width of column if using small numbers to make a larger viewable area on your computer screen. If you decide to do this, you should make sure your variable name is still identifiable in the **Data View** sheet.

✓ If some of the characters are no longer viewable in the **Data View**, holding the mouse pointer over the variable name will show the full variable label, providing you have entered one as explained previously.

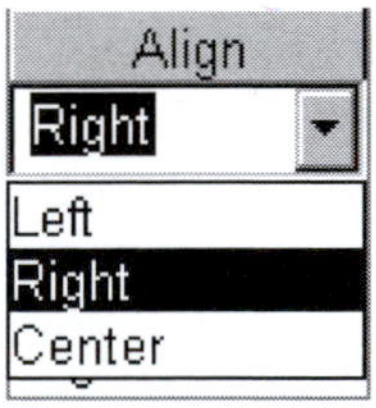

Align can be used if you wish to realign the way that the data is viewed in the SPSS **Data View** sheet. The options to choose from are left, right and centre. Using this option has no bearing on your statistical analysis but is cosmetic in terms of viewing your raw data.

The **Measure** column is where you identify which level of data for each variable is. In our example 'gender' is nominal data so **Nominal** should be selected from the drop-down list.

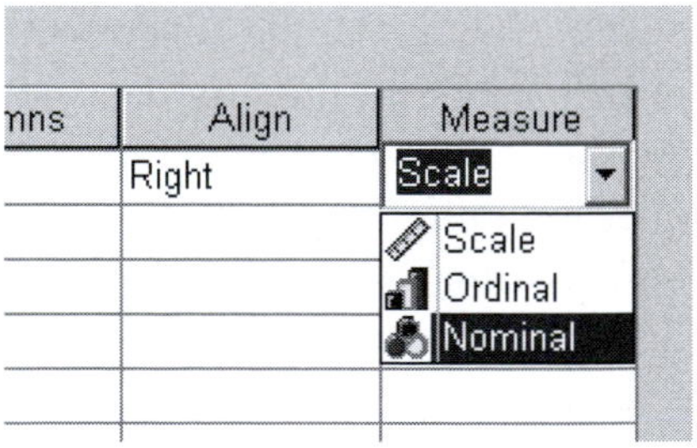

✓ SPSS groups interval and ratio data as **Scale**. This is because the same statistical tests are applied to both interval and ratio levels of data.

The **Variable View** sheet below is an example of what you should see if you have set up the variables for the homework scenario described above.

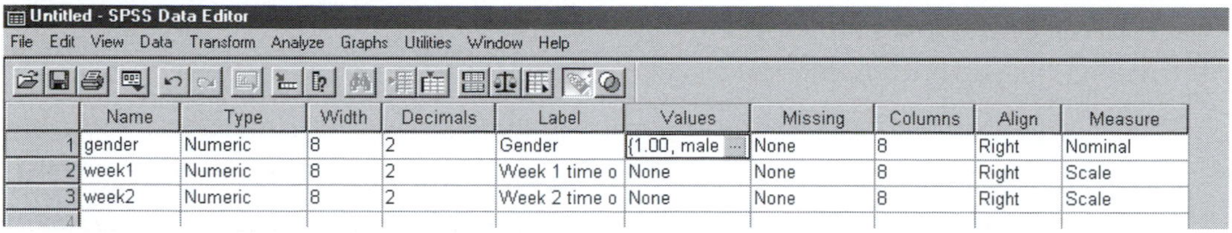

• Once the variables have been set up and labelled, click on the **Data View** tab to enter your raw data.

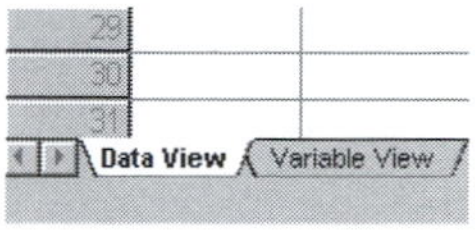

Entering data

In our scenario we obtained the homework times for ten males and ten females. We have decided arbitrarily to call each male number 1 and each female number 2. Therefore, we must enter in the first column a number 1 in the first 10 rows and a number 2 in the rows 11 to 20 as shown below.

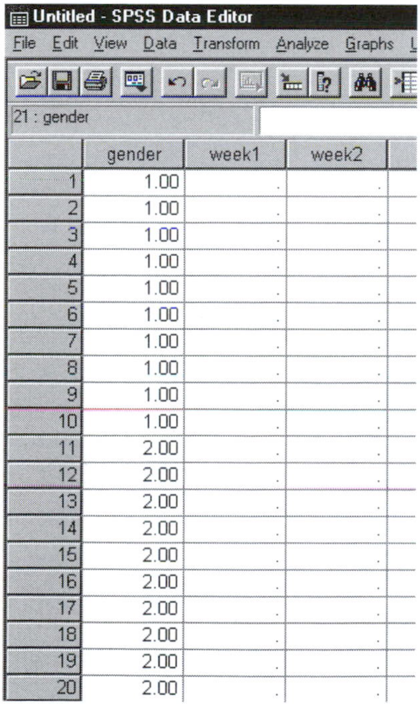

• So that we can see the labels that we have given to these values click on the **View** drop-down menu and select **Value Labels**.

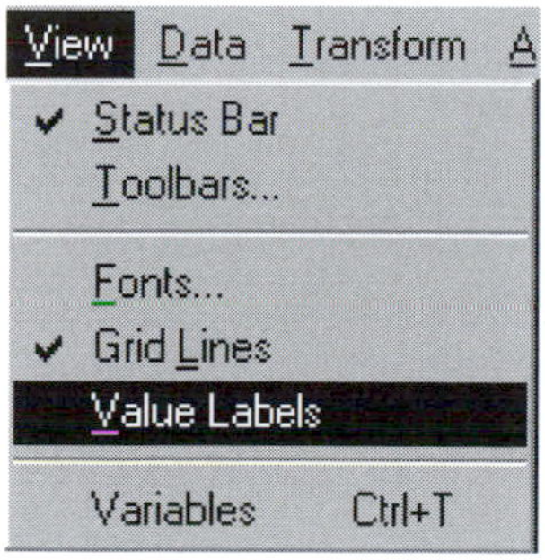

- Alternatively, click on the **Value Labels** short-cut icon.
- The labels we entered in the **Variable View** screen are now shown.

✓   To revert back to the numerical values either click the short-cut icon or go to the **View** drop-down menu and select **Value Labels** again.

After completing our first column we can then go on to enter the homework times for weeks 1 and 2.

	gender	week1	week2
1	male	45.00	51.00
2	male	56.00	53.00
3	male	67.00	65.00
4	male	123.00	105.00
5	male	89.00	98.00
6	male	99.00	96.00
7	male	115.00	122.00
8	male	136.00	125.00
9	male	102.00	100.00
10	male	39.00	39.00
11	female	124.00	136.00
12	female	99.00	87.00
13	female	135.00	115.00
14	female	145.00	156.00
15	female	89.00	91.00
16	female	97.00	100.00
17	female	112.00	104.00
18	female	85.00	79.00
19	female	156.00	142.00
20	female	130.00	119.00

Grouping variable

Independent measures

You must assign a separate name for each condition when setting up the SPSS Data Editor

Saving your data

Saving in SPSS is similar to other applications. When you save your data, SPSS saves the information on both the **Data Editor** and **Variable View**.

- Go to the **File** drop-down menu and select **Save As**.
- Locate where you want to save your data; we have chosen the 3½ disk.
- Name the file; we have called ours 'homework data'.
- You will notice that the **Save as type** is called a **.sav** file.
- Then click on **Save**.
- At the top left-hand side of the **Data View** screen you will notice the title of your file.

✓ It is a good idea to save your work regularly. As with other applications you can now just click on the save icon. 🖫

The SPSS output file

When you undertake any analysis, SPSS switches to the **SPSS viewer** screen where results tables and graphs are output. So far no tests have been run to produce any output, so the screen shown below is only for illustration.

✓ The **SPSS Viewer** file has some similar drop-down menus to the **Data Editor** but some functions can only be performed in the **Data Editor**.

Output Navigator   *Displays output of analysis*

The Output Navigator displays the output in an outline view. You are able to hide, collapse and move items within this screen.

✓ The **SPSS Viewer** and the **Data Editor** screens contain separate files. Therefore, when using the **Save** command each of these must be saved separately.

Saving your output

- Go to the **File** drop-down menu and select **Save As**.
- Locate where you want to save your data, we have chosen the 3½ disk.
- Name your file, we have called ours 'homework results'.
- You will notice that the output **Save as type** is called a **.spo** file.
- Then click on **Save**.

Save As

Save in: 3½ Floppy (A:)

File name: homework results

Save as type: Viewer Files (*.spo)

Save

Cancel

At the top left-hand side of the **SPSS Viewer** screen you will notice that the title of your file changes from Output1 to homework results.

FAQ

Whenever I try to enter a variable name I get the following alert message, what am I doing wrong?

SPSS for Windows

Variable name contains an illegal first character.

OK

*An illegal first character has been entered. SPSS will not let you enter a number, hyphen or other non-letter-based character as the first character of a variable name. SPSS will also not allow you to enter certain characters as part of the variable name, such as * ! ?*

I have entered my variable name, but the grey bit with 'var' now has 'var0000', I think I have done something wrong.

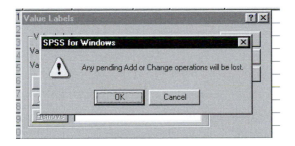

Yes, you have done something wrong but it only takes a minute to correct it. All you have done is typed in your variable name in the Data View screen rather than in the Variable View screen. One way to correct this is to click on the 'var0000'. This will highlight the column black and then press delete on the keyboard, this will delete the whole column. Now, switch to Variable View and type the variable name in the correct place.

I have tried to assign value labels but this message has appeared, what should I do next?

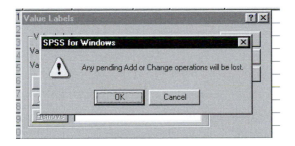

You have added your numerical value and the label but selected OK instead of selecting Add and then OK. Press the Cancel command and then press Add and OK.

I have saved both of my data and output files as 'homework'. When I want to open them again, how will I know which is which?

*The data and the output file names have a different ending. With the Data Editor the file name ends with .sav and the **SPSS viewer** the file name ends with .spo. Also if you are opening the files from your disk you can see a difference in the* *icons. The data file looks like a miniature spreadsheet, whereas the output file looks like a small bar chart.*

I have entered my data as shown below, and know that I want to find differences between males and females but have no idea how I am going to do it.

	males	females
1	25.00	29.00
2	23.00	28.00
3	31.00	21.00
4	41.00	26.00
5	27.00	39.00

You have entered your data incorrectly, remember that gender is nominal data and therefore needs a grouping variable. Refer to the beginning of this chapter on how to enter data.

I have two grouping variables: gender and eye colour. I have used the values 1 and 2 for my gender variable, do I need to assign different numbers for the different eye colours; I have three colours?

Not necessarily, whichever numbers you assign are unique to that individual variable. You can use the numbers 1, 2 and 3 for the eye colour or completely different numbers. As long as you give each number a label in each variable's Value Label section you will be fine.

Chapter 3

Descriptive statistics

Introduction to descriptive statistics

It can be very tempting sometimes to undertake inferential statistics (such as comparing males and females) straight away. But we should not overlook the use of descriptive statistics. They give us a way of accurately describing large datasets quickly and easily. The most common descriptive statistics used are the measures of central tendency (mean, median and mode) and the measures of dispersion (standard deviation, standard error and variance).

Many of the inferential statistics procedures will show some descriptive statistics in the output, however these are not always shown in the format you would prefer and they don't always show all of the descriptive statistics you might require. This is why many SPSS users choose to produce descriptive statistics separately from the inferential statistics. There are also many different ways of obtaining descriptive statistics. There is not a right way or a wrong way; it simply comes down to personal preference on a) procedure and b) the way the statistics are formatted in the output. This chapter aims to show the main descriptive statistics procedures, but once you have become familiar with these it is recommended that you explore the program's menus to find what works best for you.

Sending variables across to a different box

Within many screens in SPSS you need to send the required variables from one box to another. This can be achieved by:

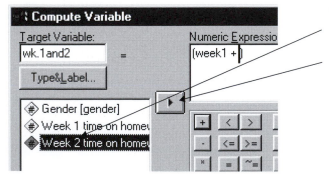

- Highlighting the variable by clicking on it with the mouse and then clicking on the arrow. Your variable will then appear in the new box.

Data entry

	gender	week1	week2
1	1.00	45.00	51.00
2	1.00	56.00	53.00
3	1.00	67.00	65.00
4	1.00	123.00	105.00
5	1.00	89.00	98.00
6	1.00	99.00	96.00
7	1.00	115.00	122.00
8	1.00	136.00	125.00
9	1.00	102.00	100.00
10	1.00	39.00	39.00
11	2.00	124.00	136.00
12	2.00	99.00	87.00
13	2.00	135.00	115.00
14	2.00	145.00	156.00
15	2.00	89.00	91.00
16	2.00	97.00	100.00
17	2.00	112.00	104.00
18	2.00	85.00	79.00
19	2.00	156.00	142.00
20	2.00	130.00	119.00

Enter the dataset as shown in the example. In this chapter we will be using the same dataset as the one entered in Chapter 2.

✓ See Chapter 2 for full data entry procedures.

Frequency command

The **Frequency** command allows you to analyse a full range of descriptive statistics including the measures of central tendency, percentile values, dispersion and distribution.

- From the **Analyze** drop-down menu, select **Descriptive Statistics** and then **Frequencies**.

- Select **Gender** and click on the arrow button between the variables list and the **Variable(s)** box to send it across.
- Ensure that the **Display frequency tables** box is ticked.
- Then click **OK**.

SPSS output

The first table in your output file shows the **Statistics** table.

Statistics

Gender

N	Valid	20
	Missing	0

SPSS essential

- **N** tells us how many cells in the **Gender** column we have entered values for (**Valid**) and how many values are **Missing**. This is especially useful for variables which contain scores or answers to questions that may not have been completed, as it will tell you exactly how many cases/scores this applies to.
- From our table we can see that there were no missing values.

The table headed **Gender** gives a frequency breakdown for males and females.

Gender

		Frequency	Percent	Valid Percent	Cumulative Percent
Valid	male	10	50.0	50.0	50.0
	female	10	50.0	50.0	100.0
	Total	20	100.0	100.0	

SPSS essential

- The **Frequency** column shows a frequency count for each gender and also includes the total count for both.
- The table also shows values for **Percent**, **Valid Percent** and **Cumulative Percent**. The different types of percentage here can be very helpful. **Percent** shows the total frequency percentage of cases/scores for each variable. **Valid Percent** gives the actual frequency percentage of the cases/scores taking into account any missing values. **Cumulative Percent** shows the combined percentage for successive categories, beginning with the category that accounts for the largest percentage of the data.

✓ Be careful if your data contains missing values as you will need to decide whether to report the percent or valid percent or both.

The **Frequencies** command also allows you to carry out other descriptive statistics as shown below.

- From the **Analyze** drop-down menu, select **Descriptive Statistics** and then **Frequencies**.

✓ If you have produced any prior analysis, there may be variables listed in the **Variable(s)** box on the right hand side of the **Frequencies** window. If this is the case, click on the **Reset** button.

- Select the variables you wish to include in the descriptive analysis. If you are following the example above send 'week1' and 'week2' to the **Variable(s)** box.
- Click on the **Statistics** button of the **Frequencies** window.

- Here you can choose from a range of descriptive statistics. We have chosen the **Mean, Median, Mode** and **Std. deviation** (standard deviation).
- Click on the **Continue** button.
- Deselect the **Display frequency tables** option. As we are only interested in the measures of central tendency here, frequency tables are not required.
- Click on **OK**.

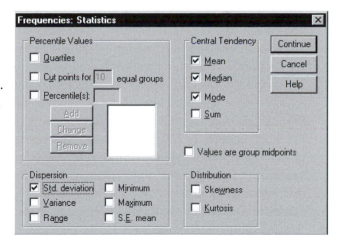

> ✓ SPSS offers options for **Percentile Values** so that you can divide your data into different groups, either quartiles where your data is divided into four equal groups or you can select a specified number of equal groups. Alternatively you can add different percentiles (for example, the ninetieth percentile), in this case SPSS output would show the value at the ninetieth percentile.

SPSS output

The table headed **Statistics** lists the descriptive statistics chosen from the options.

Statistics

		Week 1 time on homework	Week 2 time on homework
N	Valid	20	20
	Missing	0	0
Mean		102.1500	99.1500
Median		100.5000	100.0000
Mode		89.00[a]	100.00
Std. Deviation		32.6195	30.9367

[a]. Multiple modes exist. The smallest value is shown

SPSS essential

- The **Statistics** table shows the descriptive statistics for the time in minutes spent on homework for week 1 and week 2. The table is structured so that the variable names are in columns and the descriptive statistics are in rows.
- By looking at the **Statistics** table we can see that the **Mean** time that all 20 pupils spent on homework in week 1 was 102.1500 minutes, whereas in week 2 only 99.1500 minutes were spent studying.
- We can also see that the **Median** time spent on homework is very similar for both of the weeks (week 1: 100.5000 minutes and week 2: 100.0000 minutes).
- In our example the **Mode** is not a relevant statistic because multiple modes exist. If you are interested in the mode you may want to produce a frequency table to see what the other modes are.
- The **Std. Deviation** shows that there is a larger spread of scores in 'week1' than in 'week2' homework times.

You may wish to support your descriptive statistics with some charts. The **Charts** button is very useful for producing more than one chart at a time, including bar charts, pie charts and histograms. Histograms can help identify if your variables are normally distributed. In our example we want to explore the distribution in scores of our homework times in both weeks.

- From the **Analyze** drop-down menu, select **Descriptive Statistics** and then **Frequencies**.
- Send the variables 'week1' and 'week2' to the **Variable(s)** box.
- Click on the **Charts** button.

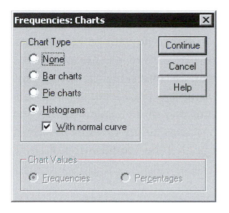

- Select the **Histograms** radio button and also click in the box for **With normal curve**.
- Click **Continue**.
- As we only want the Charts on this occasion deselect the **Display frequency tables** and then click **OK**.

SPSS output

As we have selected 'week1' and 'week2' SPSS generates a histogram for both variables.

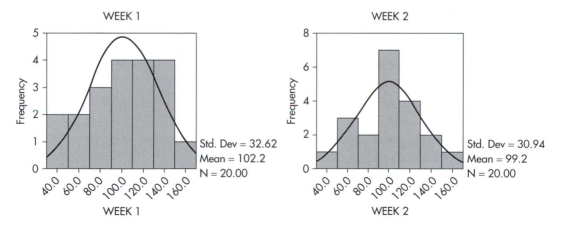

SPSS essential

- Histograms are useful for checking for normal distribution. If the bars of the histogram follow a similar pattern to the bell curve shown above, then this indicates the scores are drawn from a normally distributed population. The importance of this is that if you wish to carry out a parametric test, then the data should be normally distributed to meet the assumptions for that test.
- The output for a histogram also shows the **standard deviation**, the **mean** and the number of participants.
- Although the above distributions look as if they are approaching normal distribution, and therefore meet the assumptions for a parametric test, you can carry out the **One-sample Kolmogorov–Smirnov** test, which will test for normal distribution. The procedure for this is shown below.

The above examples show that our samples look as if they could well be drawn from normal distributions. If the data is negatively or positively skewed we are much less confident that the distribution of the population is normal. By observing the histograms below we can see that the one on the left shows that the sample is negatively skewed with the majority of the scores/cases falling towards the higher end of the scale. The second histogram has a positive skew, with the majority of scores/cases falling towards the lower end of the scale. With histograms like these, it is possible that the samples do not come from normally distributed populations.

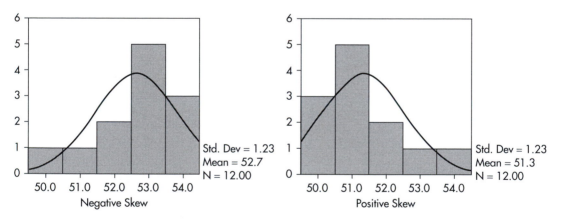

Procedure for the one sample Kolmogorov–Smirnov test

The one sample Kolmogorov–Smirnov test, more commonly known as the K–S test, takes the observed cumulative distribution of scores and compares them to the theoretical cumulative distribution for a normally distributed population.

- From the **Analyze** drop-down menu select **Nonparametric Tests** and then **1-Sample K-S**.

- Select 'week1' and 'week2' and send them to the **Test Variable List**.
- The **Test Distribution** box should have **Normal** ticked. If not select **Normal**.
- Click on **OK**.

SPSS output

One table is produced which details the normality of both of our variables.

One-Sample Kolmogorov–Smirnov Test

		WEEK 1	WEEK 2	
N		20	20	
Normal Parameters[a,b]	Mean	102.1500	99.1500	} *Essential*
	Std. Deviation	32.6195	30.9367	
Most Extreme	Absolute	.100	.109	
Differences	Positive	.071	.082	} *Advanced*
	Negative	−.100	−.109	
Kolmogorov–Smirnov Z		.445	.489	} *Essential*
Asymp. Sig. (2-tailed)		.989	.970	

[a]. Test distribution is Normal.
[b]. Calculated from data.

SPSS essential

- The first part of the **One-Sample Kolmogorov–Smirnov Test** output table shows **N** (the number of participants), the **Mean** and the **Standard Deviation**.
- We have ticked a **Normal Distribution** with which to compare our data, this is confirmed by the superscripted [a]. The superscripted [b] indicates that the observed distribution corresponds to a theoretical distribution that is normally distributed.
- To check this for yourself, **Asymp. Sig. (2-tailed)** values should be > 0.05 to indicate that the observed distribution corresponds to the theoretical distribution. That is, your data is not significantly different to a normal distribution at the $p < 0.05$ level of significance.
- From the table we can see that both variables have **Asymp. Sig. (2-tailed)** values > 0.05, therefore both weeks of homework times can be assumed to be normally distributed (week 1: $p = 0.989$, week 2: $p = 0.970$).

SPSS advanced

- The **One-Sample Kolmogorov–Smirnov Test** output reports where the **Most Extreme Differences** are. These indicate the difference between the observed cumulative distribution and the theoretical cumulative distribution. The larger the difference, the more likely the distributions will be different to a normal distribution.

Descriptives command

The **Descriptives** command is an alternative way to produce basic descriptive statistics. However, it does not give as many options as the **Frequencies** command. As before we are interested in observing the descriptive statistics for our homework time variables.

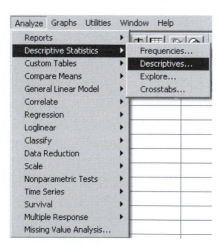

- From the **Analyze** drop-down menu select **Descriptive Statistics** and then **Descriptives**.

- Select variables 'week1' and 'week2'.
- Send them to the **Variable(s)** box.
- Click **OK**.

SPSS output

The following table shows the **Descriptive Statistics** for the variables 'week1' and 'week2'.

Descriptive Statistics

	N	Minimum	Maximum	Mean	Std. Deviation
Week 1 time on homework	20	39.00	156.00	102.1500	32.6195
Week 2 time on homework	20	39.00	156.00	99.1500	30.9367
Valid N (listwise)	20				

SPSS essential

- The **Descriptive Statistics** table consists of the number of participants (**N**) and the **Minimum** and **Maximum** time spent on homework each week. Also shown is the **Mean** time spent doing homework for each week and the **Standard Deviation**.
- By observing the table above we can see that the **Mean** for 'week1' (102.1500 minutes) is higher than for 'week2' (99.1500 minutes).
- 'week1' also has a larger dispersion of scores as shown by the **Std. Deviation** (32.6195) than 'week2' (30.9367).

Basic tables

Sometimes we may wish to examine the scores of one variable grouped by a second variable. If this is an essential part of your analysis you can obtain this in a number of ways. One option is to use the **Split File** command (for procedure details see Chapter 5). A second option is to use the **Basic Tables** command.

✓ Any tables produced using the **Basic Tables** command will only make sense if the data has been given suitable labels in the **Variable View** screen when setting up the dataset.

	Name	Type	Width	Decimals	Label	Values	Missing	Columns	Align	Measure
1	gender	Numeric	8	2	Gender	{1.00, male}...	None	8	Right	Nominal
2	week1	Numeric	8	2	Week 1 time o	None	None	8	Right	Scale
3	week2	Numeric	8	2	Week 2 time o	None	None	8	Right	Scale

homework.sav - SPSS Data Editor
File Edit View Data Transform Analyze Graphs Utilities Window Help

✓ It is not too late to go back and alter these at any time. If the **Basic Tables** you produce don't make sense because of bad labelling, alter the labels here and then run the command again.

Procedure for Basic Tables

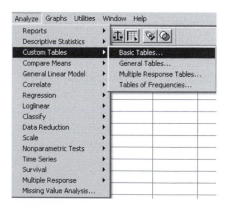

- From the **Analyze** drop-down menu, select **Custom Tables** and then **Basic Tables**.

- Select 'week1' and 'week2' and send them to the **Summaries** box.
- Select 'Gender' and send it to the **Subgroups Down** box.
- Click on the **Statistics** button.

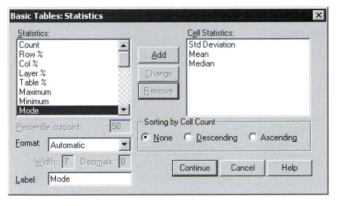

- The **Statistics** box offers a selection of descriptive statistics to choose from.
- For this example, click on **Std Deviation**.
- Click on the **Add** button and it will appear in the **Cell Statistics** box.
- Do the same for the **Mean**, **Median** and **Mode**.
- Click on the **Continue** button and then **OK**.

SPSS output

The basic table shows the requested descriptive statistics for the variable 'gender'.

			Std Deviation	Mean	Median	Mode
Gender	male	Week 1 time on homework	33.80	87.10	94.00	39.00
		Week 2 time on homework	30.87	85.40	97.00	39.00
	female	Week 1 time on homework	24.50	117.20	118.00	85.00
		Week 2 time on homework	25.44	112.90	109.50	79.00

SPSS essential

- The table shows the **Std Deviation**, **Mean**, **Median** and **Mode** for each variable and is split so that differences between males and females can be seen.
- If we look at the table above we can see that **Mean** homework time for females in week 1 (117.20 min) and week 2 (112.90 min) is greater than that for males (week 1: 87.10 and week 2: 85.40).
- The **Std Deviation** for the males is larger in both weeks than the females, indicating a larger spread of scores within the male participants.

✓ By sending the grouping variable to different **Subgroups** boxes different formats of table will be generated such as the differences in the tables of means below.

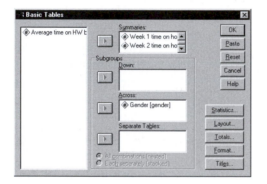

This table was produced by placing 'gender' in the **Across Subgroups** box.

		Gender	
		male	female
Week 1 time on homework		87.10	117.20
Week 2 time on homework		85.40	112.90

Gender	male	Week 1 time on homework	87.10
		Week 2 time on homework	85.40
	female	Week 1 time on homework	117.20
		Week 2 time on homework	112.90

This table was produced by placing 'gender' in the **Down Subgroups** box.

Placing 'gender' in the **Separate Tables Subgroups** box will produce an individual table of descriptive statistics for each group.

FAQ

I want to select more than one variable from the variable list but I can't if they are not next to each other, is there a way of doing this?

If you want to select more than one variable at a time, but they are not next to each other in the list of variables, hold down the Ctrl key on your keyboard and then click on each of the variables you wish to include in your analysis.

I am confused as to why the arrow on the button between the variable selection windows keeps changing direction, why is this?

The arrow button will point in the opposite direction of the selected variable, or if no variables are selected it will point towards the empty variable(s) box. This is to give you an indication of where the selected variable(s) will go when the button is clicked on.

I have tried to produce some descriptive statistics through the Frequencies command but don't want any frequency tables. I have deselected the Display Frequency Tables box and this error message has appeared.

SPSS is just letting you know that you need to select some form of command to produce some output. Press OK and then remember to select your required descriptives. In future it might be an idea to select your Descriptives or Charts first before deselecting the Display Frequency Tables box.

Details on the use of descriptive statistics can be found in Chapter 2 of Hinton (2004).

Chapter 4

Illustrative statistics

Introduction to illustrative statistics

Illustrative statistics are a visual representation of data. Along with descriptive statistics they can be useful tools for summarising and comparing some or all of your data. It is often easier to see general trends in a graph rather than trying to interpret numerical information. The procedures and screen shots that are detailed in this chapter are created using version 11 of SPSS. The procedures for creating illustrative statistics in version 12 are the same, although the graphs produced may look slightly different with respect, for example, to the scale chosen. Any major differences between the two versions regarding illustrative statistics will be described in separate sections.

There are three ways of obtaining illustrative statistics in SPSS.

1   All types of graphs can be obtained using the **Graphs** drop-down menu.
2   You are also able to produce some graphs using the **Frequencies** command.
3   Finally, many statistical test procedures have chart options; these are briefly covered in the accompanying chapters.

This chapter focuses on some of the options available within the **Graphs** drop-down menu. The methods used to create several different types of graph are similar. This chapter will therefore describe a procedure for an example graph, and indicate which other types of chart can also be created through a similar procedure. The chapter is organised into the following sections:

* graphs examining distributions of scores
* graphs created for data that have a grouping variable
* graphs created for data that have several measurements from the same person, i.e. a repeated measures design
* graphs for data with a mixed design, i.e. datasets with both grouping variables and repeated measures variables
* editing graphs in SPSS
* introduction to graphs that are produced through the **Gallery** and **Interactive** options in SPSS.

Graphs displaying distributions of scores

Graphs can be useful tools in making judgements regarding the size and distribution of a dataset, and may also highlight any potential anomalies within a dataset such as skewed distributions and potential outlying data points. These irregularities may affect the decision on which statistical test to perform.

Scenario

In this chapter we will use the homework example from Chapter 2. In this example a teacher noted the number of minutes that ten boys and ten girls aged 9 years, spent on their homework over a 2-week period. We can produce a histogram to show the distribution of scores each week and compare these to the normal distribution.

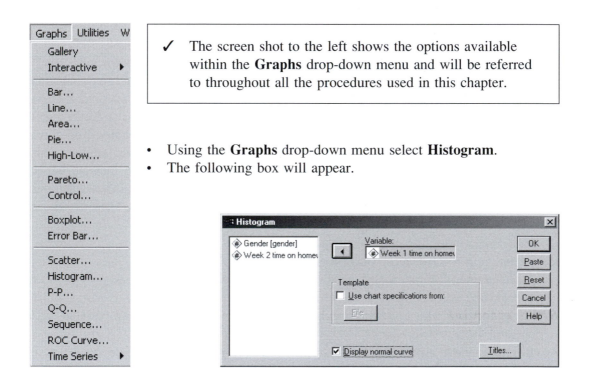

✓ The screen shot to the left shows the options available within the **Graphs** drop-down menu and will be referred to throughout all the procedures used in this chapter.

• Using the **Graphs** drop-down menu select **Histogram**.
• The following box will appear.

• Send the desired variable across to the **Variable** box, and place a tick in **Display normal curve**.
• Click on **OK** and your histogram will appear in the Output screen.

✓ Generating histograms using this method will only allow single charts to be created. You can produce more than one histogram at once by using the **Frequency** command, see Chapter 3 for details.

SPSS output

SPSS produces a histogram with the variable (week 1) as the *X*-axis and the frequency (minutes studied) as the *Y*-axis.

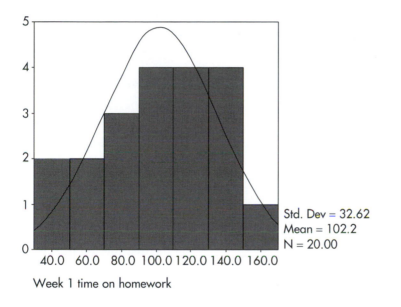

Std. Dev = 32.62
Mean = 102.2
N = 20.00

Week 1 time on homework

SPSS essential

* The histogram output displays the **Standard Deviation**, **Mean** and **Number of Participants (N)**.
* By looking at the histogram above and the superimposed curve we can evaluate the distribution of our scores. If the bars of the histogram follow a similar pattern to the bell shaped normal distribution we can assume that the scores obtained come from a normally distributed population.

A second common way to illustrate distributions of data is through the use of the **Boxplot** command. Boxplots can be used to illustrate distribution of scores on a single variable in a similar fashion to a histogram and can assist in determining the distribution of the data. Boxplots are also useful for indicating outliers and extreme scores. In addition boxplots can be used to compare the distributions of groups on a single variable, or for a comparison of scores from the same sample of participants on more than one measurement, i.e. a repeated measures design.

The following procedure will take an example of generating a boxplot for the distribution on a single variable.

- From the **Graphs** drop down menu select **Boxplot**.
- The **Boxplot** box will appear.
- As we want to display the distribution on a single variable, select the **Summaries of separate variables** option, as we have no grouping variable.
- Click on **Define** and the following box will be shown.

- Send the variable to be illustrated to the **Boxes Represent** box.
- As our example is focusing on the distribution of scores from, week 1, this is the only variable selected.
- Click **OK**, and the illustrations that are generated in the Output screen are shown in the next section.

✓ The procedure for a comparison of scores from the same sample of participants on more than one measurement is the same. For example, if we wanted to compare the distribution of scores in week 1 and week 2 both variables would be selected and sent across to the **Boxes Represent** box.

SPSS output

The first table to be produced is the **Case Processing Summary** table.

Case Processing Summary

	Cases					
	Valid		Missing		Total	
	N	Percent	N	Percent	N	Percent
Week 1 time on homework	20	100.0%	0	.0%	20	100.0%

SPSS essential

• The **Case Processing Summary** table indicates the number and percentage of missing scores in our dataset.
• As we can see from this table, no scores in our dataset are missing and therefore we are considering all 20 participants when making judgements about the distribution of the scores in our dataset.

The graph that follows illustrates the distribution of the scores in the form of a boxplot.

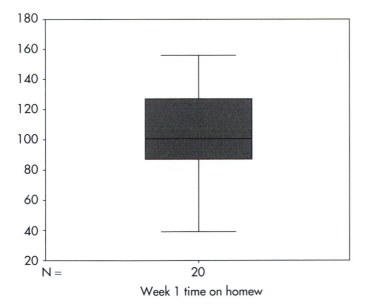

SPSS essential

- The black line in the centre of the box indicates the median value.
- The shaded box (showing red on screen) indicates where 50 per cent of the data falls, i.e. the data that lies between the twenty-fifth and seventy-fifth percentile.
- The lines extending from the shaded box are commonly referred to as 'whiskers' and connect the highest and lowest scores that aren't considered to be outliers.
- Outliers are those scores that are more than 1.5 box lengths from the twenty-fifth or seventy-fifth percentile and are therefore not considered as falling inside the range of scores to be displayed in the distribution. These will therefore not be connected by the whiskers, and will instead be shown as a circle.
- Extreme values are those scores that are more than three box lengths from the twenty-fifth or seventy-fifth percentile and are shown as a star.
- If the dataset is normally distributed, the boxplot will be symmetrical. The median line will be in the centre of the box, and the whiskers extending from the top and bottom half of the box will be of equal lengths.
- In the example above we can see that our data is approaching a normal distribution as the boxplot is fairly symmetrical. The top whisker is slightly shorter than the bottom one, indicating that 50 per cent of the data is falling slightly towards the upper end of the measurement scale. There is no indication of any outliers or extreme scores, and therefore we are confident that our distribution is adequate. This supports our previous histogram.
- If we are concerned about the distribution of our data after visually checking the graph, there are a number of ways to test for this. For example, we could carry out a Kolmogorov–Smirnov test, which will test statistically for normal distribution. Further details of this test can be found in Chapter 3.

✓ Outliers and extreme scores may be an indication of an error in data entry.

Boxplots can also be used to illustrate the distributions of two or more groups of data. For example, more data has now been added to the original homework dataset and we now wish to further investigate the distribution of homework times across our two groups of participants, males and females. The new data is shown below.

	gender	week1
1	male	45.00
2	male	56.00
3	male	67.00
4	male	123.00
5	male	89.00
6	male	99.00
7	male	115.00
8	male	136.00
9	male	102.00
10	male	39.00
11	female	124.00
12	female	99.00
13	female	135.00
14	female	145.00
15	female	89.00
16	female	97.00
17	female	112.00
18	female	85.00
19	female	156.00
20	female	130.00
21	male	64.00
22	male	77.00
23	male	.
24	male	69.00
25	male	99.00
26	female	327.00
27	female	109.00
28	female	256.00
29	female	170.00
30	female	98.00

We can now create a boxplot which will display the distributions of the variable 'week1' for each of our two groups as defined within the variable 'gender'.

- Choose **Boxplot** from the **Graphs** drop-down menu to generate the box shown.
- As we want to compare the distribution of the female scores and the male scores on the same graph we need to select **Summaries for groups of cases**. This is because we have a defined grouping variable of gender between which we want to compare the distributions of scores.
- Click on **Define** to show the following box.

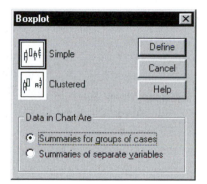

✓ As we can see from the dataset the homework time for participant 23 is missing. This will be discussed later.

- The variable that we are displaying the distribution of is 'week1' and should be sent to the **Variable** box.
- We want to generate a boxplot for each gender group. The variable 'gender' should therefore be sent to the **Category Axis** box. This will ensure that the two genders will be placed on the X-axis, and a boxplot detailing the distribution of both groups on the variable 'week1' will be produced.
- Click on **OK** and the boxplot will be shown in the Output window.

47

SPSS output

Again, the first table to be produced is the **Case Processing Summary**. This gives a description of the dataset, and an indication of the number and percentage of missing scores in our dataset.

Case Processing Summary

		Cases					
		Valid		Missing		Total	
	Gender	N	Percent	N	Percent	N	Percent
Week 1 time on homework	male	14	93.3%	1	6.7%	15	100.0%
	female	15	100.0%	0	.0%	15	100.0%

SPSS essential

- As we can see from the table above there is one missing value for the males, therefore we are considering only 14 of the 15 participants in the male group when making judgements about the distribution of the male scores in our dataset.
- There may be a number of valid reasons why this data is missing or there may be an error in data entry.

The graph that follows illustrates the distribution of the scores for each group in the form of a boxplot. The same format is taken when interpreting boxplots produced in

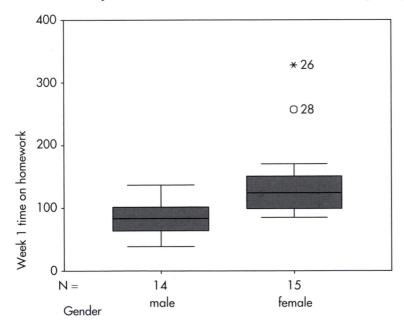

SPSS for multiple boxplots, as that taken for boxplots showing the distribution of scores on a single variable. That is, the (red) box indicates where 50 per cent of the data lies, and the whiskers connect the lowest and highest scores that are not considered to be outliers. The black line shows the median values.

SPSS essential

- As we can see from the above example, the distributions of males and females on the variable 'week1' is quite different.
- By observing the female participants' distribution of homework times we can see that they spend more time on homework than the male participants.
- The female data also highlights an outlier, which is shown by a circle. SPSS shows that the case number of participant 28 is the outlier.
- The female distribution of homework times also shows an extreme value, which is shown to be participant number 26.
- By observing the above boxplot we can see that the red box (50 per cent of the distribution) for the male scores is smaller than that for the females, indicating a smaller spread of scores among the males.
- While the two groups score on different parts of the scale, if the outlier and extreme value were removed both boxplots would be approximately symmetrical. This indicates that both groups have approximately normal distributions on the variable 'week1'.

✓ It would be a good idea to check the missing value and the reasons behind the outlier and the extreme score. These can be corrected if they are as a result of input errors or other factors that make the data inappropriate. However, if these values are valid then they would be kept in the dataset.

Graphs for data with an independent design

In this section we will be exploring how to produce graphs using a grouping variable. In our current homework time example we have a grouping variable of gender.

Producing a variety of graphs in SPSS, which have a grouping variable, follows a similar procedure. We will use a bar chart as an example, although generating other types of graphs, such as pie charts and line charts will be similar.

In our example we want to compare the mean time spent on homework between males and females in week 1. A bar chart will clearly show this and the procedure is as follows.

- From the **Graphs** drop-down menu, select **Bar**.
- **Simple** is already selected as default and is the most appropriate selection for our example as we want just two bars, one for male mean scores and one for female mean scores.
- In the **Data in Chart Are** section, click on the **Summaries for groups of cases** radio button. We need to select this as we have a grouping variable of 'gender' and by selecting this option we will be able to split the variable measuring homework time between the two groups.
- Click on the **Define** button.

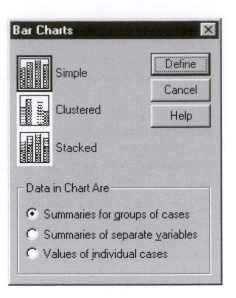

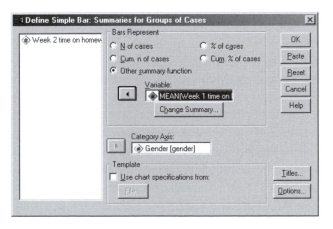

- Select **Gender** and send it to the **Category Axis** box. This will ensure that our two groups will appear on the *X*-axis as independent mean scores.
- In the **Bars Represent** section, click on the **Other summary function** radio button. The **Variable** box will now be active.
- Select 'week1' and send it to the **Variable** box.
- Click on **OK**.

✓ Remember that the dependent variable needs to be sent to the **Variable** box and the grouping variable must be sent to the **Category Axis**.

Some useful option buttons

✓ Clicking on the **Change Summary** button allows you to change the summary that the bars represent to alternative descriptive statistics, for example if you need to compare the median values.

✓ The **Titles** button allows you to add a title and sub-title to your chart. However, if you intend to paste the chart into a report, it is advisable to title it in your word-processing package to ensure the fonts and headings look the same.

✓ The **Options** button offers you choices on excluding missing values.

SPSS output

Once you have clicked on **OK** SPSS generates your bar chart.

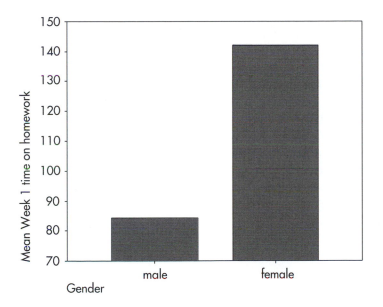

SPSS essential

- The output will produce a bar chart that shows gender on the *X*-axis and the mean amount of time spent on homework across week 1 on the *Y*-axis. The bar chart shows that females spent a higher mean time on homework than the males.

✓ Sometimes the axes selected by SPSS can be deceptive. The axis can be adjusted using the **Chart Editor**. Instructions for this and other changes are given at the end of this chapter. These changes should always be made in SPSS before transferring to a word-processing program.

Clustered and stacked bar charts

Clustered and stacked bar charts can be used to display categories of one variable summarised within categories of another variable.

	experien	machine	errors
1	novice	old	4.00
2	novice	old	5.00
3	novice	old	7.00
4	novice	old	6.00
5	novice	old	8.00
6	novice	old	5.00
7	novice	new	5.00
8	novice	new	6.00
9	novice	new	5.00
10	novice	new	6.00
11	novice	new	5.00
12	novice	new	6.00
13	experien	old	1.00
14	experien	old	2.00
15	experien	old	2.00
16	experien	old	3.00
17	experien	old	2.00
18	experien	old	3.00
19	experien	new	8.00
20	experien	new	9.00
21	experien	new	8.00
22	experien	new	8.00
23	experien	new	7.00
24	experien	new	9.00

Scenario

A new manager of a factory is keen to reduce the number of errors made at his factory. Staff were divided into those who were experienced and those who were novices. Also it was noted whether the machine that each member of staff used was old or new. The number of errors was recorded.

Procedure for clustered and stacked bar charts

- From the **Graphs** drop-down menu, select **Bar**.
- Select **Clustered**.
- In the **Data in Chart Are** section, click on the **Summaries for groups of cases** radio button.
- Click on the **Define** button.

- Select 'experien' and send it to the **Category Axis** box. This will ensure that the two groups will appear on the *X*-axis.
- In addition to grouping the scores by experience, we also want to separate the mean scores by the other independent variable, which is whether the person was operating an old or a new machine.

- We therefore need to send the second grouping variable 'machine' to the **Define Clusters by** box.
- We now select the **Other summary function** radio button within the **Bars Represent** option. This will make the **Variable** box active.

- We send the dependent variable 'errors' the **Variable** box. Note that it now shows Mean (errors). The bars on the graph will represent the mean errors for each group.
- Once all our variables are in the correct place click on **OK**.

SPSS output

The chart that we have asked SPSS to generate is shown below.

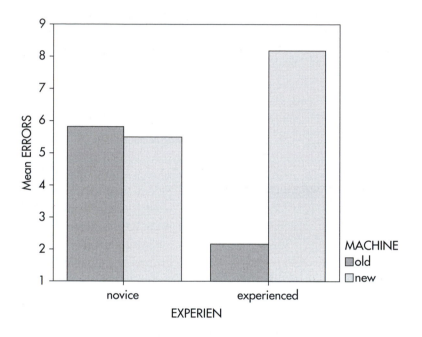

As can be seen, we have generated a chart that separates the scores of the two groups of participants, experienced and novice operators. In addition to this, within each group of experience, we have also separated the mean scores for those operators who were using either old or new machinery. For example, the first bar represents the mean number of errors made by those novices who were using old machines.

SPSS essential

- We can see from the above chart that there does appear to be a pattern emerging between the two groups in the number of errors made while using the machines.

- Within the novice group we can see that there is not much difference in the number of errors made when using the old or the new machine.
- We can also see that the experienced operators made more errors than the novice operators when using the new machinery, but fewer errors when using the old machinery.

Graphs for data with a repeated measures design

Graphs that are produced with a repeated measures design all follow a similar procedure in that after you have chosen the graph from the drop-down menu you must select the **Summaries of separate variables** option. This is shown with the error bar chart in the example below.

Scenario

A team coach wanted to know what effect weather conditions made to the time it took to complete a 5 km run. Twelve runners completed a 5 km run in bad weather conditions and again the following week when the weather was a lot milder. The times were rounded to the nearest minute and were entered into SPSS.

Data entry

	wet	dry
1	26.00	22.00
2	17.00	17.00
3	20.00	19.00
4	22.00	20.00
5	19.00	18.00
6	18.00	17.00
7	24.00	21.00
8	19.00	19.00
9	19.00	18.00
10	26.00	23.00
11	28.00	25.00
12	18.00	18.00

Enter the dataset as shown in the example.

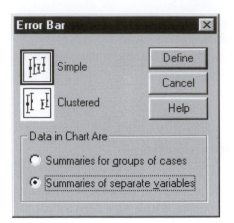

- From the **Graphs** drop-down menu select **Error Bar**.
- **Simple** is already selected as default and is the most appropriate selection for our example.
- In the **Data in Chart Are** section, click on the **Summaries of separate variables** radio button. We need to select this option because we have two different variables that we want to examine.
- Click on the **Define** button.

- Select both weather conditions and send them to the **Error Bars** box.
- Click on **OK**.

	Define Simple Error Bar: Summaries of Separate Variables

✓ By clicking on the **Bars Represent** button you can change the error bars to standard error of the mean.

✓ Details of the **Change Summary**, **Titles** and **Options** buttons have been discussed on page 51.

SPSS output

The Error bar chart is then produced as shown below.

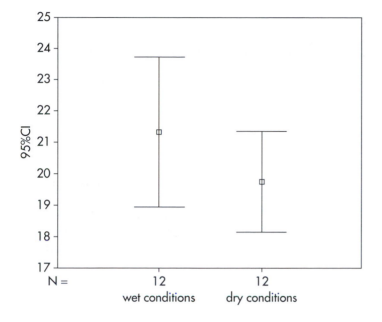

SPSS essential

- By examining the output you can see that the two variables are on the *X*-axis and the number of minutes that it took to complete the 5 km run on the *Y*-axis.
- The square in the middle of the error bar represents the mean.
- The two whiskers that accompany the mean are the 95 per cent confidence intervals. For more details of confidence intervals see Chapter 6.
- By looking at the above graph we can see that in the wet weather conditions the runners had a slower mean running time with a wider confidence interval than in the dry conditions.

Graphs for data with a mixed design

In a mixed design we have an independent variable and a repeated measures variable. We therefore need to be careful when producing graphs that we have selected the appropriate variable for each axis.

Scenario

Novice and experienced workers operate machines in a factory and their errors are monitored over a 3-week period.

	workers	week1	week2	week3
1	novices	7	6	5
2	novices	4	4	3
3	novices	6	4	4
4	novices	7	6	5
5	novices	6	5	4
6	novices	4	2	2
7	experien	7	3	2
8	experien	8	4	2
9	experien	6	2	1
10	experien	9	6	3
11	experien	7	4	3
12	experien	10	6	3

Enter the dataset as shown in the example.

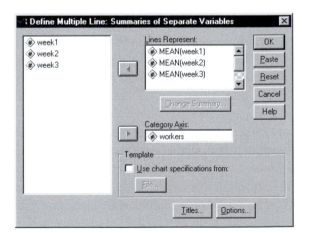

- From the **Graphs** drop-down menu, select **Line**.
- As we have more than one variable to be plotted on our chart we need to select a **Multiple** line chart. This will ensure that points for each variable mean will be plotted.
- Because we have a repeated measures element within our design we must choose the option of **Summaries of separate variables**. This will allow such a chart to be generated.
- Click on **Define**.

- Our independent measures variable 'workers' should be sent to the **Category Axis** box to ensure that the two group means will be taken and plotted independently of each other.
- Our repeated measures variable 'time' has three levels of measurement: week 1, week 2, and week 3. These should be sent to the **Lines Represent** box.
- Click on **OK**.

✓ Details of the **Change Summary**, **Titles** and **Options** buttons have been discussed on page 51.

SPSS output

We have generated a graph in SPSS that plots the mean number of errors made by the two groups of workers over a 3-week period, as shown below.

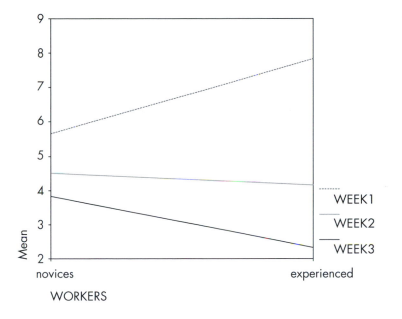

SPSS essential

- We can see from the above chart that there does appear to be a pattern in the number of errors made by workers over the 3-week period.
- In week 1 the experienced operators were making more errors than the novices. This trend was not evident at the week 2 measurement, with the two groups of workers making a similar number of errors.
- By week 3 the trend had been reversed, and now experienced operators were making fewer errors than their novice counterparts.
- All workers were, however, making fewer errors in the third week than they had in weeks 1 and 2.

Transposing axes (SPSS versions 11 and earlier)

When generating the above chart while undertaking a two factor analysis of variance there is the option to generate the chart by specifying which variable you wish to appear on which axis. Generating the plot through the above command will automatically select the axes for you. However, if you did wish to examine the relationship by having the time period measurements on the X-axis, and the groups of workers on the lines then the following procedure should be adopted.

While this is part of the editing function on SPSS, which will be explained later in this chapter, transposing axes is mainly specific to multiple line charts and clustered bar charts.

- Double click on your chart to activate the **Chart Editor**.
- The active window will open on top of your original graph, which will appear greyed out underneath as shown below.

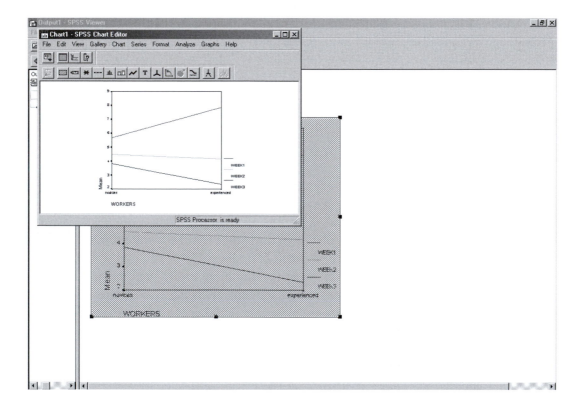

- In the **Chart Editor** window select **Transpose Data** from the **Series** drop-down menu.
- This will swap the assignment of the variable axis in the chart.
- If you are happy with the axis change, close down the **Chart Editor** and your original graph should reflect the changes. The original graph and the new graph are shown below.

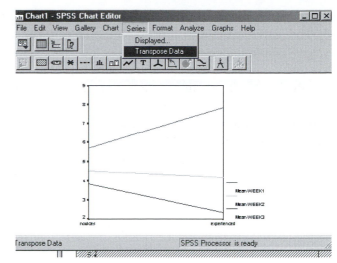

By comparing the original line chart on the left with our transposed axes chart on the right we can see that the repeated measures variable is now shown as the category axis and the independent variable as separate lines.

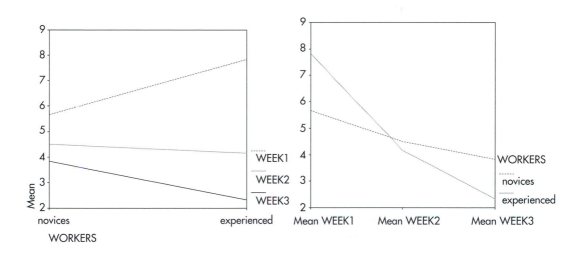

Transposing axes (SPSS version 12)

Transposing axes with SPSS version 12 requires a different procedure to that described above.

- Double click on your chart to activate the **Chart Editor**.
- The active window will open on top of your original graph, which will appear greyed out underneath as shown below.

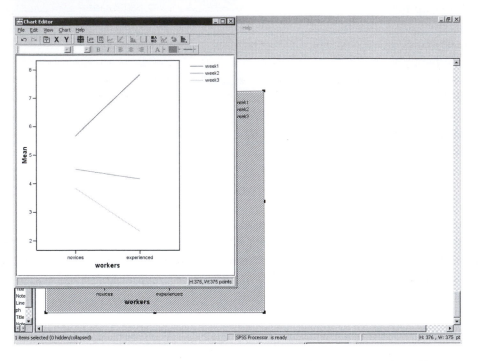

- In the **Chart Editor** window select the lines to be transposed by clicking on one of them.
- The lines become highlighted as shown by a thicker blue line around the lines and the legend.
- Right click and select **Properties Window**.
- The following window will then appear.

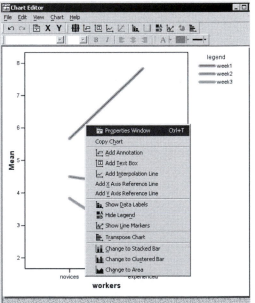

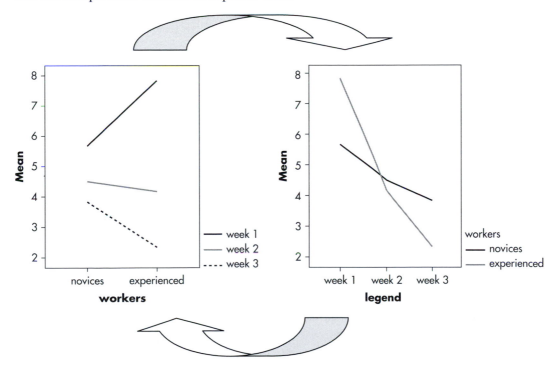

Properties

| Chart Size | Lines | Categories |
| Interpolation Line | Variables | Line Options |

Y-Axis: Mean

Z-Axis:

X-Axis: workers

Group by: legend

Variables:

Apply   Close   Help

- Select the **Variables** tab.
- As we can see the 'workers' are currently on the *X*-axis and the weeks appear as the legend.
- These need to be swapped around by clicking and dragging the variables in the **Variables** box and then reassigning them to the opposite axis.
- Click on **Apply** and then **Close**.
- Then close the **Chart Editor** window.

By comparing the original line chart on the left with our transposed axes chart on the right we can see that the repeated measures variable is now shown as the category axis and the independent variable as separate lines.

Graphs illustrating frequency counts

So far the graphs which we have described have concerned dependent variables measured on a continuous scale. If your data is nominal such charts will not be appropriate. Examples of nominal data include ethnicity, favourite political party, type of car or any variable that makes up a category and can be measured by a frequency count. One way to display this information is with pie charts.

Scenario

	vehicle
1	car
2	car
3	lorry
4	other
5	bus
6	van
7	van
8	lorry
9	lorry
10	car
11	car
12	car
13	car
14	bus
15	van
16	van
17	other
18	car
19	car
20	car

A group of school children were asked to conduct a traffic survey in their village. They recorded the first 20 types of vehicle that passed by their school. The categories they used were car, bus, lorry, van and other (farm vehicles, milk floats, etc.). The data is shown on the left.

✓ The data displayed is shown in the value label format rather than as a numerical value, see Chapter 2 for the full data entry procedure.

- From the **Graphs** drop-down menu select **Pie** and the box on the right will appear.
- As our example surveys groups of vehicles we need to select the option **Summaries for groups of cases**.
- Click on **Define**.

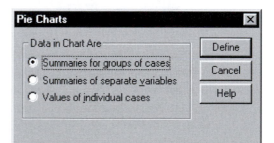

Define Pie: Summaries for Groups of Cases

Slices Represent

- ⦿ N of cases
- ○ Cum. n of cases
- ○ Other summary function
- ○ % of cases
- ○ Cum. % of cases

Variable:

Change Summary...

Define Slices by:
⊕ Type of Vehicle [vehicl

Template

☐ Use chart specifications from:

File...

OK
Paste
Reset
Cancel
Help

Titles...
Options...

- Select the variable 'vehicle' and send it to the **Define Slices by** box. This will ensure that each type of vehicle is grouped and the total counts of each vehicle appear as one slice.
- As we are interested in the frequency of each vehicle passing through the village, the default setting of **N of cases** is appropriate.
- Click on **OK**.

✓ The pie chart default option is number of cases (frequency count). This can be changed to the options presented in the **Slices Represent** box.

SPSS output

The pie chart generated by SPSS can be seen below.

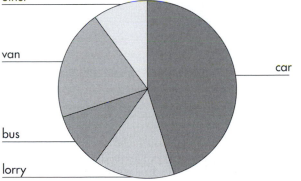

other

van

car

bus

lorry

SPSS essential

• The **Pie Chart** clearly shows that the majority of vehicles that passed through the village were cars, then vans, then lorries.
• As a default the value labels are used to lablel the pie chart segments. However, we can also show the values or percentages using the SPSS **Chart Editor**, following the procedure below.

Editing graphs (SPSS versions 11 and earlier)

The procedure for editing all graphs in SPSS follows a similar structure.

• Double click on the chart to activate the SPSS **Chart Editor**.
• The active window will open on top of the original graph, which will appear greyed out underneath.
• The element of the chart that you want to edit should now be selected in the **Chart Editor** by double clicking on it.
• In our example we want to display the percentage of the whole that each segment accounts for.
• We therefore need to double click on one of the labels to display the following box.

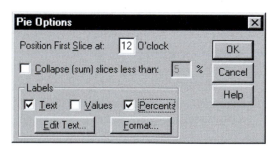

• The **Pie Options** window will now open.
• In the **Labels** section, put a tick in the **Percents** box.
• Click on **OK** and close the **Chart Editor** window.

The pie chart should now have been updated, and in addition to showing the text labels, the percentage is now displayed as well. This can be seen below.

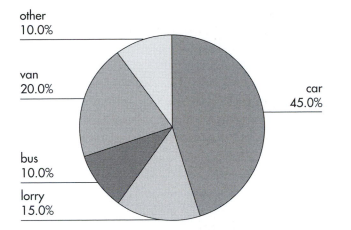

✓ Other types of chart can be edited in a similar manner. To make all changes, the **Chart Editor** window must first be active, and then the area of the graph to be changed should be double clicked on, making the amendments as necessary.

Editing axes (SPSS versions 11 and earlier)

When SPSS produces charts, it does not always have the scale of the axis starting at zero. If you do not examine the range of the axis carefully, the chart may lead you to believe that the difference between variables is larger than it really is. The example below shows the difference in the mean amount of time spent on homework between males and females over the period of a week. There is only a 30-minute difference between males and females but because the full range of minutes in the axis is not shown, this difference can appear very large. We can alter the axis as follows.

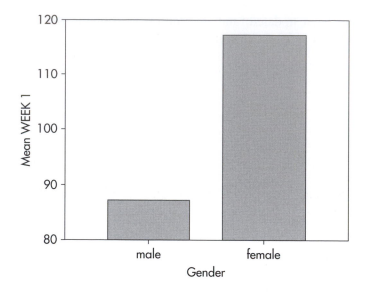

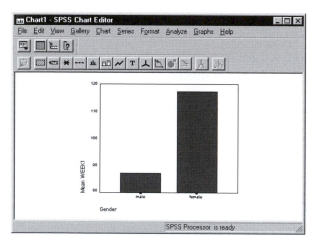

- When viewing the chart in **SPSS viewer**, double click on it.
- This will launch the SPSS **Chart Editor**.
- Double click on the *Y*-axis to open the **Scale Axis** window.

- In the **Range** box change the minimum value to 0.
- You can also change the **Axis Title** to something more appropriate.
- Click on **OK**.
- The chart with the adjusted axis should now be visible in the **Chart Editor** window.
- Close the **Chart Editor** window to update this SPSS output.

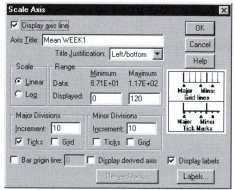

✓ In this example the increments pre-set by SPSS for the scale are appropriate. However, sometimes you may need to change these as well. If you do change the increments make sure that the maximum value selected for the scale is divisible by the increments.

SPSS output

The bar chart now shows the adjusted axis, which gives the full range of minutes spent on homework for the week from zero to 120.

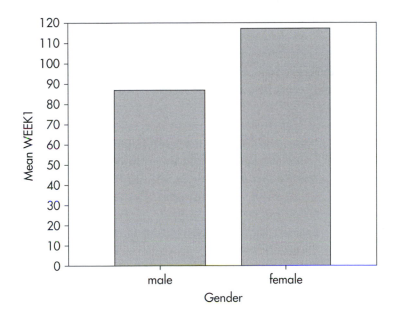

SPSS essential

• The above bar chart still shows the same information as the original one. However, because the axis now shows the full range of minutes, a more accurate reflection of the difference in time spent doing homework between the two genders is portrayed.

Editing graphs (SPSS version 12)

Editing all graphs in SPSS (version 12) follows a similar procedure and we will use the pie chart example in this section.

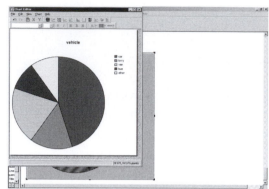

- Double click on the chart to activate the SPSS **Chart Editor**.
- The active window will open on top of the original graph, which will appear greyed out underneath.
- In the **Chart Editor** window click on the segments that you wish to edit.
- With a pie chart a thick blue line highlights each individual segment as well as the legend.
- In our example we want to display the percentage of the whole that each segment accounts for.
- We therefore need to right click and select **Show Data Labels**.
- The following window will appear.

- Select the **Data Value Labels** tab.
- Click on 'Percent' and then the green arrow next to the **Available** box will become active. Click on the arrow to send 'Percent' to the **Contents** box.
- Use the same procedure to send 'vehicle' to the **Contents** box.
- Click on **Apply** and then **Close**.
- Then close the **Chart Editor** window.

The pie chart should now have been updated and, in addition to showing the text labels for the segments, the percentage is now displayed.

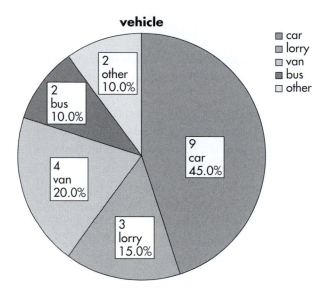

vehicle

- car
- lorry
- van
- bus
- other

2
other
10.0%

2
bus
10.0%

4
van
20.0%

9
car
45.0%

3
lorry
15.0%

✓   Other types of chart can be edited in a similar manner. To make all changes, the **Chart Editor** window must first be active, and then the area of the graph to be changed should be double clicked on, making the amendments as necessary.

Editing axes (SPSS version 12)

Sometimes we may wish to modify the scale selected by SPSS. This can be achieved by changing the increments on the scale. To do this double click on the chart, which will launch the SPSS **Chart Editor**. Click on the scale, the numbers will become highlighted with a blue line. Right click your mouse and select **Properties window** and select the **Scale** tab.

- To change the minimum or maximum values of the scale deselect the **Minimum** or **Maximum Auto** value then enter the required value in the **Custom** box.
- You may also change the increments in a similar manner.
- Select **Apply** and then **Close**.
- Close the **Chart Editor** window to update the SPSS output.

Interactive graphs and gallery

A useful feature of the **Graphs** command is the **Gallery** option, which offers help on the different chart types and gives advice on when to use different graphs for different types of data.

As you become more familiar with SPSS illustrative statistics procedures, you may wish to customise your graphs using the **Interactive** option, which is again found under the **Graphs** drop-down menu. An example of the interactive graph option is shown at the end of Chapter 15.

FAQ

I'm trying to create a bar chart but it does not display the information the way I want it to.

*Make sure that you are using the most appropriate chart for your research design. Remember, if you have an independent measures design (i.e. you have a grouping variable) you need to select **Summaries for groups of cases**; if you have a repeated measures variable you need to select **Summaries of separate variables**. Choosing the wrong option will create a graph which may not display the data in the way you envisioned.*

I've created a graph and have made some changes to the scale. However, now that I have finished editing my graph is still grey.

Check on the task bar at the bottom of the screen that the Chart Editor window isn't still open. Close this and the graph should now be OK.

Working with your dataset

O NCE YOU HAVE ENTERED your data into SPSS and conducted some preliminary analysis you may wish to make changes to your dataset. SPSS has the facility to simply and quickly transform your data into a different format by adding scores together or recoding data into a new variable. You may find that you need to add extra cases or an extra variable, which you want to include in the middle of your dataset. Alternatively, you may want to move some data or change the order of it. The first part of this chapter aims to give you a general introduction to working with your dataset.

Second, SPSS is very versatile at retrieving data and producing outputs for use with other applications. For example, you may have you previously entered data into Microsoft Excel and now want to conduct some analysis in SPSS. This is very simple to achieve. Similarly, once you have completed your analysis, SPSS output tables and graphs can be easily imported into another application such as Microsoft Word.

Transforming your data

The **Transform** drop-down menu offers a variety of commands which allow you to transform your data, such as adding scores together or recoding data into a new variable. We will be describing some of the most common procedures starting with the **Compute** command. This command does exactly what its name says; it enables the user to perform arithmetical operations that usually result in a new variable being produced. For example, you may have collected data from a questionnaire and need to add the scores for all the questions into a 'total' column; this is possible within the **Compute** procedure.

Scenario

A teacher wanted to see whether there was a difference in the amount of time boys and girls spent on homework. He asked ten boys and ten girls aged 9 years to make a note of the number of minutes they spent studying over 2 weeks (as discussed in Chapter 2). We can use this dataset to calculate the mean time that each child spent on their homework across the 2 weeks. We generated these mean times using the **Compute** command in SPSS.

	gender	week1	week2
1	male	45.00	51.00
2	male	56.00	53.00
3	male	67.00	65.00
4	male	123.00	105.00
5	male	89.00	98.00
6	male	99.00	96.00
7	male	115.00	122.00
8	male	136.00	125.00
9	male	102.00	100.00
10	male	39.00	39.00
11	female	124.00	136.00
12	female	99.00	87.00
13	female	135.00	115.00
14	female	145.00	156.00
15	female	89.00	91.00
16	female	97.00	100.00
17	female	112.00	104.00
18	female	85.00	79.00
19	female	156.00	142.00
20	female	130.00	119.00

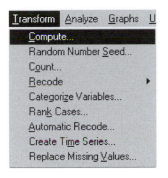

- Click on the **Transform** drop-down menu.
- Select **Compute**. The **Compute Variable** box is then shown.

- We want to create a new variable for our calculated mean. Therefore, in the **Target Variable** box type in a new name for your variable. We have called ours 'wk.1and2'.

✓ Remember the rules for the naming of variables, see Chapter 2 for more details. In our example the name that we have chosen has a full stop. Full stops can be useful in the middle of variable names when we may want to use a hyphen but cannot because of the naming rules. Remember though, you cannot use full stops at the end of variable names.

- We now need to create the numeric expression for whatever **Compute** command we wish to do.
- In our example the expression would be (week1 + week2)/2 in order to generate the mean homework time. We can type this equation in, or alternatively we can send the weeks in the left-hand box to the **Numeric Expression** box and click on the appropriate function keys, i.e. + or /.

✓   More complex expressions can be created using the **If** option in which you can specify case selection.

---

	gender	week1	week2	wk.1and2
1	male	45.00	51.00	48.00
2	male	56.00	53.00	54.50
3	male	67.00	65.00	66.00
4	male	123.00	105.00	114.00
5	male	89.00	98.00	93.50
6	male	99.00	96.00	97.50
7	male	115.00	122.00	118.50
8	male	136.00	125.00	130.50
9	male	102.00	100.00	101.00
10	male	39.00	39.00	39.00
11	female	124.00	136.00	130.00
12	female	99.00	87.00	93.00
13	female	135.00	115.00	125.00
14	female	145.00	156.00	150.50
15	female	89.00	91.00	90.00
16	female	97.00	100.00	98.50
17	female	112.00	104.00	108.00
18	female	85.00	79.00	82.00
19	female	156.00	142.00	149.00
20	female	130.00	119.00	124.50

homework.sav - SPSS Data Editor
File Edit View Data Transform Analyze Graphs Utilities Wi

- Once your numeric expression has been entered, click **OK**.
- A new variable should now have been added to your dataset, with the variable name as specified in the **Compute Variable** box.

Log transformation

There will be occasions when your data doesn't satisfy the assumptions of the test you want to use. A solution to this in certain circumstances is to transform the data. A logarithm transformation will 'squash' your data together and can be used to deal with data that is skewed or has outliers. One problem for a number of tests is that if the standard deviations of the different groups are very different you should not do the test. A log transformation can improve this situation. This is what we shall look at in our example.

A researcher was testing to see if there was a difference in the amount of time it took expert typists and novice typists to type a piece of text.

However, when the researcher found that the standard deviation for the novices was six times larger than that for the experts he realised that this would fail the 'equal variances' assumption required for the *t* test, which he wanted to perform. Therefore, the researcher decided to conduct a log transformation.

This can easily be achieved using the **Compute** command.

	group	minutes
1	Novice	20.00
2	Novice	25.00
3	Novice	36.00
4	Novice	26.00
5	Novice	28.00
6	Novice	23.00
7	Novice	28.00
8	Novice	26.00
9	Expert	9.00
10	Expert	11.00
11	Expert	11.00
12	Expert	10.00
13	Expert	9.00
14	Expert	10.00
15	Expert	10.00
16	Expert	10.00

- Click on the **Transform** drop-down menu.
- Select **Compute**. The **Compute Variable** box is then shown.

- In the **Target Variable** box type the name of our new column. We have called ours 'lnmin'.
- Then from the **Functions** command (which is in alphabetical order) select '**LN(numexpr)**' and send it to the **Numeric Expression** box.
- Send your variable 'minutes' across to the **Numeric Expression** box, this will change the question mark to the variable name; **LN(minutes)**.

Untitled - SPSS Data Editor

File   Edit   View   Data   Transform   Analyze   Graph

3:

	group	minutes	lnmin
1	Novice	20.00	3.00
2	Novice	25.00	3.22
3	Novice	36.00	3.58
4	Novice	26.00	3.26
5	Novice	28.00	3.33
6	Novice	23.00	3.14
7	Novice	28.00	3.33
8	Novice	26.00	3.26
9	Expert	9.00	2.20
10	Expert	11.00	2.40
11	Expert	11.00	2.40
12	Expert	10.00	2.30
13	Expert	9.00	2.20
14	Expert	10.00	2.30
15	Expert	10.00	2.30
16	Expert	10.00	2.30
17			

Now the dataset will display the transformed data and the test can be conducted using this new variable.

The difference in the size of the standard deviation for the novice typists is now only twice as big as the expert on the transformed variable. We are now more confident that a statistical test can be performed more appropriately.

Recoding data

From the homework example previously discussed we have compared our two groups of children (male and female) within our dataset. We are also able to create and compare different groups. For example, the school advice was that each pupil should be studying for an hour per week. Therefore the teacher decided to investigate which students did more than 60 minutes studying a week and who studied less than the recommended amount. To recode the number of hours into two groups the following procedure can be performed.

Transform   Analyze   Graphs   Utilities   Window   Help

Compute...
Random Number Seed...
Count...
Recode   ▶   Into Same Variables...
Categorize Variables...   Into Different Variables...
Rank Cases...   46.00
Automatic Recode...   59.50
Create Time Series...   66.00
Replace Missing Values...   114.00

- Go to the **Transform** drop-down menu and select **Recode**.
- Two options are available. We want to recode **Into Different Variables** as we want to preserve our original individual raw scores, which would be lost if we chose to recode into the same variables.
- The **Recode into Different Variables** box will then appear.

- Send the variable that you wish to change to the **Numeric Variable** box.
- As we are recoding our raw scores into a different variable, our new variable will need to have a name and label assigned to it.

- Click on **Change**. This should replace the question mark following the arrow with our variable 'H.work'.
- Click on **Old and New Values**, here we must specify the boundaries of our groups.

- The default selection is for single values to be recoded. As we are specifying a range of values for each group, select the **Range** option.
- Enter the lowest value in the first box and the highest value for group 1 in the second box. A new value for our first group now needs to be entered.
- Once this is complete click on **Add**. The **Old --> New** box will confirm that scores from 0 to 60 will be recoded into group 1.

As we are only recoding for two groups, all other values of homework time will be in the second group.

- Click on **All other values** and recode them as the value 2.
- Click on **Add**, then **Continue**.
- Then click on **OK**.

Recode into Different Variables: Old and New Values

Old Value
- ○ Value:
- ○ System-missing
- ○ System- or user-missing
- ○ Range:
  [ ] through [ ]
- ○ Range:
  Lowest through [ ]
- ○ Range:
  [ ] through highest
- ● All other values

New Value
- ● Value: [ ]   ○ System-missing
- ○ Copy old value(s)

Old --> New:
```
0 thru 60 --> 1
ELSE --> 2
```
[Add] [Change] [Remove]

☐ Output variables are strings   Width: [8]
☐ Convert numeric strings to numbers (5->5)

[Continue] [Cancel] [Help]

A new column will be added to the end of your dataset which assigns scores to either group 1 or group 2. You now need to go into the **Variable View** window and assign value labels to these numbers as detailed in Chapter 2.

Replacing missing values

There may be a case when you have a couple of missing values in your data and you wish to replace these with the mean of that column. One way that this can be achieved is by first working out the mean of the variable and then re-entering the data into a new column. Alternatively, you can use the **Replace Missing Values** command.

Scenario

A factory manager was concerned about the amount of over-time his employees were working and the effects that this may have on their working practices. Fifteen employees were selected from the workforce and the total number of hours overtime they worked per week were recorded. The number of errors made when using machinery in the same week were also recorded.

However, when making the observations, the number of errors made by worker 10 was missed. We can therefore use the **Replace Missing Values** command to generate a mean score in order to include this in the calculations of our inferential statistics.

	overtime	errors
1	5.00	2.00
2	7.00	1.00
3	8.00	3.00
4	4.00	5.00
5	3.00	3.00
6	.00	5.00
7	2.00	3.00
8	2.00	5.00
9	5.00	7.00
10	5.00	.
11	8.00	3.00
12	8.00	2.00
13	4.00	4.00
14	4.00	2.00
15	3.00	3.00

• Select **Transform** and **Replace Missing Values**.

• Highlight the variable with the missing values in it and send it across to the **New Variable** box. In our case the number of errors variable has a missing value.

• Enter a **Name** for our new variable ('errors_1' is given by default by SPSS).

• The default setting is to generate a mean score for the missing data points from the whole series.

• Click on **OK**.

SPSS then generates a new column with the mean value for the errors produced in the place of any missing scores.

Inserting a variable

You may have entered all your data and decided that you would like to insert a variable in the middle of it. This can be simply achieved.

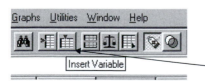

• Left click with your mouse on the column on your data sheet to the right of where you would you would like your variable to be entered.

• Select the **Data** drop-down menu and **Insert Variable**.

• Alternatively click on the **Insert Variable** icon.

> ✓ The new variable is always inserted to the left of the variable that you have selected.

Inserting a case

Also, if you have entered your data but need to add a new case, i.e. all the data for one participant, in the middle of the dataset this can be done at any time. To insert the new case:

- Left click your mouse below the row in which you want your case to appear.
- Go to the **Data** drop-down menu and select **Insert Case**.
- Alternatively click on the **Insert Case** icon.

> ✓ The new case is always inserted above the row that you have selected.

Go to case

With very large datasets if you want to look at more detail at a certain case or row, rather than scroll down the data you are able to go directly to that case.

- Go to the **Data** drop-down menu and select **Go to Case**.
- Alternatively, select the **Goto Case** icon.
- The **Go To Case** box will appear.

- Enter the **Case Number** that you would like to go to.
- Select **OK**.

Go To Case	☒
Case Number [21]	OK

Your cursor will then go to the case or row that you have entered.

Split file command

Sometimes we may wish to compare groups of participants within our dataset in order to generate the descriptive statistics of separate groups for comparison purposes. In our example above we may wish to compare the male and female students' mean time spent on homework across the 2 weeks.

- Go to the **Data** drop-down menu and select **Split File**.
- The **Split File** box will then appear.
- The default setting will be **Analyze all cases, do not create groups**.

- ✓ Two options are available to us, the difference in options refers to the organisation of the output tables.
- ✓ By selecting **Compare groups** results for both males and females will appear on the same output table.
- ✓ By selecting **Organize output by groups** the groups' results will be displayed on two separate tables, one for each group.

In our example we want to compare our two groups of children on their homework times. We have selected **Compare groups**, which allows the results of both groups to be displayed on the same table.

- When one of these options has been selected, the **Groups Based on** box will change from grey to white enabling us to send over the grouping variable with which we want to compare results.
- Once this is complete click on **OK**.

Split File On

You can ensure that your command has been carried out by the **Split File On** confirmation at the bottom right-hand corner of the screen.

✓ The default option is for the dataset to be sorted by the grouping variables. This will rearrange the dataset and place all the people in one group together on the sheet. If your dataset is already arranged like this then no immediate change will be apparent.
✓ If you do not want SPSS to rearrange your dataset according to the grouping variable then select the **File is already sorted** option.

Your dataset is now ready for you to carry out your analysis. The **Split File** command offers you the opportunity to generate a variety of descriptive and illustrative statistics where you can compare the grouping variables (nominal data) that you have selected.

In our example we are going to generate basic descriptive statistics for our variable of mean homework time. Descriptive statistics have been carried out as described in Chapter 3. The output produced by this command when the **Split File** option is activated is shown below.

✓ You do not have to include the grouping variable in the **Descriptive Statistics** command box. The procedure should be carried out as usual and SPSS will automatically know to split the file for the two groups in the final output.

SPSS output

As we can see from the **Descriptive Statistics** table, the means and the standard deviations of the amount of time spent on homework across the two weeks ('wk.1and2') are shown separately for the two groups of children.

Dependent variable (scores)

Descriptive Statistics

Gender		N	Minimum	Maximum	Mean	Std. Deviation
male	WK.1AND2	10	39.00	130.50	86.7500	31.5940
	Valid N (listwise)	10				
female	WK.1AND2	10	82.00	150.50	115.0500	24.3829
	Valid N (listwise)	10				

Independent variable

SPSS essential

- From our example we can see that the female students, with a mean of 115.0500 minutes, are studying for a longer period than the male students with a mean of 86.7500 minutes.
- To find out if these mean scores are significantly different from each other an independent samples *t* test should be performed, see Chapter 7.

However, care must be taken when calculating inferential statistics, which should be carried out on the complete dataset and not on split parts. You must therefore ensure that the **Split File** command is not in operation when performing such tests. Look at the bottom right-hand corner of the screen to check this.

- To unsplit your data go to the **Data** drop-down menu and select **Split File**.
- Select the option for **Analyze all cases, do not create groups**, or click on **Reset**, then click on **OK**.

Weight cases command

If you have a large dataset of frequency counts, rather than entering the raw scores for each individual case, each combination of scores is entered along with the total frequency count for that group. This is achieved by using the **Weight Cases** command. For SPSS to associate the frequency counts with the variables the following procedure should be followed.

Scenario

A researcher wanted to test the difference of opinion between conservatives and liberals on some new taxation legislation. In a survey 120 people were identified as conservatives and 80 as liberals. A question on the survey asked whether the respondent agreed with a new taxation legislation ('for'), disagreed with it ('against'), or had no opinion or did not know about it ('don't know').

The results of the survey are shown below. We can see from the way that this has been entered how many people voted for what party and what their opinions were on the new tax legislation. For example, we can see that 78 conservatives were for the new tax legislation.

• Go to **Data** and **Weight Cases**.

• The variable we want to weight the categories by is 'Frequency', therefore, in the **Weight Cases** window, select the **Weight cases by** option and send the variable Frequency over to the **Frequency Variable** box.

• Click on **OK**.

✓ You can be sure that the procedure has been carried out successfully as a message saying **Weight On** will be displayed in the bottom right-hand corner of the screen.

Importing data from Excel

In some cases datasets may be created in an application other than SPSS, with a view to transferring these to SPSS at a later date. In order to do this a few rules must be followed.

- All data needs to be entered numerically. This will ensure that SPSS can read the data. If data is written in non-numeric forms, this will be recognised by SPSS as string data and the options available for your further analysis will be limited.
- All labelling of values must be done once the data is transferred into SPSS using the **Variable View** window.
- Make the first row of your dataset into the variable names. This will enable you to translate these straight over to become the variable names in the SPSS columns.
- Any variable names that you choose must be compatible with the SPSS rules regarding naming variables. Please see Chapter 2 for further details of these.

Arial		10	**B** *I*
	G29	▼	=

	A	B	C
1	Gender	week1	week2
2	1	45	51
3	1	56	63
4	1	67	65
5	1	123	105
6	1	89	98
7	1	99	96
8	1	115	122
9	1	136	125
10	1	102	100
11	1	39	39
12	2	124	136
13	2	99	87
14	2	135	115
15	2	145	156
16	2	89	91
17	2	97	100
18	2	112	104
19	2	85	79
20	2	156	142
21	2	130	119

In order to transfer data from Excel to SPSS follow the procedure below. Continuing with our previous example of gender and the number of hours children spent doing homework in a week, the data would be entered into Excel as shown here.

- Gender is entered as values 1 and 2 in preparation for its transfer to SPSS.
- The first row in the spreadsheet details the variable names.
- Save this dataset, close it, make a note of where you have saved it and then open SPSS.

- Now we are in our new data entry sheet.
- Go to the **File** drop-down menu and choose **Open Data**.

File	Edit	View	Data	Transform	Analyze	Graphs
New	▶					
Open	▶			Data...		
Open Database	▶			Syntax...		
Read Text Data				Output...		
Save	Ctrl+S			Script...		
Save As				Other...		

Open File

Look in: Data Files

File name:

Files of type: SPSS (*.sav)

SPSS (*.sav)
SPSS/PC+ (*.sys)
Systat (*.syd)
Systat (*.sys)
SPSS portable (*.por)
Excel (*.xls)
Lotus (*.w*)
SYLK (*.slk)
dBase (*.dbf)
Text (*.txt)

Open
Paste
Cancel

- Find the place where your data has been saved.
- Under the section **Files of type** 'SPSS (*.sav)' files will be the default option. This is because SPSS assumes that the file to be opened will be an SPSS file.
- Using the arrow at the side scroll down the file types until you find the file type in which you have saved your work.
- In our example this is an '**Excel (*.xls)**' file.

Once the file type has been selected click on your saved file, which should now be shown in the box above, and click on **Open**. The **Opening Excel Data Source** box will then appear.

Ensure that the **Read variable names from the first row of data** box is selected if you have set up your Excel sheet with the first row being the variable names. The cell ranges to be imported into SPSS are confirmed in the worksheet box. Click on **OK**, and your data should be imported as shown below.

Opening Excel Data Source

C:\WINDOWS\DESKTOP\Data Files\Data.xls

☑ Read variable names from the first row of data.

Worksheet: Sheet1 [A1:C6]

Range:

OK   Cancel   Help

	gender	week1	week2
1	1	45	51
2	1	56	63
3	1	67	65
4	1	123	105
5	1	89	98
6	1	99	96
7	1	115	122
8	1	136	125
9	1	102	100
10	1	39	39
11	2	124	136
12	2	99	87
13	2	135	115
14	2	145	156
15	2	89	91
16	2	97	100
17	2	112	104
18	2	85	79
19	2	156	142
20	2	130	119

- As shown, the variable names have been entered into SPSS as they fitted the rules of naming set up by SPSS.
- As no decimal places were used in the Excel sheet, SPSS has set the dataset to no decimal places.
- Now the data is in SPSS we need to assign value labels to our values in the gender variable column.
- This is done through the **Variable View** window. Details of this can be found in Chapter 2.

Copying and pasting between applications (SPSS versions 11 and earlier)

Once you have carried out all your statistical analysis in SPSS you may need to transfer the output into word-processing packages such as Microsoft Word, particularly any graphs that you have created. To do this follow the procedure below.

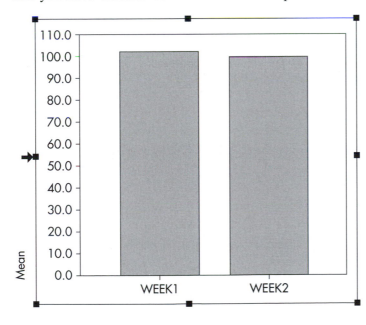

- Click once on the output that you want to copy so that a black square is highlighted.
- Go to the **Edit** drop-down menu and select **Copy Objects**.
- Open your word-processing program document and click on **Paste**.

> ✓ If you want to copy more than one object at once hold down the control key when selecting your objects, which will allow you to highlight more than one thing, then proceed as above.
> ✓ If you want to copy your entire output into a Word document, then choose **Edit** and **Select All** (or **Ctrl** and **A** on the keyboard), and proceed as above.

Copying and pasting between applications (SPSS version 12)

The procedure for copying charts and tables to Microsoft Word using SPSS version 12 is similar to that described above. However, rather than choosing **Copy Objects** when transferring charts, you must select **Copy**. This will ensure that the chart will transfer to Microsoft Word and be visible.

When copying tables, either **Copy** or **Copy Objects** can be used. When using **Copy Objects** the table will appear in the Word document exactly as it appears in the SPSS output. Once transferred to Word using this procedure, the table cannot then be edited. When copying tables using the **Copy** command, the table will appear in Word as it does in the SPSS output, but double clicking on the table once in Word will allow editing. This includes deleting or adding columns and rows, and editing text and titles.

FAQ

I have recently compared two groups in my dataset using the Split File command but now I am ready to carry out an independent t test the output has produced this Warnings table. What should I do?

Warnings

> Independent samples tests are not performed for Gender because this variable is specified both as a grouping variable and as a split variable.
> This command is not executed.
> The Independent Samples table is not produced.

The first thing to check would be that the Split File command is not still active. Check the bottom right-hand corner of the screen for confirmation of this. As a further check, go back into the Split File box and either click on reset, or select the Analyze all cases, do not create groups option.

I have tried to import data created in Excel; the data transfers OK, but the variable names will not import and I have to reassign them once in SPSS. What is going wrong?

Check that the names which you assign to your variables in Excel are compatible with the variable-naming rules stipulated by SPSS. Remember, SPSS will not allow spaces, several keyboard characters, or names with more than eight characters. See Chapter 2 for more details of this.

If you have complied with the rules of naming but SPSS will still not import your names, check that you have selected the option when importing data which will assign the first row of your Excel spreadsheet as the variable names (see page 88).

I have completed my analysis and have transferred my graphs to my report, but I am having problems formatting them as they moved around the page, and do not always reliably copy.

This is likely to be a consequence of using Copy and not Copy Objects. When transferring tables and graphs between applications, we advise that you use Copy Objects and then paste into your Word document as this will lead to fewer formatting problems.

Chapter 6

Introduction to statistical tests

ONCE WE HAVE TYPED our data into SPSS and produced descriptive statistics we usually wish to analyse the data to test certain hypotheses. For example, we may have input the data from a questionnaire about stress at work. Now we wish to test whether people in customer relations posts are more stressed than people in technical posts. In addition, we may wish to look at the relationship between levels of stress and work performance. Therefore we need to know which statistical tests to undertake.

Different statistical tests

We need to be aware of which type of statistical test we wish to perform on our data. A number of statistical tests will examine *differences* between samples: they will compare samples to infer whether the samples come from the same population or not (e.g. *t* tests). Other tests examine the *association* between samples, such as a *correlation* (e.g. Pearson's correlation) or tests of *independence* (as in the chi-square test). Before we look at the specific tests it is worth considering how the tests of statistical significance have been constructed.

Introduction to parametric tests: the logic of significance testing

The following gives a brief description of the logic of significance testing. It is clearly not presented as a full account (which can be obtained from the many statistics textbooks that are available, e.g. Hinton, 2004) but as an introduction (or reminder) of the background to the tests that can be undertaken with SPSS.

While there are a number of different statistical tests available there is a common logic to significance testing, particularly for tests comparing samples. The following example shows the logic of a one-tailed test. The explanation includes the reason why it is called a one-tailed test.

In performing a significance test we calculate the value of a particular statistic (t, F, r, etc.) based on our samples. For a given sample size, and making certain assumptions, statisticians have worked out for us the distribution of the statistic if the samples were drawn from the same population. This is the distribution of the statistic when the null hypothesis is true. This is called Distribution A in Figure 6.1. When we calculate the value of the statistic for our samples we have to decide if it belongs to Distribution A, or to a second distribution (Distribution B). The statistic belongs to Distribution B when the

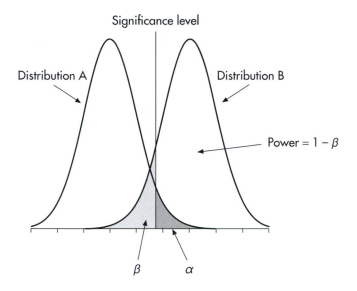

FIGURE 6.1 A one-tailed statistical test

samples come from different populations (and the null hypothesis is false). To make this decision we choose a cut-off point on the scale (called the significance level). This is shown by the vertical line in Figure 6.1.

If the calculated value of the statistic falls to the left of the significance level in Figure 6.1 then we say that we cannot reject the null hypothesis and claim that the value belongs to Distribution A. If the value of the statistic falls to the right of the significance level in Figure 6.1, then we reject the null hypothesis and claim that the value belongs to Distribution B. As the distributions overlap we cannot select a significance level that separates them completely. This means that sometimes we will claim that the statistic belongs to one distribution when it really belongs to the other. Conventionally, we choose the significance level so that the value of $\alpha = 0.05$. This places 95 per cent of Distribution A to the left of the significance level, with only 5 per cent of Distribution A the 'wrong' side of the line. This sets up the risk of making a Type I error, claiming a difference when there is not one, at a probability of 0.05 ($p = 0.05$). This gives us a risk of only 5 in 100 of falsely claiming a statistically significant result.

Having set the significance level using Distribution A, we can see that this leaves parts of Distribution B on either side of the significance level. This means that we can also make a Type II error, claiming no difference when there really is a difference in the populations the samples come from. The probability of making a Type II error is shown by β on Figure 6.1. If the value of our statistic belongs to Distribution B but lies within the area marked by β we will mistakenly claim it comes from Distribution A as the value is to the left of the significance level.

The above example is known as a one-tailed test as we make our decision about the significance of our statistic at only one end, or tail, of Distribution A. With a two-tailed test we argue that a difference could arise when the value of our statistic comes from either Distribution B, which overlaps the upper end of Distribution A, or from a third distribution, Distribution C, which overlaps the lower end of Distribution A. This is shown in Figure 6.2. In this case we have to set a significance level at both tails of Distribution A. To give an overall value of $\alpha = 0.05$, the size of each of the tails of Distribution A cut off by the significance level is set at 0.025.

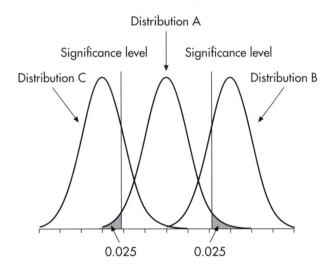

FIGURE 6.2 A two-tailed statistical test

If we return to Figure 6.1 we can see that, if the whole area under a distribution curve is set to 1, then the amount of Distribution B to the right of the significance level is $1 - \beta$. This is the probability of claiming a statistically significant difference between our samples when there really is one. Here we are making a correct claim of statistical significance. This is referred to as the *power* of the statistical test. It follows from the above logic that a one-tailed test is more powerful than a two-tailed test. Furthermore, we can see that a statistical test with very low power is unlikely to detect statistical significance even when the samples come from different populations. This is because β will be large and most of Distribution B will be the 'wrong' side of the significance level.

The conventional level of significance is specified as $p = 0.05$ (which sets the risk of falsely rejecting the null hypothesis at 5 per cent, or 1 in 20). So when the calculated value of a statistic has a probability of less than 0.05 we write this as $p < 0.05$. Other significance levels may be chosen to indicate that a value is highly significant. So we sometimes employ the $p = 0.01$ or even $p = 0.001$ levels of significance. When a result has a probability less than these values we write the finding as $p < 0.01$ or $p < 0.001$, as appropriate.

Things to consider before analysing your data

The above logic of significance testing requires us to make certain assumptions about our data. The reason for this is that we use information from our samples to estimate population values (called *parameters*). For example, we will use sample means and standard deviations to estimate the mean and standard deviation of the population the samples are drawn from. Thus a number of tests are referred to as *parametric tests*. In order to undertake parametric tests appropriately there are a few things we need to consider.

Is your sample unbiased?

Essentially this means that the sample properly represents the population. Normally, we argue that the sample should be randomly selected from the population. If the sample is biased then the sample values will not be good estimators of the population values.

What measurement scale is your data?

Parametric tests require *interval* data – where the consecutive numbers on the measuring scale are at equal intervals. (Interval data measured on a scale with a genuine zero is called *ratio* data. Speed is an example of ratio data as zero means no speed at all. Temperature scales are interval but not ratio as zero on the scale does not mean no temperature.) We are also assuming the scales are continuous: that is, there are no gaps or breaks within them. For example, time, distance and temperature are all interval scales. Without interval data we cannot meaningfully calculate statistics such as the mean and standard deviation using the raw scores.

Are the scores from each sample drawn from normally distributed populations?

A number of our statistical tests require us to make this inference. The statistical test assumes it to be the case and if it is not then the result may underestimate or overestimate the value of the statistic. This can be checked by plotting your data on a histogram or boxplot (See Chapter 4) or by more precisely by conducting a one sample Kolmogorov–Smirnov test (see Chapter 3) which statistically tests the normality of the data.

Do the data meet the homogeneity of variances assumption?

For the tests to operate appropriately we are assuming that any manipulation we perform (such as the effect of noise on performance) affects each member of the population to the same extent and so does not affect the overall spread (*variance*) or shape of the distribution of the population scores. Therefore the population variances should be the same, and our samples should have similar variances as we use these to estimate their population values. Sometimes this gets quite complex for repeated measures elements, see Chapter 9 for more details.

You may wish to consider using a nonparametric test if you have concerns about your data, for example if you have

- ordinal data where the scores provide an order but the scale does not have equal intervals, such as a rating scale, or
- the scale is not continuous, or
- data that is not normally distributed, or
- data that violates the homogeneity of variances assumption.

An example of a nonparametric test is the Mann–Whitney *U* test, a nonparametric equivalent of the independent *t* test.

We would normally prefer to conduct a parametric test as this type of analysis is more powerful and uses the actual scores; whereas nonparametric tests make fewer assumptions about the data but usually perform an analysis on the ranking of the scores rather than on the scores themselves.

Concerns about significance testing

You might wonder why a book explaining how you can perform significance tests using SPSS would want to give reasons for not undertaking them! We are not doing this. If you look at journal articles in any area of the social sciences you will see the results of significance tests in most of them. So we are not saying 'don't perform significance tests'. What we are saying is 'be aware of their limitations'.

There has been a debate in the literature about statistical significance tests. It has been argued that tests of significance are not always the best way to make inferences from your data. There is also a concern that statistical significance is not the most important thing to report in explaining research data. Consider two studies with almost identical data. A *t* test is performed on both datasets. In the first case the calculated *t* value has a probability of 0.049 (of occurring when the null hypothesis is true). Here we say the result is statistically significant as the probability is less than the significance level of 0.05. In the second study the *t* value has a probability of 0.051. Here we say the result is not statistically significant as the probability is greater than 0.05. Even though the datasets are almost identical we are making opposite conclusions. So reporting 'significant' or 'not significant' is a problem here.

One answer is to report the actual probability values, rather than only saying a result is or is not statistically significant. In this way the reader can compare the probability value to the significance level. In fact, SPSS gives you the probability value rather than the significance level. Even though it often heads a column in a table with the term 'sig. level' it presents the actual probability, such as $p = 0.028$, rather than reporting $p < 0.05$. We recommend that you report the probability in terms of the significance level, for example, $p < 0.05$ or $p > 0.05$. (There may be cases when the values are close to significance, for example $p = 0.049$, where you wish to indicate this in your report, so for these particular cases you may wish to include the actual probability value as well as its significance.)

✓ You will notice that sometimes SPSS gives a probability value of $p = 0.000$. Actually the probability value cannot be zero. This value means a p value has been rounded down to three decimal places. As we must not wrongly report a p value of 0.000 we can change the last zero to a one and state that $p < 0.001$.

✓ Alternatively, you can obtain the actual p value by clicking once on the table, place the mouse over the 0.000 and then double click to obtain the actual probability value. However, reporting that $p < 0.001$ is usually sufficient.

Confidence intervals

An alternative to giving the statistical significance of a finding is to report confidence intervals as these may provide a more appropriate conclusion to the analysis. A confidence interval (CI) defines a range of values within which we are confident (with a certain probability) that our population value lies: for example, if we have a sample we can work out the confidence interval of the mean. This is an estimate of the population mean. With a mean of 4.00, our confidence interval might be 3.50 to 4.50 with $p = 0.95$. This tells us that, for 95 out of 100 samples, the confidence interval contains the population mean. So we can use this as an estimate of the population mean. One way of reporting this value is as follows:

Mean = 4.00 (95%CI: 3.50 to 4.50)

or   95% CI of the mean = 4.00 ± 0.5

Remember, significance testing is all about estimating population values and a confidence interval is a different way of doing this. Clearly, a narrow confidence interval provides a better estimate of the population mean than a wide one.

In a difference test, such as the *t* test, the difference in sample means is an important statistic. So SPSS prints out the confidence interval of the difference in sample means, and this gives you an estimate of the difference in population values. Consider a paired samples *t* test with a difference in means of +3.00. The calculated *t* value (of 1.588, $df = 19$, $p = 0.129$, two-tailed test) is not significant at the 0.05 level of significance. The confidence interval of this difference in means, +3.00 (95%CI: −0.954 to 6.954), indicates that the difference in means for the populations could be nearly as high as +7 but might be nearly as low as −1, so we cannot reject the possibility that it might be zero. Therefore, the confidence interval finding supports the results of the significance test.

✓ It is always a good idea to look at the confidence intervals in your SPSS output as well as checking the statistical significance of your results. Many of the SPSS outputs will include confidence intervals as part of the results table.

✓ You can produce the confidence interval of a mean for a data set by using the **Analyze** command. Select **Descriptive Statistics** and then **Explore**. Send the variable across to the **Dependent List** and the confidence interval of the mean will be reported (along with other useful descriptive statistics).

✓ An error bar chart can be produced to display the sample mean and confidence intervals. See Chapter 4 for the procedure.

Power

A second concern arises when we produce a statistic with a probability greater than the significance level, for example $p > 0.05$. In response to this, it is often reported that we 'accept the null hypothesis', indicating that our samples come from the same population. However, this is not true. The failure to achieve statistical significance may arise for a number of reasons. Our test may be so lacking in power that we are unlikely to find statistical significance even when our samples come from different populations. We may have too few participants in the study, which will reduce the power of the test. Alternatively, we may be looking for a very small effect and our analysis is unable to detect it.

Some of these problems can be made clear by an analogy. Imagine digging for treasure on a small deserted island. There are two possibilities: either the treasure is there or it is not. However, you are only able to make a judgement about whether the treasure is there or not based on the result of your dig. Even if you find nothing after a set time digging, it doesn't mean the treasure is not there. It simply means that you have not found it.

Consider digging on the island for an afternoon with a bucket and spade. If you find a treasure chest then that's great (and very lucky). But if you don't find anything then it might be that the equipment is not adequate for the job. Now contrast this with using a mechanical excavator that can shift tonnes of earth in an afternoon. Here the chances of finding the treasure chest are much greater. And if you don't find it you can be more confident (but not certain) that the treasure is not there. In our statistics tests this is a difference of power. Many researchers undertake statistical tests without checking the power of their tests in advance which may simply not be up to the job. As a rule of thumb a test that has a power of $1 - \beta = 0.8$ is seen as a test of high power, 0.5 as medium power and 0.2 as low power. Unfortunately, SPSS cannot work out the power of your test before you perform it (see the SPSS advanced box below) but SPSS does allow you, in a few tests, to report the power of your test or the effect size, *post hoc* (at the end of the analysis).

Power is influenced by both sample size and effect size. Taking our treasure hunting analogy once more, if we have lots of people digging then we have a greater chance of finding the treasure than when we only have a few. So, the larger the sample size the more powerful the test. Also the larger the effect size (for example the difference between the population means) the more likely we are to find it. If the treasure chest is the size of a matchbox we might not detect it even with our mechanical excavator. However, if it is the size of a house we are much more likely to find it.

Finally, ask yourself the question 'Am I on the right island?' It does not matter how many people and mechanical excavators you have if you are on the wrong island. It doesn't matter how powerful your statistical test if you are asking the wrong research question. In research we need to know if we are asking the right questions, testing the appropriate hypotheses. There may be little point in digging on an island you selected on a whim if the treasure map identifies a different island! Know something about the topic you are researching. Read about the effects other researchers have found and develop an understanding of what to expect in research on this topic. Remember, it is your treasure map and it will guide you on what equipment to use on your dig.

SPSS advanced

Unfortunately, SPSS does not conduct a power analysis in advance of your statistical analysis as part of the package. However, there are programs available that can do this for you. It only takes a few moments to undertake the power analysis and the outcome tells you what sample size you need for the test you want to do.

- You set the power of your test. You may choose a high power (0.8) if you want to increase the chances of finding an effect, if it is there.
- You set your significance level (α). Are you going to test significance at $p = 0.01$, which reduces the risk of a Type I error but also reduces the power, or at a conventional $p = 0.05$?
- You select the test you intend to perform, for example independent measures t test.
- You must estimate the size of the effect you are looking for. Past studies in the literature, or even a pilot study, can provide this information, forcing you to learn about the scores to expect in a study on your topic.
- You can set the sample size for the power you want. The outcome of a power analysis will tell you how many participants you need in the samples to achieve this level of power. This is very helpful information as it not only stops you from selecting too few participants but also too many. Often there is the belief that 'the more the merrier' in statistical analysis but you only really need a large enough sample size to do the job. On our desert island we do not want so many excavators that they cannot move – we just need an optimum number for the size of the island. More will be a waste of time and resources.

Conclusion: advice on significance testing

Even though we have explained the concerns about significance testing above, we now wish to move on to undertake these tests. Significance testing provides us with statistically very useful information but we can be a little more sophisticated in interpreting our results if we acknowledge the concerns listed above. So we offer some advice on interpreting the results of our significance tests by taking account of these concerns.

A statistically significant result

When the result of our test is statistically significant we reject the null hypothesis. We claim the sample differences are large enough to indicate differences in the populations we are examining or that the level of association indicates an association in the populations.

However, we can be a little more sophisticated and consider the risks of Type I and Type II errors for a moment and, before making too much of your claim, you can consider several things.

- What is the actual probability value you have produced? How significant is your probability value? What size of effect has been found by other studies on this topic?

The finding may be statistically significant but is it important? Is this effect large or small according to the literature on this topic?

- SPSS usually provides us with confidence intervals with our significance tests. This gives us an estimate of the population values. Examine these values to see the estimated range.
- Imagine you found a difference in your sample of 6 and the confidence intervals went from 5 to 7, this means that we are 95 per cent confident that the population value lies between the upper and lower limits, so in the worst case scenario our difference would still be 5 which could still be a big difference.
- If the range was large, for example, between 0.5 and 6.5, and our value is 3.5, you would be less sure as to where the true population value lies, as it could be anywhere between these limits. Indeed, there is the possibility that the population value is as low as 0.5, and though the test result may be significant this difference may not be of any practical worth.

A statistically non-significant result

When the findings are non-significant (for example $p > 0.05$), we report that we have not found evidence to indicate a difference (or association) in the populations. This is usually referred to as 'accepting the null hypothesis'.

We can consider the result a little more carefully. We do not want to make a Type II error. Remember our treasure-hunting example: just because we have not found the treasure does not mean that it is not there. So when we get a non-significant result consider two things.

- Did we perform a powerful enough test to find an effect? Were we looking for a big enough effect? Did we have enough participants to make it a powerful enough test? In the analysis of variance SPSS allows you to check the effect size and the power of your test after you have performed it.
- Look at your confidence interval to see if it supports the results of the significance test. In a t test we would expect the confidence interval to be around the zero value for a non-significant finding.

FAQ

On my output table my significance level is 0.000 and I have a two-tailed hypothesis, so I have to divide that value by two, surely the answer will still be 0.000?

It is important to remember that the p value is never 0.000. SPSS rounds the value to three decimal places, for example the actual p value could have been 0.0002. Whether you have a one- or two-tailed hypothesis and SPSS displays a p value of 0.000 you will always need to change the last zero to a one, so that $p < 0.001$.

I have been told to report my p value, but I can't find it on my output table.

The p value is the probability value which is called the significance level. On your output tables always look for the Sig (1-tailed) or Sig (2-tailed) values.

In my statistics class we calculate the value by hand and then check the back of our statistics book where we compare the obtained value with the critical value to see if it is significant or not. I have carried out a statistical test in SPSS and can't seem to find the critical value.

When you perform your inferential statistics with SPSS, it shows the actual probability value, and you then need to decide yourself if the test has produced a significant result (i.e. is your probability less than 0.05 – the conventional 5% significance level). For example, if SPSS shows a probability value of 0.03, we can conclude that this value is statistically significant as $p < 0.05$.

I have a p value of 0.06 in my SPSS output. Surely I must accept the null hypothesis?

You can not reject the null hypothesis at the 0.05 level of significance. However, consider the power of your test. Power is influenced by the size of effect you are looking for and the number of participants you are using. You may have too few participants for the effect you are looking for.

Further details of the logic of hypothesis testing can be found in Chapter 4 of Hinton (2004), with a discussion of 'power' in Chapter 9.

Chapter 7

t tests

$\mathbf{T}$HE t TEST IS ONE OF THE MOST popular tests for comparing two samples. There are many situations where we want to see whether an experimental manipulation has an effect or not: does a new reading scheme improve children's reading? Does a new work practice in a factory improve output? In these cases we are comparing a *control group*, who perform the task in the usual way, with an *experimental group*, who perform the task under the same conditions as the control group with one exception, our experimental manipulation (i.e. the new teaching scheme or the new work practice). If the two groups perform differently then we can attribute the difference to the effect of our manipulation.

We are often comparing two groups: do men and women differ on a particular task? Is a task performed more accurately in the morning than the afternoon? Here again we are comparing two samples to see whether a difference arises from our experimental manipulation: does *gender* (men versus women) affect performance on the task? Does *time of day* (morning versus afternoon) affect accuracy of performance on the task? In all these cases the t test allows us to see whether there is a difference between the performances of the two groups.

We do need to be careful that we have undertaken the study appropriately because the t test is simply a statistical technique and won't tell us when we have made a mistake. For example, the t test will tell us whether there is a difference in the performances of the two groups but not what caused the difference. If you set up the study so that the only difference between the groups is your experimental manipulation then you can be confident that this caused the difference in performance. However, if you designed it poorly and the groups differ in a number of ways you will not know which of these differences is responsible for any differences in the performance. We need to make sure that the groups are selected so that the only difference between them is the one we are interested in (the experimental manipulation) and there are no other *confounding* variables. Also, there are a number of assumptions underlying the t test and we need to make sure that our data satisfies these assumptions otherwise the result may not be meaningful.

The t test relies on a number of assumptions as it is a parametric test.

- The samples are randomly and independently chosen from their populations. This is important as the t test uses the samples to estimate details of the populations they come from (such as the population mean and variance, referred to as *parameters*) and if the samples are selected in a biased way it will affect the accuracy of the estimations.

- The data collected must be interval or ratio, from continuous distributions and normally distributed populations. There is some debate as to the importance of these assumptions but they do underlie the logic of the test. As long as the distributions are approximately normal the results may still be meaningful, particularly for large samples (over 30), so you can go ahead with the test. However, gross violations of this assumption can lead to meaningless results.

- The data from the two samples come from populations with equal variances (the *homogeneity of variance assumption*). The *t* test uses this assumption in its calculation by 'pooling' the variances of the two samples to estimate the (equal) population variance. If the assumption is invalid the calculation is not meaningful. But, as the *t* test is 'robust', it is still likely to make sense even when the variances differ somewhat (for small samples, say 10, even with one sample variance up to three times the other, the *t* test may still be interpreted correctly). So, usually, we report the *t* test result for assumed equal variances, but large differences in the sample variances should not be ignored. In many studies we are assuming that our manipulation has a constant effect and so the sample variances should be the same. Our advice is, when you find unequal variances, if you can understand why the variances might differ and it makes sense to continue with the *t* test, then choose the result of the test where equal variances are not assumed.

Essentially the *t* test compares two results. The first is the difference between the mean scores of the two samples. The second is an estimate of what it would expect the difference in means to be when the null hypothesis is true. If the difference in means is not bigger than the expected difference then we cannot reject the null hypothesis: we have not found evidence that our experimental manipulation is having an effect. If the difference in means is larger than the expected difference then we can see whether it is large enough to reject the null hypothesis and claim that our experimental manipulation is having a statistically significant effect.

Independent samples *t* test

The independent samples *t* test is undertaken when the samples are unrelated, with different participants in each sample, such as the daytime and night-time driving tasks discussed below. This test is also called the unrelated *t* test or the independent measures *t* test. (With related samples, such as the same group of participants tested at two different times of the day, the paired samples *t* test should be used.)

Scenario

A driving simulator was used to investigate the number of errors made during daytime and night-time driving tasks. It was predicted that more errors would be made on the night-time test. The number of errors performed was calculated for each person.

Data entry

Enter the dataset as shown in the example. For independent samples we have to input a grouping variable to indicate which sample a score comes from. In this case we have included a variable named 'driving', and have given the night drivers a value label of '1' and the day drivers a value label of '2'. The number of errors on a driving simulator is input into a variable we have labelled 'errors'. So row 1 shows a night driver who made nine errors and row 7 shows a day driver who made eight errors.

| driving independent t-test - SPSS |
| File Edit View Data Transform An |

	driving	errors
1	night	9
2	night	10
3	night	8
4	night	9
5	night	9
6	night	7
7	day	8
8	day	7
9	day	5
10	day	6
11	day	5
12	day	4
13	day	5
14	day	6
15		

✓ See Chapter 2 for the full data entry procedure.
✓ To see the value labels go to the **View** drop-down menu and select **Value Labels**.

✓ *Random allocation of groups* should be addressed when calculating an independent *t* test. In order to ensure this, the independent variable must allow such random allocation. In the above example, the participants are randomly allocated to either a day or a night driving condition.

Test procedure

- The aim is to carry out an independent samples *t* test. All inferential statistical tests are found under the **Analyze** command.
- The rationale of the *t* test is to test for significant differences in the means of two samples, therefore choose **Compare Means**.
- Our study is an independent measures design (comparing night-time and daytime driving), therefore choose **Independent-Samples T Test**.

- The *dependent variable* is 'errors' and this should be sent to the **Test Variable** box.
- The *independent variable* is 'driving' and this should be sent to the **Grouping Variable** box.
- Once 'driving' is in the **Grouping Variable** box we are prompted to **Define Groups**.

- The values which were assigned to day and night driving in the data entry procedure need to be input in the **Define Groups** box.
- To complete the test, click on **Continue** and then **OK**.

SPSS output

The first table that SPSS produces is the descriptive statistics, or **Group Statistics**, table.

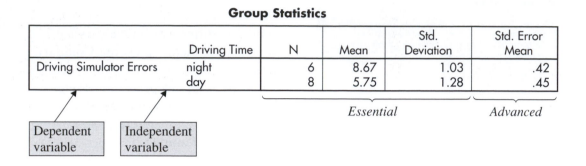

Group Statistics

	Driving Time	N	Mean	Std. Deviation	Std. Error Mean
Driving Simulator Errors	night	6	8.67	1.03	.42
	day	8	5.75	1.28	.45

Essential   *Advanced*

Dependent variable   Independent variable

SPSS essential

*   Number of participants (**N**) will be included in your descriptive statistics results.
*   By observing the **Means** it can be seen that night driving produced more errors on the driving simulator but this difference may not be significant. To ascertain if this result is significant or due to chance the **Independent Samples Test** table must be examined.
*   The **Std. Deviation** shows that the night-driving participants have a wider spread of scores than the day-driving group.

SPSS advanced

*   The **Std. Error Mean** is an estimate of the standard deviation of the sampling distribution of the mean based on the sample we tested. That is, it is the standard distance, or error, that a sample mean is from the population mean.
*   The standard error of the mean is a useful figure as it is used in the computation of confidence intervals and significance tests, such as the *t* test.
*   In our example the standard error of the mean shows that if we had obtained all the means of every sample of six night-driving participants and analysed them, we estimate that the standard deviation of those means would be 0.42. Similarly, if we took all samples of eight day drivers we estimate the standard deviation of the means would be 0.45.

The **Independent Samples Test** table displays the inferential statistics.

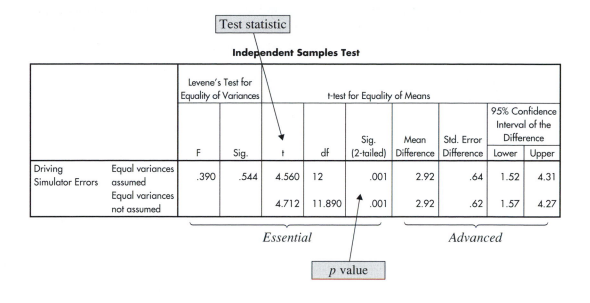

Test statistic

Independent Samples Test

		Levene's Test for Equality of Variances		t-test for Equality of Means						
									95% Confidence Interval of the Difference	
		F	Sig.	t	df	Sig. (2-tailed)	Mean Difference	Std. Error Difference	Lower	Upper
Driving Simulator Errors	Equal variances assumed	.390	.544	4.560	12	.001	2.92	.64	1.52	4.31
	Equal variances not assumed			4.712	11.890	.001	2.92	.62	1.57	4.27

Essential   *Advanced*

p value

✓   The *p* value in an **Independent Samples Test** table is for a two-tailed hypothesis shown in the column '**Sig. (2-tailed)**'. If your hypothesis is one-tailed divide this figure by two.

SPSS essential

- It can be seen from the above table that two lines of values are generated by SPSS; **Levene's Test for Equality of Variances** indicates which should be used. One of the criteria for using a parametric *t* test is the assumption that both populations have equal variances. If the test statistic *F* is significant, Levene's test has found that the two variances do differ significantly, in which case we must use the bottom values. In the example above it can be seen that $F = 0.390$, $p > 0.05$, therefore, as the variances are not significantly different, we can accept the equal variances assumption and use the top line values.

✓ If Levene's test statistic is significant it is a matter of academic judgement whether we accept the values on the bottom line, or whether we take this violation of the parametric test assumptions as a justification to do the nonparametric Mann–Whitney U test instead. If you do find an unexpected violation of the homogeneity of variance assumption (i.e. other studies of this type in your field have not found it), then be careful in interpreting the results of your study, and if you do report a t value, make sure it is the '**Equal variances not assumed**' value in the SPSS table.

- For our two-tailed hypothesis the conventional way of reporting the findings is to state the test statistic (t) with the degrees of freedom in brackets after it and the probability of this value at our chosen significance level (p). An example can be seen below. If we calculate $t = 4.560$ with 12 degrees of freedom and a probability of 0.001 we would report this as $t(12) = 4.560$, $p < 0.001$.
- In our test we predicted that more driving errors would be made on the night-time test, which is a one-tailed hypothesis. For a two-tailed hypothesis you state that there will be difference between the means but you do not predict the direction of the difference. If you make a one-tailed prediction you need to divide the '**Sig. (2-tailed)**' (p value) in half. If there is a significant difference between the means you need to ascertain if the means are showing the difference in the direction you predicted. In our example we need to make sure that the mean error score for the night drivers is in fact bigger than for day drivers.

  Our hypothesis is one-tailed, as we are predicting a direction of the difference in means (the daytime will be better), which would make our p value $= \dfrac{0.001}{2} = 0.0005$.

  As our probability of 0.0005 is smaller than our significance level of 0.001, we use the less than sign ($<$) to indicate that our result is significant at the 0.001 significance level.

✓ Don't be concerned if you have a negative t value for a two-tailed hypothesis. Whether it is positive or negative is dependent on which group's scores were entered into the t test equation first. We entered the night driving errors first which were the larger values so our t value was positive.

SPSS advanced

- The **Mean Difference** is the difference between the means of our two groups.
- Imagine that the null hypothesis is true, then the real difference in populations means is zero. If we selected all samples of size 6 and size 8 and worked out the difference in their means we could find out what the differences in means would be by chance alone. The **Std. Error Difference** estimates the standard deviation of all the differences in sample means when the null hypothesis is true. This indicates the difference in the means we would expect by chance if the null hypothesis is true. In our case the standard error difference is estimated to be 0.64. The *t* test compares the difference in our means with the standard error difference:

$$t = \frac{\text{Mean Difference}}{\text{Standard Error Difference}}$$

- As our difference in means of 2.92 is 4.5625 times bigger than the standard error of the difference, then our mean difference is large enough to be significant at the $p < 0.001$ level.
- The **95% Confidence Interval of the Difference** indicates that we are 95 per cent confident that the true population mean difference will be between the upper and lower limits.
- The *t* test tells us whether our difference is significant or not. However, the confidence interval provides us with more information about the size of the difference.
- The confidence interval provides us with an estimate of the real difference in the population. By observing our output we can see that the lower limit is 1.52 and the upper limit is 4.31, which indicates that we can be confident that the true population mean difference falls between these two values. Therefore, in the worst case scenario, the night drivers are still making 1.5 more errors than the day drivers, which is still an important difference.

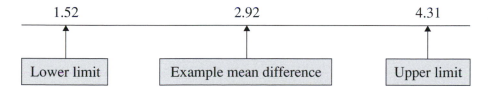

- Confidence intervals are often used as a supplementary or alternative indicator of statistical significance. Here is an example of how this could be reported:

   Difference in means = 2.92 (95%CI: 1.52 to 4.31).

> ✓ The default confidence interval given by SPSS is 95 per cent. This can be manipulated by going into the **Options** command in the *t* test procedure and selecting the required level.
> ✓ An appropriate illustrative statistic for an independent samples *t* test is a bar chart. See Chapter 4.
> ✓ To illustrate the confidence intervals for each sample mean an error bar graph can be produced. See Chapter 4.

The paired samples *t* test

The paired samples *t* test is undertaken when the samples are related, usually with the same participants in each sample. This test is also called the related *t* test or the repeated measures *t* test. (With unrelated samples, such as *men* and *women*, the independent samples *t* test should be used.)

Scenario

A teacher wondered if the children in her class worked better in the morning or in the afternoon. She decided to test this out by using a mathematics test as this required the children to concentrate. She chose a random sample of eight children from the class and gave them two tests matched on their difficulty. The test gave a score out of ten, the higher the score the better the performance.

> ✓ *Counterbalancing* should be applied to paired sample tests. For the scenario above the samples were balanced on the two versions of the test, with half the children being tested in the morning first and half tested in the afternoon first, to control for carry-over effects. Remember that this is not shown in the dataset in SPSS, but it is assumed that the samples are unbiased.

Data entry

Enter the dataset as shown in the example. We have named the samples 'am' and 'pm' with the labels 'Morning' and 'Afternoon'.

> ✓ If you do not want to show any decimal places change the decimal places to zero in the **Variable View**. See Chapter 2 for the full data entry procedure.

Untitled - SPSS Data Editor

File Edit View Data Transform A

9 : pm

	am	pm
1	6	5
2	4	2
3	3	4
4	5	4
5	7	3
6	6	4
7	5	5
8	6	3

Test procedure

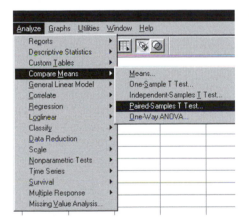

- The aim is to carry out a paired samples *t* test. All inferential statistical tests are found under the **Analyze** command.
- The rationale of the *t* test is to look for significant differences between the means of two samples, therefore choose **Compare Means**.
- The design of our study is repeated measures (comparing the scores of one group of participants over two conditions) therefore choose **Paired-Samples T Test**.

- Highlight the two variables and send them to the **Paired Variables** box.
- Both variables will now appear on the same line.
- To complete the test click **OK**.

Paired-Samples T Test

Morning [am]
Afternoon [pm]

Paired Variables:
am -- pm

OK
Paste
Reset
Cancel
Help

Current Selections
Variable 1:
Variable 2:

Options...

✓ If SPSS does not allow you to select both variables at the same time, click on one variable first, release the mouse button and then click on the second variable. Both variables should now be visible in the **Current Selections** box and SPSS will now allow them to be sent to the **Paired Variables** box. The reason SPSS will only allow the variables to be sent across in pairs is because there may be more than two variables to choose from and it allows you to run multiple paired samples tests, ensuring SPSS knows which variables to pair together.

✓ If you want to carry out more than one *t* test at once, several other combinations of pairs can be sent over at this point.

✓ It can often be difficult to select two variables that are not next to each other. Click on one variable, hold down the **Ctrl** key and then click on the other variable.

SPSS output

The first table that SPSS produces is the **Paired Samples Statistics** table detailing the descriptive statistics.

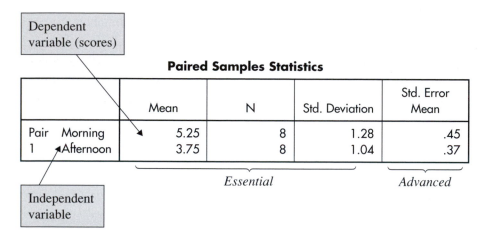

Paired Samples Statistics

		Mean	N	Std. Deviation	Std. Error Mean
Pair 1	Morning	5.25	8	1.28	.45
	Afternoon	3.75	8	1.04	.37

Dependent variable (scores)

Independent variable

Essential   *Advanced*

SPSS essential

• The number of participants (**N**) will be included in your descriptive statistics results. You can check you have input the correct number of scores.

• By observing the **Means** it can be seen that when the children took the mathematics test in the morning they got more questions correct (5.25) than when a similar test was taken in the afternoon (3.75). These differences seem to be supporting our hypothesis, but to ascertain whether this result is significant or due to chance the **Paired Samples Test** table must be examined.

- The **Std. Deviation** shows that the spread of scores in the morning is slightly larger than that in the afternoon.

SPSS advanced

- The **Std. Error Mean** is an estimate of the standard deviation of the sampling distribution of the mean. A small value tells us that we would expect a similar mean if we did the test again but a large value indicates a lot of variability predicted in the means. If we were able to test all samples of size $N = 8$ in the morning and plot their means we estimate the distribution would have a standard deviation of 0.45, and for samples of size $N = 8$ tested in the afternoon we estimate the distribution of the means would have a standard deviation of 0.37.
- The standard error of the mean is a useful figure as it is used in the computation of significance tests comparing means, such as the *t* test, and in the calculation of confidence intervals.

There is no *SPSS essentials* section for the **Paired Samples Correlations** table as it is usual to calculate a paired samples *t* test without performing a correlation so this section is *SPSS advanced* only. Indeed, the results of a *t* test are almost always reported without any details of the correlation. So, for most academic disciplines, it is perfectly acceptable to ignore this part of the output and move on to the *t* test results. However, it does tell us some useful information about our results so you might be interested in reading the next section and making up your own mind.

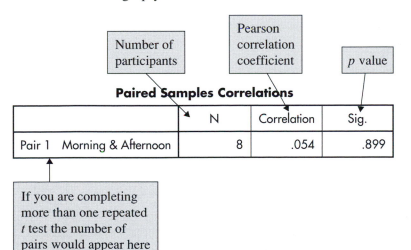

Number of participants

Pearson correlation coefficient

p value

Paired Samples Correlations

	N	Correlation	Sig.
Pair 1 Morning & Afternoon	8	.054	.899

If you are completing more than one repeated *t* test the number of pairs would appear here

SPSS advanced

- The **Paired Samples Correlations** table shows the Pearson correlation coefficient and its significance value. This test is conducted to show if the results found are consistent. We are predicting that a change in the time of day will have the same effect on all participants, they will all be worse in the afternoon by the same amount. There will be a consistent effect on them: we would expect that a participant who performed better than average on the test in the morning would still do better than average in the afternoon and someone near the bottom of the group in the morning would still be near the bottom of the group in the afternoon.

- From our example $r = 0.054$, $p = 0.899$, which is not found to be significant as $p > 0.05$. Our participants are therefore not behaving consistently as their scores in the morning test are not significantly correlated with their scores in the afternoon test. Though our participants are behaving inconsistently it is still worth looking at the difference in the means. This difference will tell us if there is an overall drop in scores between morning and afternoon, however, it won't be quite so easy to interpret with inconsistent participants.

✓ A scatterplot shows the data in its graphical form. It could also be used to check for any outliers, it is these outliers that might make inconsistent data appear more consistent. See Chapter 15 for details.

The next table that SPSS produces is the **Paired Samples Test** table, which informs us if there is a significant difference between our means or not.

Test statistic | p value

Paired Samples Test

		paired Differences						
				95% Confidence Interval of the Difference				
	Mean	Std. Deviation	Std. Error Mean	Lower	Upper	t	df	Sig. (2-tailed)
Pair 1 Morning–Afternoon	1.50	1.60	.57	.16	2.84	2.646	7	.033

Advanced   Essential

✓ The *p* value in a **Paired Samples Test** table is for a two-tailed hypothesis shown in the column '**Sig. (2-tailed)**'. If your hypothesis is one-tailed divide this figure by two.

SPSS essential

- The conventional way of reporting the findings is to state the test statistic (*t*), degrees of freedom (df), and probability value (*p*). We can report our results as follows.

$$t(7) = 2.646; \ p < 0.05$$

✓ Remember to check the mean scores on the **Descriptive Statistics** table to ensure that a significant difference is going in the direction predicted in the hypothesis.

SPSS advanced

- The **Paired Differences** show the differences between the scores of our two samples.
- The **Mean** displays the difference between the means of the two samples (5.25 − 3.75 = 1.50).
- As our samples are paired, we can find a difference score for each participant, subtracting their score in the first sample from their score in the second sample. The **Std. Deviation** indicates the standard deviation of all the difference scores.
- The **Std. Error Mean** estimates the standard deviation of all the differences between sample means for samples of size $N = 8$ when the null hypothesis is true. This indicates the difference in the means we would expect by chance if the null hypothesis is true. Our mean difference is 1.50, which is much bigger than the standard error of the mean of 0.57, suggesting that the data does not support the null hypothesis. Our calculated *t* value is the ratio of these two values:

$$t = \frac{1.50}{0.57} = 2.646$$

- The **95% Confidence Interval of the Difference** indicates that we are 95 per cent confident that the true (population) difference in means will be between the upper and lower limits. The sample mean difference falls between these two values.

- The confidence interval does not include zero and therefore even in the worst case (for our prediction), at the lower end of the confidence interval, there is still an expected difference, albeit a small one.

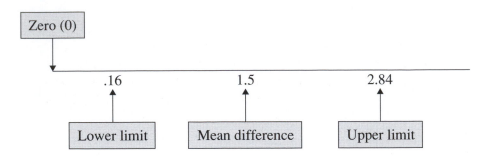

- This measure is often used as a supplementary or alternative indicator of statistical significance. A suggested way of reporting these findings is as follows:

    Difference in means = 1.50 (95%CI: 0.16 to 2.84)

✓ The default confidence interval given by SPSS is 95 per cent. This can be changed by going into the **Options** command in the *t* test procedure and selecting the required level.

✓ An appropriate illustrative statistic for a paired *t* test is a bar chart. See Chapter 4.

✓ To illustrate the confidence intervals for each sample mean an error bar graph can be produced. See Chapter 4.

FAQ

I have got a minus value for my t, what does this mean?

Don't worry, it just indicates that your first condition has a smaller mean than the second condition. If you had entered the conditions in the opposite order you would have obtained a positive t value. The significance value stays the same.

I am confused, what happens if the correlation is significant but the paired samples t test isn't significant or vice versa, how do I explain it?

The outcome of our statistics could potentially follow one of four routes.

1. *Both the correlation and test statistic t are significant, indicating a consistent and significant difference. This is easy to explain as it is the effect we are predicting.*
2. *The correlation is not significant but the test statistic t is significant, indicating that while a significant difference between the means has been found, the differences in scores for each participant are not consistent. This is harder to explain. We predicted that there would be differences between the means (which we found) but this cannot be attributed to a consistent effect of the independent variable (morning/afternoon) on the participants, so other factors may be influencing our outcome.*
3. *The correlation is significant but the test statistic t is not significant. This is easy to explain. The participants are behaving consistently and scoring very similarly in the two samples, so we have not found the effect we are predicting.*
4. *Both the correlation and test statistic t are not significant. This may not be easy to explain, but with the participants behaving inconsistently across the two samples and no significant difference in their mean scores it is really not worth worrying about.*

I am calculating an independent t test and my independent variable is gender, is this OK?

Technically, gender as a grouping variable cannot be randomly allocated and hence does not meet the assumption that your participants are randomly assigned to conditions or groups. However, in practice this variable is treated like many of the most interesting variables, for example ethnicity or age. These are the variables we wish to study and are therefore used as independent variables, with the acknowledgement of the potential issues concerning random allocation.

I have worked out the t test by hand and get a calculated value of t, I then have to look it up in a critical value table. Do I have to do any further analysis with the t value SPSS produces?

*SPSS produces the calculated t to three decimal places. It also gives you the precise probability value '**Sig. (2-tailed)**'. If you have a one-tailed hypothesis you must always half this figure. If this p value is less than or equal to your chosen significance level (e.g. 0.05) then it is significant.*

For example, if we found p = 0.094 this is non-significant. However, if our hypothesis was one-tailed our p value would be 0.047. This is significant at the 0.05 level.

If we worked out the above example by hand our calculated t value would be 1.82. By observing the critical values table (for a two-tailed hypothesis), we can see that 1.82 is not greater than the table value of 2.179 at the 0.05 significance level, therefore we cannot reject the null hypothesis. However, for a one-tailed hypothesis the critical value is 1.78. As our calculated t 'meets or beats' this value we could therefore reject the null hypothesis.

I have found a significant t value and my hypothesis is one-tailed. Does this mean that I can accept my experimental hypothesis and reject my null hypothesis?

Remember, even if your t value is significant, you need to check the means to ensure that the difference is in the correct direction to support your experimental hypothesis.

I have tried to do an independent t test but get this warning. What am I doing wrong?

Warnings

The Independent Samples table is not produced.

Group Statistics

	FEMALE	N	Mean	Std. Deviation	Std. Error Mean
MALE	1.00	0[a]	.	.	.
	2.00	0[a]	.	.	.

[a]. t cannot be computed because at least one of the groups is empty.

Have you set up the data correctly? Remember, for an independent t test both groups' scores need to be in one column. See Chapter 2, Data entry.

Details on how the independent and repeated measures *t* tests are derived and how to calculate them by hand can be found in Chapter 8 of Hinton (2004).

Chapter 8

Nonparametric two sample tests

WHEN WE WISH TO COMPARE two samples the test of choice is usually the t test. However, the t test is a parametric test which makes certain assumptions about our data (see Chapter 7). When these assumptions are not met the t test may not be appropriate so we perform nonparametric tests which do not require these assumptions. A common occasion when we might use a nonparametric test is when our data is ordinal rather than interval. If we measure such things as time, speed or accuracy we can be confident that the data is interval. This means that we are measuring our results on a scale with equal intervals. For example, the difference between 23 and 24 seconds is 1 second and the difference between 56 and 57 seconds is also 1 second. A second is always the same size wherever it is measured on the scale. However, when we produce *ratings* as our data, the data may not be interval. When we ask a teacher to judge the politeness of the children in a class or a boss to rate the management potential of the staff we have ratings. The teacher or the boss are not like clocks and speedometers, in that they may not use interval scales. The teacher might rate all the children very highly on a 0 to 10 point scale and never score a child below 7. The boss might rate one staff member as one point higher than another but believe that there is a big difference between them and rate two others quite differently despite seeing them as similar. With ratings we cannot trust that the data is from an interval scale. However, we can trust the order of the ratings. That is why nonparametric tests do not analyse the raw scores but rank the data and analyse the ranks.

Mann–Whitney *U* test (for independent samples)

The Mann–Whitney test is a nonparametric equivalent of the independent samples t test. We use a nonparametric test when the assumptions of the t test are not met. The t test requires interval data and the samples to come from normally distributed populations, with equal variances in both groups. The most common use of the Mann–Whitney test is when our data are ordinal. A rating scale is usually treated as ordinal, particularly if we are concerned that the full range of the scale is not being used by the participants. If we were interested in seeing whether there was a difference between men and women in their enjoyment of the city they all live in, we might give them a 0 to 10 scale and ask them to rate their satisfaction with the city on this scale. We decide the scale is not an interval scale as our (diplomatic) participants do not rate the city very low even when they are unhappy living in it.

As we are not assuming that the ratings come from an interval scale we are not going to work out means and standard deviations of the raw data (because we do not believe that this will give us meaningful values). So the first thing the Mann–Whitney test does is rank the complete set of scores from the lowest to the highest. If all the women rate the city highly, and the men do not, we would expect all the top ranks to be from the women and the bottom ranks to come from the men's scores. If the men favoured the city more than the women we would expect the reverse. If there was no difference between the samples then we would expect the men's and women's ratings to be spread amongst the ranks.

The problem arises when there is some separation of the samples (for example the women generally give the higher ranks) but there is also some mixing of the samples amongst the ranks (for example a few of the men rate the city highly). The Mann–Whitney test provides us with a statistic that allows us to decide when we can claim a difference between the samples (at our chosen level of significance). It calculates two U values, a U for the men and a U for the women. If both values are about the same it means that the samples are very mixed amongst the ranks and we have no difference between them. If one U is large and the other small then this indicates a separation of the groups amongst the ranks. Indeed, if the smaller of the two U values is zero it indicates that all of one sample are in the top ranks and all the other sample in the bottom ranks with no overlap at all. To test the significance of our difference we take the smaller of the two U values and examine the probability of getting this value when there is no difference between the groups. If this probability is lower than our significance level ($p < 0.05$ normally) we can reject the null hypothesis and claim a significant difference between our samples.

With large samples the distribution of U approximates the normal distribution so SPSS also gives a z score as well as the smaller of the two U values. We need to be careful if we get a lot of tied ranks, particularly with small sample sizes as these make the outcome of the Mann–Whitney test less valid. (A z score is a standard score, if you require further information on this please see a statistics book, e.g. Hinton (2004).)

Scenario

Two social clubs, the Hilltop Social Club and the Valley Social Club, decide to join forces and hire a coach to take them to see a Shakespearian play in the nearby city. One of the club secretaries decides to find out how much the members enjoyed the play so, on the coach home, asks everyone to rate their enjoyment of the play on a scale of 0 to 100. The members of Valley Social like to see themselves as very cultured people so the club secretary predicts that they will rate their enjoyment of the play higher than the members of Hilltop.

Data entry

Enter the dataset as shown in the example. See Chapter 2 for the full data entry procedure. Because of the independent groups design one column will be the grouping variable and the other column the rating score for each person.

		Mann-Whitney - SPSS Data Editor
	club	rating
1	Hilltop S	23
2	Hilltop S	54
3	Hilltop S	35
4	Hilltop S	42
5	Hilltop S	14
6	Hilltop S	24
7	Hilltop S	38
8	Valley S	46
9	Valley S	45
10	Valley S	62
11	Valley S	62
12	Valley S	75
13	Valley S	50
14	Valley S	80
15	Valley S	55
16	Valley S	33

> ✓ Remember that to see the numerical values instead of the value labels you need to go to the **View** drop-down menu and deselect **Value Labels**.

Test procedure

• Go to **Analyze** and select **Nonparametric Tests** from the drop-down menu.
• SPSS refers to the Mann–Whitney as **2 Independent Samples**. Choose this to bring up the **Two Independent Samples Tests** box.

• The dependent variable 'rating' should be sent to the **Test Variable List** box.
• The independent variable 'club' should be sent to the **Grouping Variable** box.
• SPSS then requires the user to define the range of values used when setting up the dataset to define the groups.
• To do this click on **Define Groups**.

- The values given to the groups in this example are 1 and 2.
- Enter these in the respective boxes then click on **Continue**.
- Ensure that **Mann–Whitney U** is selected under **Test Type**, then click on **OK**.

✓ Through the **Options** button you can select the means and standard deviations for the variables. While these descriptive statistics can be performed on ordinal data sets, we recommend a degree of caution when examining and interpreting them.

SPSS advanced

It is unlikely that you will be required to use test types other than the Mann–Whitney U. However, a brief description is given below of further analyses that you may wish to use to examine the nature of your data.

- The **Kolmogorov–Smirnov** test is used in a variety of analyses, but in the case of Mann–Whitney and two sample tests, it is used to determine whether the two sets of scores come from the same distribution.
- The **Wald–Wolfowitz runs** test is used to show how many 'runs' we have in the rank ordering of the data (a run is a series of ranks from the same group). As we go through the ranks, we can see if consecutive ranks come from the same group. If one group has all the bottom ranks and the other group has all the top ranks, we only have two runs. In our data, the number of runs is six indicating some mixing of the groups. With 16 participants, the worst mixing would give us 16 runs.
- The **Moses extreme reactions** test takes one of the groups as a control group and the second as an experimental group, and checks to see whether the experimental group has more extreme values than the control group.

SPSS output

The first table generated by SPSS is a description of the data giving the **Mean Rank** for each group and the **Sum of Ranks** for each group.

Ranks

	N	Mean Rank	Sum of Ranks
Hilltop Social Club	7	5.00	35.00
Valley Social Club	9	11.22	101.00
Total	16		

✓ It may be worth consulting a statistics book to refresh your memory on how to work out a Mann–Whitney test by hand to enable a fuller understanding of this table, for example Hinton (2004).

SPSS essential

- **N** indicates the number of participants in each group, and the total number of participants.
- The **Mean Rank** indicates the mean rank of scores within each group.
- The **Sum of Ranks** indicates the total sum of all ranks within each group.
- If there were no differences between the groups' ratings, i.e. if the null hypothesis was true, we would expect the mean rank and the sum of ranks to be roughly equal across the two groups.
- We can see from our example that the two groups do not appear to be equal in their ratings of the play.

In order to determine whether the difference in these rankings is significant, the **Test Statistics** table below must be observed.

Test Statistics[b]

		Test statistic
Mann–Whitney U	7.000	
Wilcoxon W	35.000	
Z	−2.595	
Asymp. Sig. (2-tailed)	.009	
Exact Sig. [2*(1-tailed Sig.)]	.008[a]	

[a]. Not corrected for ties.
[b]. Grouping Variable:

SPSS essential

- The test statistic generally reported is the **Mann–Whitney U** which is 7.000 in the above example.
- The probability value is ascertained by examining the **Asymp. Sig. (2-tailed)**. A figure of less than 0.05 is considered to be indicative of significant differences.
- In the above example $U = 7.00$; $p = 0.009$
- We can conclude that there is a significant difference between the ratings of Hilltop and Valley social clubs.
- Because our experimental hypothesis was one-tailed, the p value would be halved, to check that the difference is in the correct direction.

$U = 7.00$; $p = 0.0045$, therefore $p < 0.001$

- We can see by examining the mean ranks that Valley reports a higher mean ranking of the play than Hilltop, thus supporting our hypothesis.

SPSS advanced

- The **Mann–Whitney U** test statistic should be reported for samples of $N < 20$ in each group.
- The z score should be reported when $N > 20$ for both groups, as the distribution of U approximates the normal distribution, particularly for sample sizes of 20 and over.
- SPSS also generates a **Wilcoxon W** test statistic, which can be used if the populations being compared are not normal. Rather than ranking the two groups separately, this test combines the two groups into one for ranking purposes, then compares the total ranking from each group to ascertain if they are significantly different from each other. This test is the Wilcoxon rank-sum test for two independent samples and is different from the Wilcoxon signed-ranks test for paired data discussed later in this chapter.
- The **Asymp. Sig. (2-tailed)** level is an approximation that is useful when the dataset is large, and is used when SPSS cannot give an exact figure or takes too long to work out the significant value.
- The **Exact Sig.** is based on the exact distribution of the test statistic (in this case U). This should be reported when the dataset is small, poorly distributed or contains many ties. Reporting this significance level reflects a more accurate judgement of significance when working with datasets of this nature.

✓ Remember that in order to perform a nonparametric analysis we are working with ranks and not the raw data. Therefore, we are unlikely to trust the means and standard deviations as a proper representation of our findings. If you want to plot the raw data see Chapter 4 for more details on how to do this.

Wilcoxon signed-ranks test (for related samples)

The Wilcoxon signed-ranks test is the nonparametric equivalent of the related t test and is used when we do not believe that the assumptions of the t test are met. As the samples are related we have matched scores in the two samples. For example, a group of people rate their wakefulness on a ten-point scale in the morning and again in the afternoon. Our two samples are the ratings in the morning and the ratings in the afternoon, with each participant providing a score in each sample. As the samples are matched, the Wilcoxon test produces a 'difference score' for each participant, with each person's score in one sample taken from the same person's score in the second sample.

If all these differences go in the same direction (they are either all positive or all negative) and if there is a large enough sample size then this is convincing evidence that there is a difference between the groups. However, if some differences are positive and some negative then it is harder to judge if there is a consistent difference between the groups. To work this out the Wilcoxon test ranks the size of the differences (ignoring the sign of the difference) from lowest to highest. Then the ranks of the positive differences are added up and the ranks of the negative differences are added up. The smallest of these two totals is taken as the calculated value of the Wilcoxon statistic T.

If most of the differences go one way with only a few differences in the opposite direction, with the discrepant differences being small, this will result in a very small T. When we calculate T by hand we can then compare the calculated value with the critical values of T, at an appropriate significance level, in a statistics table. However, SPSS calculates a z score as there is a relationship between T and z (with the distribution of T approximating the normal distribution, particularly for sample sizes of 25 and over).

While we do not require the assumptions of a parametric test we do need to be aware of two things before deciding if the test is valid. When the difference between scores is zero, this indicates that a person has given the same score in both samples. As this provides us with no information about which sample has the larger scores we have to reject the individual's scores from the data and reduce the sample size by one. If our samples get too small we may not be able to claim a difference between them. Also, nonparametric tests work more accurately without tied ranks, so if there is a large number of tied ranks and if the sample size is small we must be careful that the analysis is appropriate.

Scenario

An interview panel of ten interviewers was asked to rate the two final candidates on a scale of 1 to 20 in terms of their suitability for a vacant post. Is one candidate rated significantly higher than the other by the interviewers?

Data entry

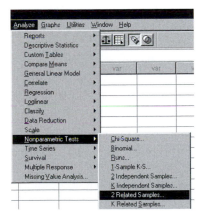

Enter the dataset as shown in the example. Because of the repeated measures design we can see that each interviewer (as shown in the rows) has two ratings.

> ✓ Because each number is a rating, there will be no decimal numbers, therefore the **Decimals** option in the **Variable View** can be set to zero. See Chapter 2 for more details on the data entry procedure.

Test procedure

- Go to **Analyze** and select **Nonparametric Tests** from the drop-down menu.
- SPSS refers to the Wilcoxon test as **2 Related Samples**. Choose this to bring up the **Two Related Samples Tests** box.

- Select both variables and send them over to the **Test Pair(s) List** box.
- Both variables will now appear on the same line.
- Check that Wilcoxon is selected under **Test Type**, and then click on **OK**.

✓ If SPSS does not allow you to select both variables at the same time, click on one variable first, release the mouse button and then click on the second variable. Both variables should now be visible in the **Current Selections** box and SPSS will allow them to be sent to the **Test Pair(s) List**.

✓ If you want to carry out more than one Wilcoxon test at once, several other combinations of pairs can be sent over at this point.

✓ It can often be difficult to select two variables that are not next to each other. Click on one variable, hold down the **Ctrl** key and then click on the other variable.

✓ Through the **Options** button you can select the means and standard deviations for the variables. While these descriptive statistics can be performed on ordinal datasets, we recommend a degree of caution when examining and interpreting them.

SPSS advanced

You are unlikely to use test types other than **Wilcoxon**, however below is a brief description of some of the uses for the other test statistics.

- The **Sign** test examines whether the median difference between the pairs is zero. This is less sensitive than the Wilcoxon, and the Wilcoxon is usually preferred.
- The **McNemar** test assesses the significance of the difference between the two samples when the data consists of two categories (for example 0 and 1).
- The **Marginal Homogeneity** test is an extension of the McNemar test where there are more than two category values in the data (for example 0, 1 and 2).

SPSS output

The first table that is produced by SPSS is the table of descriptive statistics, which gives us a summary of the ranks of the candidates. As can be seen from below, the number of **negative**, **positive** and **tied** ranks is indicated, along with the **Mean Rank** and the **Sum of Ranks**.

Independent variable

Ranks

		N	Mean Rank	Sum of Ranks
CAND_2 – CAND_1	Negative Ranks	7[a]	5.86	41.00
	Positive Ranks	2[b]	2.00	4.00
	Ties	1[c]		
	Total	10		

[a]. CAND_2 < CAND_1
[b]. CAND_2 > CAND_1
[c]. CAND_1 = CAND_2

Shows how many ranks of Candidate 1 were larger than, smaller than or the same as Candidate 2

✓ It may be worth consulting a statistics book to refresh your memory on how to work out a Wilcoxon by hand to enable a fuller understanding of this table, for example Hinton (2004).

SPSS essential

- Candidate 2 has been entered into the equation first, and therefore the calculation of ranks is based on the ratings of candidate 2 minus the ratings of candidate 1.
- The **Negative Ranks** therefore indicate how many ranks of candidate 1 were larger than candidate 2.
- The **Positive Ranks** indicate the number of ranks of candidate 1 that were smaller than candidate 2.
- Finally, the **Tied Ranks** indicate how many of the rankings of candidate 1 and candidate 2 were equal.
- The **Total** is the total number of ranks, which will be equal to the total number of judges.

- Other information that can be gained from this table includes the **Mean Rank** and a **Sum of Ranks** for both the positive and negative ranks.

The table that shows the our inferential statistics is the **Test Statistics** table shown below. The first thing that can be seen is that SPSS generates a **Z** score rather than the Wilcoxon T which will be generated when working out calculations by hand.

Test Statistics[b]

	CAND_2 – CAND_1	
Z	-2.194^{a}	Test statistic
Asymp. Sig. (2-tailed)	.028	p value

[a]. Based on positive ranks.
[b]. Wilcoxon Signed Ranks Test.

SPSS essential

- From the **Test Statistics** table it can be seen that $Z = -2.194$. A two-tailed analysis is carried out by default, which has yielded $p = 0.028$, which is significant at $p < 0.05$.
- From this we can conclude that the judges rated the two candidates significantly differently, with candidate 1 being significantly favoured by the interviewers, as indicated by the positive and negative ranks.
- The findings of the Wilcoxon test should be reported as follows:

$$z = -2.194, N = 9, p < 0.05$$

(note that **N** is reported as the total number of participants minus the tied ranks).

SPSS advanced

- When a Wilcoxon is worked out by hand, the final calculation is usually a T score. However, the researcher has the option to convert this to a z score (as the T distribution approximates the normal distribution with large sample sizes), thus yielding a p value, which is based on the normal distribution. This is particularly common when working with a large dataset (when the number of participants exceeds 25).
- SPSS automatically performs this calculation irrespective of the size of the dataset.

✓ Remember that in order to analyse nonparametric data we are working with ranks and not the raw data. As it is nonparametric data we are unlikely to trust the means and standard deviations as a proper representation of our findings. If you want to plot the raw data see Chapter 4 for more details on how to do this.

FAQ

When I calculate my Mann–Whitney test by SPSS I get two significance levels – one which is labelled 'Asymp. Sig.' and the other 'Exact Sig.'. How do I know which one to report?

The asymptotic significance is based on an approximation of significance level for your dataset. The exact significance is calculated on the exact scores given in the sample. We would normally report the exact significance if this is available. (In some tests this may take too long to work out with large sample sizes, and we would then use the asymptotic value.)

I have tried to work out a Wilcoxon by hand but got a T value, which I can't seem to get from doing a Wilcoxon by using SPSS, what am I doing wrong?

You are not doing anything wrong, SPSS produces a z score, which you may recall from early statistics classes is a standardised score. Because the T distribution approximates a normal distribution, particularly with large sample sizes, SPSS chooses to use z rather than T.

Details on the logic of the Mann–Whitney or Wilcoxon test and how to calculate them by hand can be found in Chapter 17 of Hinton (2004).

Remember that in order to analyse nonparametric data we are working with ranks and not the raw data. As in nonparametric data we are not likely to find the means and standard deviations as a good representation of variability. If we want to find the...

FAQ

Chapter 9

Introduction to analysis of variance (general linear model)

Introduction

It will not take long before you find that SPSS uses the term 'general linear model' (abbreviated to GLM), both in the menu list and in the output. So it is worth taking time to explain what this means and also to explain some of the other aspects of the GLM you will encounter in your data analysis.

- First, if you knew that you had to perform an analysis of variance (ANOVA) on your data, you would notice that it does not feature in the list of options under the **Analyze** command where other major statistical procedures are found.
- There is an option to choose a simple one-way independent measures ANOVA by going through the **Analyze** and then **Compare Means** commands. However, where are the other ANOVAs hidden?

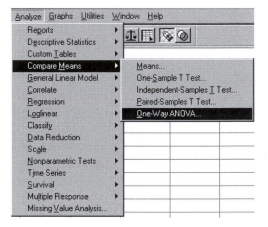

General Linear Model command

All the different forms of ANOVA can be found under the **General Linear Model** option of the **Analyze** drop-down menu. Notice from the screenshot below that the subcommands under the **General Linear Model** option still do not mention analysis of variance but have the labels **Univariate, Multivariate** and **Repeated Measures**. We shall examine the meaning of each of these in this chapter.

Data Editor

| ata | Transform | Analyze | Graphs | Utilities | Window | Help |

Reports ▶
Descriptive Statistics ▶
Custom Tables ▶
Compare Means ▶
General Linear Model ▶   Univariate...
Correlate ▶   Multivariate...
Regression ▶   Repeated Measures...
Loglinear ▶
Classify ▶   Variance Components...
Data Reduction ▶
Scale ▶
Nonparametric Tests ▶
Time Series ▶
Survival ▶
Multiple Response ▶
Missing Value Analysis...

var

A model for analysing data

A model is a way of representing a particular system. Models are extremely important for our understanding of people and events in the world. In the past, when the model of the solar system had the Earth as the centre with the sun going round it, the movement of the planets was very problematic – they appeared to move in very strange ways. However, when a new model was proposed with the sun as the centre of the solar system and the Earth and the other planets moving round it, the movement of the planets could be explained in a simpler way. This second model is so good that we can use it to send spacecraft to other planets quite successfully. So models have assumptions (the sun is the centre of the solar system) and we can use our model to make decisions (Mars will be at a certain position in 6 months' time when our spacecraft arrives). In statistics we also have models in order to allow us to make decisions about our data – whether differences between scores are genuine or simply have arisen by chance.

We can see the use of a model in the following example. A school obtains its pupils from two estates in the town: Westtown and Eastend. A researcher believes that the mathematics teacher is favouring the children from Westtown at the expense of those from Eastend. The first thing the researcher might decide to do is to check that there are no other reasons why the Westtown children might perform better than the Eastend children. Let us assume that the two estates are very similar and the people are no different in terms of social backgrounds wherever they live on the two estates. Also, there is no evidence from the school of any general discrimination against the Eastend children. Thus, we are assuming that the children enter the mathematics class without any *systematic* reasons for a difference between the Eastend and Westtown children. At the end of the year with the mathematics teacher in question the children take a mathematics test and get the following results.

Mathematics score	Home
52	Westtown
49	Westtown
51	Eastend
55	Westtown
48	Eastend
52	Westtown
49	Eastend
45	Eastend
50	Eastend
54	Westtown
50	Westtown
47	Eastend
53	Westtown
46	Eastend
48	Eastend
51	Westtown
Mean = 50	

The teacher might say 'look, the scores are showing the usual range of scores we get in children. OK, some of the Westtown children are doing better but that happens sometimes. Anyway, some of the Eastend children are doing better than others from Westtown – there's a 51 from an Eastend child and a 49 from a Westtown child.'

Let us apply a model to see if we can make a decision about whether there is a difference between the children from the two estates on the mathematics scores. From the overall data we might argue that a 'standard child' should score 50 on the test (that's our mean value). We are estimating the mean of the population of children on the test, suggesting that, no matter where a child comes from, they should get a score of 50. So the first step in the model is to argue that without any other factors being involved every child will produce a score of 50.

Now we group the children into those from Eastend and those from Westtown to see if we can make a comparison between them.

Eastend children	Westtown children
47	52
49	54
46	51
48	50
51	49
48	52
50	55
45	53
Mean = 48	Mean = 52

Notice that the means of the two groups are different, 48 and 52, so it might be that the teacher is discriminating between the children (if both means had been 50 there would have been no evidence of a difference). So we are finding variation in the scores *between the groups*. However, have these differences 'just happened' by random chance, as the teacher implied, or have they arisen through systematic discrimination by the teacher?

This is where the next step of our model comes in. Each child should score 50 on the test but doesn't because of discrimination by the teacher. The mean of 48 shows on average a 'teacher effect' of −2 for the Eastend children and the mean of 52 shows an average 'teacher effect' of +2 for the Westtown children. For our model we have to argue that the teacher effect results in consistent or *systematic variation* between the groups, so each child in the Eastend group should have the same effect of −2 and each child in the Westtown group should have the same effect of +2, to be consistent.

However, not all the children in the Eastend group have scored 48 and not all the children in the Westtown group have scored 52. To explain this by our model we can argue that there is *variation within the groups* due to *unsystematic or random variation* (such as individual differences, chance effects occurring on the day of the test and other random factors). We refer to this as 'error' variation.

Finally, we have the description of the model.

A child's score = Population mean + teacher effect + error

Now we can present the table of results in terms of the model:

Eastend children	Westtown children
$50 - 2 - 1$	$50 + 2 + 0$
$50 - 2 + 1$	$50 + 2 + 2$
$50 - 2 - 2$	$50 + 2 - 1$
$50 - 2 + 0$	$50 + 2 - 2$
$50 - 2 + 3$	$50 + 2 - 3$
$50 - 2 + 0$	$50 + 2 + 0$
$50 - 2 + 2$	$50 + 2 + 3$
$50 - 2 - 3$	$50 + 2 + 1$
Mean $= 48$	Mean $= 52$

So far so good. But there are one or two things we need to check. Remember the model is assuming the scores differ because of the teacher effect and error. The teacher effect is constant within a group so the *only* reason the scores within a group vary is because of the error. We are expecting (according to the model) that the error in each group will be the same, as the participants are randomly allocated to groups (remember we said earlier that there are no consistent differences between the people living in the two estates – it is random chance that leads one family to live on one estate and another family to live on the other). If we had a massive amount of error in one group and almost none in the other this would be very odd and it would undermine the assumption of our model. We measure variability by the statistic *variance* (the square of the standard deviation). Formally, this assumption is that each group comes from a population with equal variance. We estimate the population variance by our sample variance, so the variance of each group should be more or less the same. This is referred to as the *homogeneity of variance* assumption. Looking at the errors we can see this is fine. Finally, as we are calculating statistics such as means, standard deviations and variance, these only are meaningful if our scores come from an interval scale. Again, we are all right as the mathematics test produces interval data. All the assumptions of the model are met.

Without the model our data is simply data: a collection of numbers. By applying a model, as we did above, we give order to the data and we are able to make statistical decisions, such as inferring a teacher effect. Our model is quite simple but still requires us to make a set of assumptions such as 'all scores in a group would be the same except for error', and 'the variability of the scores in one group is the same as the variability of scores in the other group' as the error should, according to the model, be evenly spread across the groups.

Notice that we are expecting the scores in one group to consistently differ from scores in the other group because of the teacher effect. The general term for this is the *treatment effect*, as we are arguing that the groups would not differ if we had not treated them to the effect of the teacher (like giving patients with an illness a particular treatment).

So the general description of our model is as follows:

Score = Population mean + treatment effect + error

This type of model is referred to as a *linear model* and will be explored further in the following section. It is a deceptively simple model given that it allows us to undertake some very powerful statistical analyses.

Statistical tests use this model to look for systematic variation in the scores that can be attributed to a treatment effect and unsystematic or random variation that can be attributed to error. Analysing these sources of variation in the scores allows us to make a statistical decision (is there a treatment effect or not?). This is what we mean by the *analysis of variance*. The model also underlies regression analysis as well. The above example is the simplest case of the model (in fact you may recognise the analysis as an independent t test – see Chapter 8) but the ANOVA allows us to investigate the variation in the scores in data produced by any number of independent variables with any number of groups (or conditions). We can even use it to look at more than one dependent variable (see Chapter 12 for an introduction to multivariate analysis of variance).

Just out of interest the independent t test on the above data gives a value of $t = -4$, $df = 14$, $p < 0.01$, indicating a highly significant difference between the groups in the predicted direction. (A t test is a simple case of an ANOVA with only two samples. When this is the case we have the following relationship between the two: $t^2 = F$. Our result gives an ANOVA F value of 16, indicating that the variance between the groups, including the treatment effect, is 16 times bigger than the variance within the groups, the error variance, showing a large treatment effect.) We have an answer to our statistical decision: we do think the teacher is biased in favour of the Westtown children.

The general linear model

Underlying a wide range of statistical tests is the general linear model, in particular the ANOVA and regression. This allows us tremendous flexibility in analysis: we can have as many conditions (groups) as we want and indeed as many variables as we want in the analysis, and yet the same basic model structure underlies all these analyses. The model can be a little complex to explain when we have a lot of variables, so we are going to look at a simple case: the use of a linear model in examining the relationship between two variables. In this example a researcher is interested in people's use of technology in their leisure activities (computers, DVD players, camcorders, cable TV, etc). The participants were given a test of their technical skills in using these products as well as providing information on their use of them. We are going to look a tiny piece of the data: five people's responses to two variables – their Internet use in hours per week and their score out of 20 on the technical skills test. The data is shown in the table below:

Participant	Internet use (hours per week)	Technical skills test (out of 20)
1	4	4
2	3	5
3	6	9
4	7	13
5	10	14

What is the relationship between these two variables? It is not very clear from the table so a more helpful representation of the data is a scatterplot (Figure 9.1).

Notice from the graph that the relationship is not obvious. How can we model this relationship? We could simply join the points to make a W shape, as in Model A (Figure 9.2), or draw a smooth curved line that would go through all the points, as in Model B.

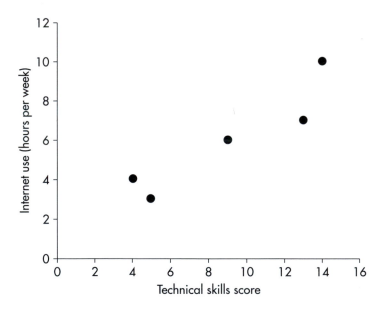

FIGURE 9.1 A scatterplot of technical skills by Internet use

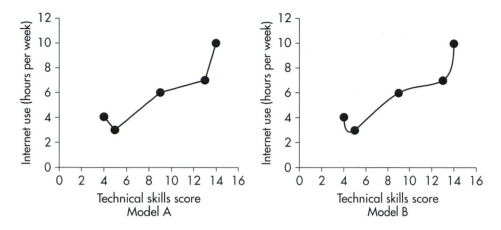

FIGURE 9.2 Two models for the data

The problem is that these models are quite complicated to describe – there is no simple mathematical description of either of them. Furthermore, there is no guarantee that any new data will fit the model. As an alternative we could argue that the relationship between the variables is a simple one, a linear relationship, but the reason the points on the graph do not follow a straight line is due to 'error'. If we look at the scatterplot again we can see that the points fall within a band from bottom left to top right, that appears to follow a line. In Figure 9.3 we have included a straight line on the graph to indicate the

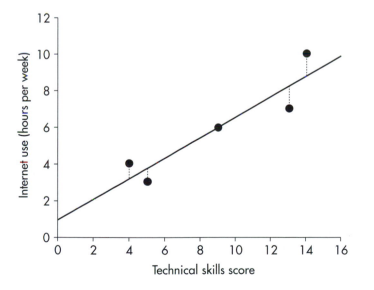

FIGURE 9.3 Fitting the data to a linear model

relationship we believe would have occurred had there been no error (our model), with the dotted lines indicating the error – the distance of each point from the line.

Mathematically we define a straight line by the formula

$$Y = a + bX$$

where 'a' is a constant called the *intercept* as this is the value of Y when the line crosses the Y-axis (when $X = 0$). If the line passes through the origin ($X = 0$, $Y = 0$) then the intercept will be zero. The constant 'b' is called the *slope* as it gives the value of the slope of the line.

We now have a situation where we are assuming that our scores are the result of a linear relationship (a linear model) plus error. We could decide either that the technical skills scores are correct and the Internet use scores contain variability due to error, or vice versa. In this example we will assume the X values (the technical skills scores) are correct and the Y values (Internet use) do not fit the model due to the error, so we have:

Observed values of $Y = a + b$ (observed values of X) + error

so:

Internet use $= a + b \times$ technical skills score + error

We are able to work out the straight line that best fits our data by finding the equation of the line that gives us the smallest overall error. This line is called the *regression line* and you can see how to calculate it in Chapter 15.

According to the regression analysis the best fit line for our data is defined by the following equation:

Internet use $= 0.951 + 0.561 \times$ technical skills score

What this is saying is that the model can explain some variability in the data (that which follows the straight line) but not other variability (the error). For example, participant 1 scored 4 on the technical skills test. Putting 4 in the above formula for our linear model we get a prediction that the participant spent 3.195 hours on the Internet (as $3.195 = 0.951 + 0.561 \times 4$). In fact they spent 4 hours on the Internet, so, according to our model, 3.195 is explained variability and 0.805 is unexplained variability or error.

The table below shows the data described in terms of the linear model:

Participant	Internet use	Internet use (explained by model)	Internet use (error)	Technical skills score (assumed to be correct)
1	4	3.195	+0.805	4
2	3	3.756	−0.756	5
3	6	6	0	9
4	7	8.244	−1.244	13
5	10	8.805	+1.195	14

Now that we have fitted the data to our linear model we can make statistical decisions about the goodness of this fit. We can examine how much of the variability in the scores is explained by the model and how much is unexplained or error variability. Again, as mentioned earlier, examining the sources of the variability in the data allows us to make statistical decisions. Is there a systematic variation in the dependent variable that results from a systematic variation in the independent variable? It is all a question of whether the data fits the model well or whether there is simply too much error for it to be a good fit. If, on fitting the model, there is very little error then the model is a good representation of the data.

We need to be aware of the assumptions we are making about our data when applying the model. We would expect there to be more or less the same variability in the scores around the regression line at each point on the line – that is, the variability due to error would be the same at each point on the line. If there was only a small error at one point and a huge amount of error at another place it would undermine the validity of the model. We expect the error to be evenly spread around the regression line as we are assuming that random factors are the only reason for the error. This is the assumption of 'homogeneity of variance' mentioned earlier; however, in the case of regression it is often referred to as homoscedasticity.

In the example above we have looked at one single dependent variable, Y, which in our case was the Internet use, and one single independent variable, X, the technical skills score. But this is the simplest case of the general linear model. We can have any number of independent variables and produce the following multiple regression equation:

$$Y = a + b_1X_1 + b_2X_2 + b_3X_3 + b_4X_4 + \ldots$$

The key point is that the general form of the function remains the same and so is termed the general linear model. This underlies all our ANOVA and regression calculations.

It may appear surprising to learn that both the ANOVA and regression analysis are based on the general linear model. Indeed, they are like two sides of the same coin. Both types of analysis are examining how much of the observed variation in the dependent variable can be attributed to variation in the independent variable and how much is due to error. That is why you will sometimes see both a regression and an ANOVA in your SPSS output.

For the data to be appropriate to this form of model we need to make certain assumptions about the 'error' that remains after we have removed the variation explained by the model:

- the errors add up to zero
- the errors are normally distributed
- the errors are independent of each other.

These assumptions are required as they indicate that the errors really are random and there is no systematic variation left unexplained in them after applying the model. If there is systematic variation in the error terms then it indicates that there is a better model for the data and the one we have found is not the most appropriate.

These assumptions underlie the assumptions that we mentioned in Chapter 6 concerning parametric tests.

> A more detailed discussion of the general linear model can be found in Chapter 23 of Hinton (2004).

Key terms in the analysis of variance

When we collect the results of a study we find that not every score is the same. There is variability in the data. We measure this variability by calculating *sums of squares*. If you look at the formula for a standard deviation or variance you notice that the top section of the formula contains the term $\sum(X - \bar{X})^2$ which is the sum of the squared deviations from the mean, or sums of squares. We can calculate the total variability in the data by working out the variability for all the scores in the study. However, we can also work out a sums of squares for each source of variability, such as variability due to the independent variable(s) or to sources of error. We can work out how much of the total sums of squares arises from each source of variation.

Next, we need to work out an average amount of variability due to each source. This is because we might get more variation from 30 participants than 10 participants, or from six conditions rather than three conditions, simply because we have more of them. We work out an average variability or *mean square* by dividing the sums of squares attributed to one source of variation by the degrees of freedom for the same source of variation. Mean square is also called *variance* (and is the square of the standard deviation). If we now compare the variance due to a particular source, such as an independent variable, with an appropriate error variance the resulting *variance ratio* will be large if there is a large systematic variation in the data due to the independent variable. If it is small (around 1) then the variability due to the independent variable is no different from the variability arising by random error. We can examine the probability of producing a variance ratio (or *F* value) of a particular size when the null hypothesis is true. We can then use the calculated value of *F* for each of our independent variables to decide if they indicate statistically significant differences between their conditions or not.

A one factor analysis of variance calculates one *F* value for the one independent variable to examine for statistical significance. However, a different error variance is produced for the one factor independent measures ANOVA and the one factor repeated measures ANOVA because the latter is able to remove systematic variation due to the participants from the error term.

A two factor analysis of variance produces three *F* values, one for each independent variable and one for the *interaction*. If we were comparing men and women on a task in the morning and the afternoon we would have two independent variables: gender and time of day. An interaction occurs when the effect of one factor is different for the different levels of the second factor. So, if women were better on the task in the morning and the men were better in the afternoon then we would have an interaction.

If we do not find an interaction in a two factor ANOVA we look at the effects of the variables separately. The *marginal means* for 'gender' would give the mean for the men across both morning and afternoon and also the women across both morning and afternoon. Similarly, the marginal means for 'time of day' would give the mean for the morning scores and the mean for the afternoon scores averaged across both the men and the women.

There are a number of other terms we need to know when using the ANOVA in SPSS:

- Groups, treatments, levels and conditions all refer to the different samples of an independent variable. So 'time of day' in the example above has two conditions, levels or groups – 'morning' and 'afternoon'.
- 'Subjects' is used to refer to the participants.
- Tables headed **Between Subjects Effects** refer to the outcome of the analysis for the independent measures factor(s).
- Tables headed **Within Subjects Effects** refer to the outcome of the analysis for the repeated measures factor(s).

Finally, the ANOVA always performs a two-tailed test as it measures the amount of variability but not the direction (i.e. which condition has the higher or lower mean). So, unless we only have two conditions, we may wish to undertake further analysis to explore where the differences lie between the different conditions with a statistically significant F value. The different comparisons you can undertake are described later in this chapter.

Univariate analysis of variance

In SPSS we select the **Univariate** ANOVA when we have a single dependent variable and our independent variables are all of an independent measures design.

When all our independent variables are independent measures, the ANOVA is relatively simple as the technique examines the variation in the data and attributes sources to the variation: how much is due to systematic variation between the conditions and how much is due to unsystematic or error variation within the conditions. If we find a relatively large amount of systematic variation compared to the error variation we can claim that there is a genuine treatment effect occurring in the data.

In this book we shall be examining the one factor and the two factor independent measures ANOVA. By taking these two examples the reader will be able to see the basic one factor analysis (a single independent variable) and an example with an interaction – the two factor analysis (two independent variables). SPSS allows you to input any number of independent variables but the logic is the same. Having undertaken a two factor ANOVA on SPSS the three and four factor ANOVAs are quite easy to perform.

Multivariate analysis of variance

We select **Multivariate** ANOVA in SPSS when we have more than one dependent variable and independent measures independent variables. For example, we are interested in the effects of age and gender on heart rate and blood pressure after a long period of sleep deprivation. Age and gender are our independent variables and heart rate and blood pressure are the dependent variables.

Multivariate ANOVA (or MANOVA as it is termed) is not commonly undertaken at undergraduate level, however an introduction to MANOVA is presented in Chapter 12. We will make reference to multivariate analysis as it is a feature of the repeated measures output considered in the next section.

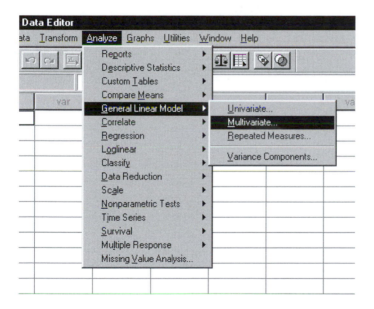

Repeated measures analysis of variance

When one or more of the independent variables is repeated measures we need to select **Repeated Measures** from the **General Linear Model** options list in SPSS.

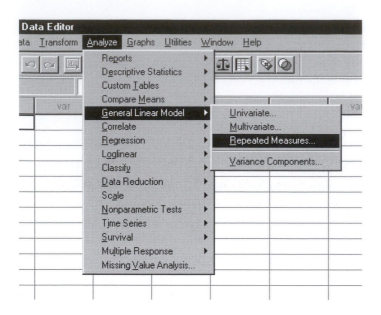

When we have a repeated measures factor the analysis is a little more complicated than when we have only independent measures. In fact, new users of SPSS undertaking a repeated measures ANOVA for the first time often are amazed at the amount of output they get with their results and find it all rather confusing: Why all these tables? Which is my *F* value?

This can be explained by an example. A researcher is interested in the effect of practice on computer games. She takes a simple flight simulator game – flying an aircraft on screen. Each participant is instructed on how to play the game, given 2 minutes to learn the controls and then has 10 minutes to play the game. The researcher records the number of errors the person makes during the 10-minute trial. The participants are tested once a day for 4 days using the same procedure. Thus, there are four conditions, trial 1 to trial 4, of the independent variable 'practice' with the dependent variable of number of errors. We would perform a one factor repeated measures ANOVA on these data.

The problem of repeated measures designs is the question of *sphericity*. Our underlying model requires certain assumptions to be met. One of these concerns the homogeneity of variance of the *differences between samples* (sphericity). This is also referred to as the homogeneity of the covariance between pairs of conditions, or the homogeneity of covariance assumption.

If we do not have sphericity then our variance calculations may be distorted and our ANOVA *F* value will be too large, so sphericity is a key assumption of the repeated measures ANOVA. Sphericity is not a problem when we have independent measures factors as it results from the fact that we have the same participants in each condition.

It is also not a problem with a repeated measures factor when we have only two conditions (as this always has sphericity). However, when we have three or more conditions of a repeated measures factor we can test for sphericity. Furthermore, there is a greater risk of violating the assumption as the number of repeated measures conditions increases.

Fundamentally, sphericity is violated when the participants have different responsiveness to the treatment effect across the conditions, or when there are different carry-over effects across the conditions for the different participants. This is referred to as a treatment by subject interaction. As an example, different people have different susceptibility to certain drugs, so one person may be unsteady on their feet after a certain amount of alcohol while another person can still walk steadily. This causes a problem for our ANOVA model, which is looking for consistency in the treatment effect across the participants across the conditions. We can look at pretend results of the flight simulator example to show this. First, with sphericity:

Participant	Trial 1	Trial 2	Trial 3	Trial 4
Peter	12	10	8	6
Paul	9	7	5	3
Mary	6	4	2	0
Variance	9	9	9	9

Note that each condition variance is the same, so we have homogeneity of variance. Now let's look at the differences between conditions for each person:

Participant	Trial 1 − Trial 2	Trial 1 − Trial 3	Trial 1 − Trial 4	Trial 2 − Trial 3	Trial 2 − Trial 4	Trial 3 − Trial 4
Peter	2	4	6	2	4	2
Paul	2	4	6	2	4	2
Mary	2	4	6	2	4	2
Variance	0	0	0	0	0	0

Here we have homogeneity of the differences between conditions. All the variances are the same. (They are zero in our example, which you would not get in real research data, but this is for illustration purposes only.) So we have sphericity; the effects of the treatments are consistent across the people and conditions. Everybody is improving in the same way with more practice on the flight simulator.

Now let's see data with sphericity violated:

Participant	Trial 1	Trial 2	Trial 3	Trial 4
Peter	12	9	6	3
Paul	9	7	5	3
Mary	6	5	4	3
Variance	9	4	2	0

Note we do not have homogeneity of variance. Now let's look at the differences between conditions for each person:

Participant	Trial 1 − Trial 2	Trial 1 − Trial 3	Trial 1 − Trial 4	Trial 2 − Trial 3	Trial 2 − Trial 4	Trial 3 − Trial 4
Peter	3	6	9	3	6	3
Paul	2	4	6	2	4	2
Mary	1	2	3	1	2	1
Variance	1	4	9	1	4	1

Here, the differences are not consistent across the people and conditions, so we do not have sphericity. We do not have homogeneity of variance of the differences between pairs of treatments: one is nine times larger than another. Peter starts badly with 12 errors and improves a lot on each trial (reducing his errors by 3), but Mary starts well (6 errors) and only improves a little each time (by 1). Paul is in the middle.

If we did a repeated measures ANOVA on this second set of data we would get an incorrect highly significant F value. So we must correct for the sphericity violation to get a more accurate value of F. That is why there is so much output for a repeated measures ANOVA because SPSS provides us with a lot of information to help us decide how to choose the correct F value. Let us take these pieces of information in turn:

1   SPSS calculates a univariate ANOVA (as we have one dependent variable) and produces a 'sphericity assumed F value' for our repeated measures factor. A value called *epsilon* is printed out and if this is 1 then the sphericity assumption is met and we can finish there and take this F value.

2   If epsilon is less than 1 then we may have a problem with sphericity. SPSS prints out a 'lower bound' or worst case for epsilon. For three conditions the worst sphericity violation will give an epsilon of 0.5. The more conditions we have the closer the lower bound gets to zero.

3   SPSS provides the result of Mauchly's test of sphericity as a check on our data. If this is significant then sphericity is violated. The difficulty with this is that Mauchly's test may miss a violation with small samples and indicate violations with large samples when they are not big enough to worry about. So we need to be sensitive to the epsilon value whatever Mauchly tells us. Certainly, an epsilon of 0.75 should be viewed as low. If the sphericity assumption has been violated we must correct our F value.

4   SPSS calculates a corrected F value according to three different correction methods. The 'lower bound' method gives a corrected degrees of freedom and F value for the 'worst case scenario' of sphericity violation. We don't use this as there are two less severe corrections: the Greenhouse–Geisser and the Huyn–Feldt. The former is more conservative than the latter, overcorrecting for sphericity. Despite this, we recommend the Greenhouse–Geisser correction when sphericity is violated, as it provides a middle position between the lower bound and sphericity assumed values.

Usually that is all we need to do. However, there is an alternative to correcting for a sphericity violation. That is to avoid the problem by performing a multivariate analysis instead of a univariate one. In the flight simulator example, instead of regarding the trials 1 to 4 as a repeated measures factor, we view trial 1 errors as the first dependent variable, the trial 2 errors as the second dependent variable, the trial 3 errors as the third dependent variable and the trial 4 errors as a fourth dependent variable. We can do this as the same participants have produced each of the three sets of results. So we get further results printed out.

5   SPSS calculates a multivariate ANOVA (or MANOVA). Again this can be calculated in a number of different ways so SPSS provides us with an F value worked out according to four different methods (Pillai's trace, Wilks' lambda, Hotelling's trace and Roy's largest root). We can then take the F value that we believe is the most appropriate to use. The authors recommend Wilks' lambda.

If it avoids the problem, why don't we simply take the multivariate F value and ignore the univariate analysis if sphericity is such a headache? The answer is that for most cases the univariate analysis is more powerful – it is better at detecting an effect when it is there. So we normally prefer the univariate correction. However, when we have a low epsilon and large samples then the multivariate test can be more powerful.

This may all sound quite confusing, particularly when we first see all the output we get with a repeated measures factor in an ANOVA. Practically, with most data it is not a problem as all the different analyses give the same result. The different forms of analysis all indicate the same thing (significant or otherwise) and this is very reassuring.

If you do find the different analyses produce different outcomes then it is worth looking at the data in more detail to see what is really going on and this may need a higher level of statistical knowledge than we are assuming in this book. You have a choice of looking deeper into the matter yourself or consulting a statistician, depending on how confident you feel in your own understanding of the data.

Contrasts and multiple pairwise comparisons

We have to remember that a statistically significant F value in an ANOVA allows us to reject the null hypothesis but does not tell us which alternative hypothesis to accept. If we have examined the effect of a particular drug on performance and included four conditions (no drug, low dose, medium dose and high dose) in our analysis then a significant F value would indicate a difference between the conditions but not where the difference lies. For example: is there a difference in performance between the no drug and the low dose conditions? Is the effect due to the high dose condition being different to the rest? We can only find this out by making comparisons between our conditions.

We can plan our comparisons in advance of the analysis, in which case we wish to make only specific comparisons rather than comparing every condition with every other one. In the above example we might be interested in comparing the no drug condition with the others to see if there is a drug effect. SPSS refers to this form of comparison as a *contrast*. Planning your comparisons is often recommended as it indicates that there is a rationale for the whole study rather than undertaking the study as a 'fishing expedition', fishing around to see which significant effects pop up. However, although referring to it as 'fishing' sounds derogatory, we may have undertaken an exploratory study and wish to make a number of comparisons after the ANOVA. These are referred to as *post hoc* tests (literally meaning 'after this'). Post hoc tests normally allow us to undertake pairwise comparisons, that is, compare one condition with another. The tests correct for the increased risk of Type I errors with multiple comparisons, and this allows us to undertake all possible pairwise comparisons if we wish to do so. Unfortunately, SPSS does not allow you to perform post hoc tests on repeated measures variables in an ANOVA (because there is some debate as to the appropriate terms to use in the analysis). However, we can examine the main effects, which also provide us with pairwise comparisons.

The different contrasts and comparisons we can use to help us to understand a significant *F* value in an ANOVA are explained in the following sections.

Contrasts

SPSS allows you to undertake the same contrasts whether you are undertaking an independent measures or repeated measures ANOVA in the **General Linear Model** command. When you click on the **Contrasts** button you will see one of the following boxes.

For the independent measures ANOVA: and for the repeated measures ANOVA:

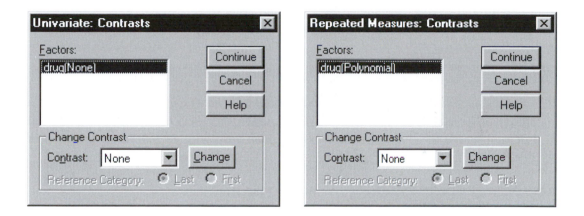

✓   Notice that the default setting for the independent measures ANOVA is no contrasts but for the repeated measures ANOVA it is polynomial.

✓   You must select the contrast you want and then press **Change**.

There are six standard contrasts that SPSS allows you to make (and there are two versions of the first two contrasts depending on whether you select **Last** or **First** as the **Reference Category**).

Deviation   The mean of each condition is contrasted with the overall mean except the last (when **Last** is selected) or first (when **First** is selected).

Simple   The mean of each condition is contrasted with the mean of the last condition (when **Last** is selected) or the mean of the first condition (when **First** is selected).

Difference   The mean of each condition is compared to the mean of the previous conditions.

Helmert   The mean of each condition is compared to the mean of the subsequent conditions.

Repeated   The mean of each condition is contrasted with the mean of the next condition, so with three conditions we have condition 1 versus condition 2, and condition 2 versus condition 3.

Polynomial   The means of the conditions are contrasted in terms of whether they fit a trend. With two or more conditions a linear trend is tested, with three or more conditions both a linear and a quadratic trend are tested, and with four or more conditions a linear, a quadratic and a cubic trend are all examined and the significance of these trends presented.

Almost all the planned contrasts that you are likely to want to perform are included in this list. In our drug example, comparing the 'no drug' condition with all the rest (the drug conditions) would be achieved by a Helmert contrast.

Post hoc multiple comparisons

If a significant *F* value has been detected during your analysis, but you do not have a specific hypothesis to test, a multiple pairwise comparison post hoc test may be carried out to ascertain where the differences lie. This is quite easy with an independent measures ANOVA as there is a handy **Post Hoc** button in the **Univariate** box.

• Select **Post Hoc**.

• Select **Tukey**.

There are a large number of post hoc tests available but a good all round test is the Tukey test. This uses a similar method to the *t* test by dividing the difference between any two means by the standard error of the difference between any two means. The Tukey uses a 'general purpose' standard error that can be used for any pair of means. When running multiple *t* tests there is always the problem of an increased risk of a Type I error. The Tukey overcomes this problem by setting an overall level of significance, for example at 0.05. That means that the risk of a Type I error has a probability of, say, 0.05 when we compare every pair of means.

However, when we try to perform a post hoc test on a repeated measures ANOVA in SPSS we cannot do it.

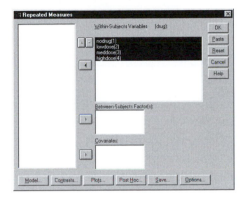

Even though there is a **Post Hoc** button in the SPSS repeated measures ANOVA box . . .

. . . you will not be able to select a repeated measures factor to perform a post hoc test on it.

However, it is important to note that if you have a mixed design ANOVA, your independent measures factor will appear in this box and can be chosen.

Main effects

We can compare the condition means of a repeated measures factor (or an independent measures factor if you wish) in an ANOVA via the **Options** button. Within the **Options** box we are able to select the **Compare main effects** option. A repeated measures example is shown below. As the pairwise comparisons of a number of means will result in an increase in the risk of a Type I error, this needs to be controlled for, and a Bonferroni correction is chosen to correct for this.

- Select **Options**.

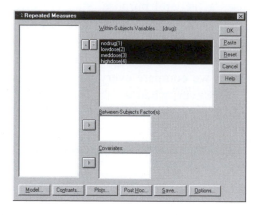

- Send the variable across to **Display Means for**.
- Tick **Compare main effects**.
- Select **Bonferroni** in the **Confidence interval adjustment**.

For a one factor ANOVA this will produce the post hoc multiple comparisons for the repeated measures factor.

When we have a multifactor ANOVA (such as a two factor ANOVA) the **Compare main effects** option will only compare the marginal means for each factor. So a two factor ANOVA with three conditions on each factor will compare the three marginal means of factor one and then the three marginal means of factor two. We should only compare the main effects if we have a significant F value for that factor in the ANOVA and not a significant interaction. (If we have a significant interaction we can look at the simple main effects and an example of this is shown in Chapter 11.)

Comparing condition means

In conclusion we can advise the following general rules of thumb with respect to comparing condition means. Remember they are only valid if you have a statistically significant ANOVA F value.

- If possible, select planned contrasts in advance for the comparisons you are interested in.
- However, if you wish to perform post hoc tests (with a one factor ANOVA or a multifactor ANOVA without significant interactions) then:
  - for independent measures factors choose a post hoc Tukey test
  - for repeated measures factors choose **Compare main effects** with a Bonferroni correction.
- If you have a significant interaction in a multifactor ANOVA you can examine the simple main effects via the SPSS syntax, see Chapter 11.

FAQ

Do I need to read all the information about the general linear model before doing my analysis of variance?

No, you will find the information for performing the analysis of variance in Chapters 10 and 11. Following the 'SPSS Essential' sections will explain the key aspects of the output. However, if you understand the model SPSS is using to analyse your data then you will have a better understanding of the output.

Why do you need a 'model' to undertake an analysis of variance?

If we assume our data is following a particular pattern we can see how well it fits that pattern. We assume that the data follows a linear pattern – the general linear model. With two variables we argue that the pattern is a straight line. When we map our data on to the model we can then find out how much of the variability in our data can be explained by the model and how much cannot be explained. Comparing these two sources of variability allows us to make statistical decisions. Without the model we could not do this.

One factor analysis of variance

W E OFTEN WISH TO COMPARE more than two conditions of an independent variable. When this is the case we can no longer use the *t* test but use the analysis of variance (ANOVA). The advantage of the ANOVA is that it allows us to include as many conditions as we wish in the one test. In the one factor ANOVA we obtain a statistic, a variance ratio referred to as *F*, which looks at the variability in the scores between the conditions compared to the variability in the scores due to random factors or error. If there is an effect of the independent variable on the dependent variable it should produce a large variability in the scores between the conditions and so produce a large value of *F*. Note here that a large value of *F* tells us that there is an effect of the independent variable on the dependent variable but not which conditions are producing it. Consider three different methods for teaching young children about arithmetic. The results of a mathematics test might show a significant *F* value in an ANOVA. However, without further investigation it could be that all three methods produce very different scores, or that two produce similar scores and the third results in different scores. The ANOVA only tells us there is a difference somewhere but a further, post hoc, multiple comparison test needs to be employed to find out exactly which conditions are producing the effect.

There are two forms of the one factor ANOVA, just as there are two forms of the *t* test. The one factor independent measures design is for situations where the scores in each condition come from different participants and the repeated measures design is for situations where the scores in each condition come from the same participants.

One factor independent measures analysis of variance

Here is an example. A company designing watches wanted to know whether there was a difference in their five new watch faces in terms of the ease of reading the second hand accurately. They set up a test presenting the watch face 50 times, with the watch showing a different time at each presentation. Each presentation lasted the same very brief interval. Participants were asked to accurately read the position of the second hand. Errors were noted. There were 100 participants randomly divided into groups of 20 for each watch-face test. As the participants took part in only one condition it was an independent measures design, with 'watch type' as the independent variable (with five conditions) and 'error scores' as the dependent variable. A one factor independent measures ANOVA was used to test the hypothesis that there was an effect of watch type on the error scores.

The ANOVA analyses the variability in the scores and links that variability to various causes such as the effect of the independent variable and also to random chance. In order to do this, there are assumptions underlying the ANOVA, which, if violated, may result in the analysis being inappropriate and inaccurate. First, it is assumed that participants are randomly allocated to conditions so we have unbiased samples. Second, it is also assumed that the scores in each condition come from normally distributed populations and are measured on an interval scale; and third, that the scores in each condition come from populations with equal variances.

	type	minutes
1	first letter	15.00
2	first letter	20.00
3	first letter	14.00
4	first letter	13.00
5	first letter	18.00
6	first letter	16.00
7	first letter	13.00
8	first letter	12.00
9	first letter	18.00
10	first letter	11.00
11	last letter	21.00
12	last letter	25.00
13	last letter	29.00
14	last letter	18.00
15	last letter	26.00
16	last letter	22.00
17	last letter	26.00
18	last letter	24.00
19	last letter	28.00
20	last letter	21.00
21	No letter	28.00
22	No letter	30.00
23	No letter	32.00
24	No letter	28.00
25	No letter	26.00
26	No letter	30.00
27	No letter	25.00
28	No letter	36.00
29	No letter	20.00
30	No letter	25.00

Scenario

A researcher was interested in the effects of hints on a person's ability to solve anagrams (an anagram is a jumbled up word). The time it took a participant to solve five eight-letter anagrams was measured. The same five anagrams were used in three conditions: first letter (where the first letter of the word was given), last letter (where the last letter was given), and no letter (where no help was given). Thirty participants were chosen and ten were randomly allocated to each condition. The number of minutes it took to solve the five anagrams was recorded.

Data entry

Enter the dataset as shown in the example.

✓ Remember that to see the value labels you need to go to the **View** drop-down menu and select **Value Labels**.
✓ See Chapter 2 for the full data entry procedure.

Choice of method

There are two procedures for completing a one way independent measures ANOVA, which produce different outputs. Both procedures give the same results, however there are different benefits with each method. Method one is quicker to generate, produces tables that are easy to interpret and allows you to perform post hoc contrasts very easily, but this procedure can only be performed with the independent measures ANOVA. Method two is the general method for all types of ANOVA. Method one may be easier for the new user to SPSS and method two may be preferred by a researcher who performs many different ANOVAs with SPSS.

Test procedure: method one

- All inferential statistics are found under the **Analyze** command.
- Select **Compare Means** and then **One-Way ANOVA**.

- The dependent variable is 'minutes' and therefore should be sent to the **Dependent List** box.
- The independent variable is 'type' and therefore should be sent to the **Factor** box.

One-Way ANOVA: Options

Statistics
- ☑ Descriptive
- ☑ Homogeneity-of-variance

☑ Means plot

Missing Values
- ⦿ Exclude cases analysis by analysis
- ○ Exclude cases listwise

Continue | Cancel | Help

- Click on the **Options** button and select **Descriptive** and **Homogeneity-of-Variance** and **Means plot**, which will produce a line graph of the means.
- Click on **Continue**.

Planned contrasts and post hoc multiple comparison tests

Ordinarily, there would be no need for you to carry out both planned contrasts and post hoc tests on your data (See Chapter 9 for more details on these). However, despite it being unnecessary to carry out both of these tests, the chapter will explain both options. In your analysis you should decide which is the most appropriate test for your data. A general 'rule of thumb' would be if you are testing a specific hypothesis, planned contrasts might be the most appropriate. If you are unsure of the directionality of your test, employing pairwise comparisons via a post hoc test may be the most suitable option. You do not do BOTH but, for illustration purposes, we shall show both.

Planned contrasts

If you wish to make use of planned contrasts with this method, the following procedure, which is unique to this method, should be adopted. It is necessary to weight the groups using coefficients that total zero. Such planned contrasts tell SPSS which groups to combine and which to compare. We choose the values of the coefficients to weight the groups according to the following rules:

1 Coefficients for groups on one side of the comparison have positive coefficients (+) and coefficients on the other side have negative coefficients (−).
2 It is necessary to weight the groups using coefficients that total zero.
3 Both sides of the coefficients are weighted equally, so if two groups are given +1 on one side of the comparison, the other side of the comparison must have a weight of −2.

- Click on the **Contrasts** button to compare effects of various groups of scores.
- Our chosen comparison is to contrast the combined effects of groups one and two against three (first and last letter against no letter).
- For this combination we need to assign the coefficient of −1 to each of the first two groups and combine their effects against the third group to which we assign the coefficient +2.
- Click on **Continue**.

```
One-Way ANOVA: Contrasts                    [×]

□ Polynomial    Degree: [Linear    ▼]    Continue
                                         Cancel
[Previous]  Contrast 1 of 1   [Next]
                                         Help
Coefficients: [        ]
  [Add]       -1
              -1
  [Change]    +2
  [Remove]
Coefficient Total: 0.000
```

✓ If you wanted to make pairwise comparisons of your data these can be most easily achieved through the **Post Hoc** command.

SPSS advanced

✓ The **Contrasts** box also gives the option to perform a trend analysis. Performing this test will give more information as to the underlying model best fitting the data. This can be achieved by selecting the **Polynomial** box and selecting the type of trend required. The common ones are outlined below:

- The *linear* model analyses the fit of the trend to a linear relationship. This can be performed on two or more conditions.
- The *quadratic* model analyses the fit of the trend to a curved line. This can be performed on three or more conditions.
- The *cubic* model analyses the fit of the trend to a wavy line. This can be performed on four or more conditions.

- SPSS can calculate the relevant trends for your data but make sure you have enough conditions which are appropriate to make sensible conclusions.

Post hoc tests

If your analysis is best served by post hoc multiple pairwise comparisons, then the post hoc option is the most efficient way to generate these as part of the ANOVA procedure.

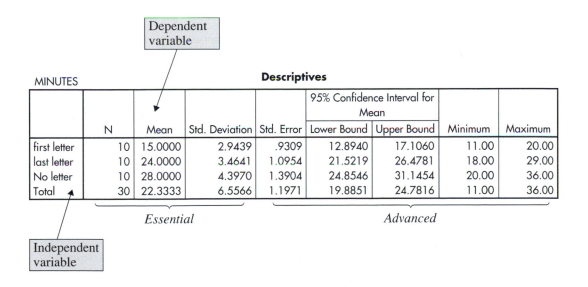

- Click on the **Post Hoc** button and put a tick in the appropriate post hoc test for pairwise comparisons. We have selected the **Tukey**.
- Click on **Continue** and **OK** to complete the ANOVA procedure.

✓ There are advantages and disadvantages of the different post hoc tests. We recommend the Tukey as it controls the overall Type 1 error rate and is reasonably powerful.

SPSS output

The first table that SPSS produces is for **Descriptive Statistics**.

Dependent variable

MINUTES

Descriptives

	N	Mean	Std. Deviation	Std. Error	95% Confidence Interval for Mean Lower Bound	95% Confidence Interval for Mean Upper Bound	Minimum	Maximum
first letter	10	15.0000	2.9439	.9309	12.8940	17.1060	11.00	20.00
last letter	10	24.0000	3.4641	1.0954	21.5219	26.4781	18.00	29.00
No letter	10	28.0000	4.3970	1.3904	24.8546	31.1454	20.00	36.00
Total	30	22.3333	6.5566	1.1971	19.8851	24.7816	11.00	36.00

Essential   *Advanced*

Independent variable

SPSS essential

- The first column of our **Descriptives** table details the number of participants (**N**) in each group.
- The table above displays the mean times taken to complete the anagrams in the three conditions. It can be seen that when participants were not given any help to solve the anagrams (no letter), they took longer to generate the solution (mean time = 28 minutes). When given the last letter, participants solved the anagrams quicker than when not given any letters (24 minutes), although not as quickly as when the first letter of the solution was given (15 minutes). These differences seem to be supporting our hypothesis, but to ascertain whether this result is significant or due to chance the ANOVA table must be examined.
- The **Std. Deviation** indicates the spread of scores in the three conditions. The largest spread of scores was found in the 'No letter' condition (4.3970 minutes).
- The table also displays the **Total** mean and standard deviations of all three conditions together.

SPSS advanced

- The **Std. Error** (standard error) is an estimate of the standard deviation of the sampling distribution of the mean.
- The **95% Confidence Interval for Mean** indicates that we are 95 per cent confident that the true (population) mean will be between the upper and lower limits. The sample means fall between these two values. See Chapter 6 for more details.

SPSS produces Levene's **Test of Homogeneity of Variances** table, which tells us if we have met our second assumption (the groups have approximately equal variance on the dependent variable).

Test statistic

Test of Homogeneity of Variances

MINUTES

Levene Statistic	df1	df2	Sig.
.355	2	27	.704

p value

SPSS essential

- If the Levene's test result is not significant ($p > 0.05$), the variances are approximately equal.
- Here, we see that the **Sig.** value is 0.704, which is greater than 0.05. We can therefore assume that the variances are approximately equal.
- If the Levene's test result is significant ($p < 0.05$) then the variances are significantly different. If this is the case then you may need to consider transformation to make your variances more homogeneous.

The ANOVA summary table is displayed next. This table contains the key information regarding our calculated F statistic.

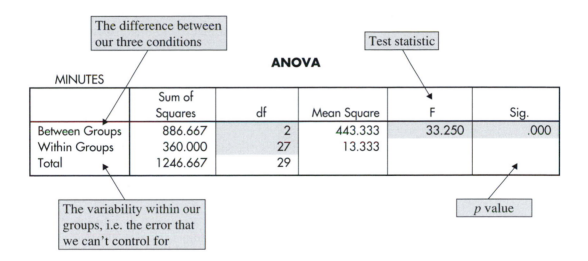

ANOVA

MINUTES

	Sum of Squares	df	Mean Square	F	Sig.
Between Groups	886.667	2	443.333	33.250	.000
Within Groups	360.000	27	13.333		
Total	1246.667	29			

The difference between our three conditions

Test statistic

The variability within our groups, i.e. the error that we can't control for

p value

SPSS essential

- The degrees of freedom (**df**) need to be reported. In ANOVAs there will be two values, one for the factor (**Between Groups**) and one for the error (**Within Groups**), so here $df = (2,27)$.
- If SPSS states that the probability (**Sig.**) is 0.000, it means that SPSS has rounded up or down the amount to the nearest number at three decimal places. However, we would always round the last 0 to a 1, so that $p < 0.001$.
- The conventional way of reporting the findings is to state the test statistic (**F**), degrees of freedom (**df**), and probability (**Sig.**).
  An example can be seen below.

$$F(2,27) = 33.250; \; p < 0.001$$

- As $p < 0.001$, this indicates that there is a highly significant difference between the three groups. However, it does not state where the significance lies.

SPSS advanced

- The **Sum of Squares** gives a measure of the variability in the scores due to a particular source of variability. The **Mean Square** is the variance (sum of squares divided by degrees of freedom). Note that there is a lot of variability due to our factor and much less due to error.

As we made a planned comparison through the **Contrasts** box, this result is shown next. The first table confirms the contrast performed. If you elected to make more than one contrast, these will appear on the same table.

Contrast Coefficients

	TYPE		
Contrast	first letter	last letter	No letter
1	−1	−1	2

The contrast selected in this example was to compare the group that had no letter hints when solving anagrams with the other two groups. The outcome of the contrast is shown in the **Contrast Tests** table below:

Contrast Tests

		Contrast	Value of Contrast	Std. Error	t	df	Sig. (2-tailed)
MINUTES	Assume equal variances	1	17.0000	2.8284	6.010	27	.000
	Does not assume equal	1	17.0000	3.1305	5.430	13.942	.000

Our analysis checked for homogeneity of variances and, as discussed earlier, we have not found any significant differences in our variances and can therefore assume that they are equal. In our example we can therefore take the top row of contrast information. If we were less sure about our variances, and found them to be significantly different in the three groups, then we would need to take the more conservative results shown in the second row.

SPSS advanced

- The **Contrast Tests** table should be read in a similar fashion to a *t* test table.
- A **Value of Contrast** of 17.000 is produced. When analysed by *t* tests, a *t* value of 6.010 at 27 degrees of freedom is found to be significant as $p < 0.001$.
- We can conclude that the time taken for the people who received no hints when completing anagrams was longer than for those who were given a hint.

We selected to make multiple pairwise comparisons between groups through the use of a Tukey post hoc test. The results appear in the **Multiple Comparisons** table.

Multiple Comparisons

Dependent Variable: MINUTES
Tukey HSD

(I) TYPE	(J) TYPE	Mean Difference (I-J)	Std. Error	Sig.	95% Confidence Interval	
					Lower Bound	Upper Bound
first letter	last letter	−9.0000*	1.6330	.000	−13.0489	−4.9511
	No letter	−13.0000*	1.6330	.000	−17.0489	−8.9511
last letter	first letter	9.0000*	1.6330	.000	4.9511	13.0489
	No letter	−4.0000	1.6330	.053	−8.0489	4.888E-02
No letter	first letter	13.0000*	1.6330	.000	8.9511	17.0489
	last letter	4.0000	1.6330	.053	−4.8880E-02	8.0489

*. The mean difference is significant at the .05 level.

SPSS essential

- The **Multiple Comparisons** table shows all the possible pairwise comparisons for our three groups of participants.
- In each comparison, one group is given the identifier 'I' and the second 'J'. This is evident in the **Mean Difference** column, which gives the resulting figure when the mean of one group (J) has been subtracted from the mean of another group (I).
- In our example, the mean of group one (first letter) was shown to be 15.0000 minutes in our descriptive statistics calculations, and the mean of the second group (last letter) 24.0000 minutes.

    15.0000 (I) − 24.0000 (J) = −9.0000

- The **Sig.** column enables us to assess if the mean differences between the groups are significant.
- We can see from our example that the difference between the first letter and last letter group is significant, as is the difference between the first letter and no letter group as the p values are small and less than 0.05.
- We have not found significant differences between the last letter and no letter group as $p > 0.05$. However, this is only just outside the realm of claiming a significant difference, so examining the confidence intervals may give more information as to the strength of this difference.

SPSS advanced

- The **95% Confidence Interval** provides us with a different method for assessing the differences in our groups. From looking at the significance level we concluded that there was no significant difference between our groups 'no letter' and 'last letter' ($p > 0.05$). However, the confidence interval calculated suggests that there may be a difference.
- The upper and lower bounds of the confidence interval are 0.0488 to -8.0489. This is quite a large range, however it does include zero just at the top of the range, despite the mean difference being -4.
- Confidence intervals are therefore a good way of complementing significance levels, particularly if the figures are found to be on the edge of significance. See Chapter 6 for more details on confidence intervals and their uses.

SPSS also calculates the homogeneous subsets (**MINUTES**) table shown below.

MINUTES

Tukey HSD[a]

TYPE	N	Subset for alpha = .05	
		1	2
first letter	10	15.0000	
last letter	10		24.0000
No letter	10		28.0000
Sig.		1.000	.053

Means for groups in homogeneous subsets are displayed.
[a]. Uses Harmonic Mean Sample Size = 10.000.

SPSS advanced

- The homogeneous subsets table (**MINUTES**) combines together those pairwise comparisons that were not found to be significantly different from each other.
- As we found in the **Multiple Comparisons** table, the group who were given the first letter of the anagram performed significantly differently from the other two groups (last letter and no letter groups). However, these last two groups did not perform significantly differently from each other.
- SPSS has therefore created two subsets from the data. Because the first letter group was found to perform differently from the other two groups, it appears in a subset on its own.
- The two remaining groups were found to be different from the first letter group, but not different from each other, and hence appear in the same subset.
- If all three groups were found to be significantly different from each other, three separate subsets would have been created, one for each group in our study.

We selected the option for SPSS to produce a plot of the means of our groups of participants, and this appears as follows:

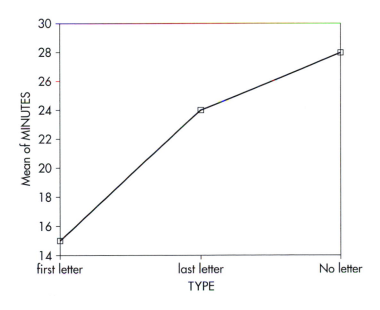

SPSS essential

- We can see from the graphical display of the means the patterns previously discussed.
- Those participants in the group that was given the first letter of the anagram as a hint completed the tasks in the shortest amount of time.
- The group that performed the worst was the one that was not given any hints regarding the anagram completions.

Test procedure: method two

- Remember all inferential statistics are found under the **Analyze** command.
- Select **General Linear Model** and then **Univariate** as we have only one dependent variable (see Chapter 9 for more details of the general linear model).

- The dependent variable is 'minutes' and this should be sent to the **Dependent Variable** box.
- The independent variable is 'type' and this should be sent to the **Fixed Factor(s)** box.

Within the ANOVA procedure you can also produce descriptive statistics.

- Select the **Options** button and place a tick next to **Descriptive statistics**.
- Place a tick next to **Homogeneity tests** and then click on **Continue**.

Also when creating ANOVAs through the **General Linear Model** method, you can generate the illustrative statistics as part of the procedure.

- Select the **Plots** button and then send the factor 'type' across to the **Horizontal Axis** box. This will produce a line chart with the three conditions on the X-axis, and a line plotting the means of the three conditions.
- Click on **Add** to send the factor to the **Plots** box, then **Continue**.

Planned contrasts and post hoc multiple comparison tests

As with the first method for generating independent factor ANOVAs in SPSS, both planned and post hoc tests can be carried out using the general linear model. Again it is only necessary to carry out either a planned contrasts or a post hoc test on your data, depending on the design and research questions surrounding your study. However, below we explain the procedure for both.

Planned contrasts

Calculating independent ANOVAs through the method described earlier allows the user to specify the contrast combination that best fits their study design. However, when calculating ANOVAs through the general linear model, pre-created contrasts are provided for you within the **Contrasts** option. These are listed in the contrasts section of Chapter 9.

Click on the **Contrasts** option on the **Univariate** box to reveal the following box.

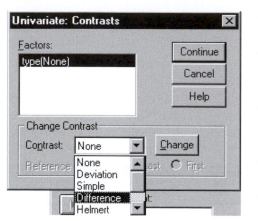

- The default option is for no contrasts to be performed in the calculation.
- By clicking on the drop-down menu next to **Contrast**, the contrast options are shown.
- In our example we wanted to compare the last group (no letter) to the first two groups (first and last letter)
- This comparison is best served by the **Difference** contrast.
- Click on **Change** and then **Continue**.

Post hoc multiple comparison tests

If your analysis would be best addressed through the use of pairwise comparisons, the post hoc tests option should be the one selected.

- Select the **Post Hoc** test button then send the independent variable to the **Post Hoc Tests for** box.
- Place a tick in the box of the appropriate post hoc test – we have selected **Tukey**.
- Click on **Continue** and then **OK** to complete the ANOVA procedure.

178

> ✓ There are advantages and disadvantages of the different post hoc tests. We recommend the Tukey as it controls the overall Type 1 error rate and is reasonably powerful.

SPSS output

The first table that SPSS produces is the **Between-Subjects Factors** table. This lists the number of participants in each group, and confirms how many groups have been used in the calculations.

The independent variable

Between-Subjects Factors

		Value Label	N
TYPE	1	first letter	10
	2	last letter	10
	3	No letter	10

The next table that SPSS produces is for **Descriptive Statistics**.

The independent variable

Descriptive Statistics

Dependent Variable: MINUTES

TYPE	Mean	Std. Deviation	N
first letter	15.0000	2.9439	10
last letter	24.0000	3.4641	10
No letter	28.0000	4.3970	10
Total	22.3333	6.5566	30

Essential

SPSS essential

- The **Descriptive Statistics** table displays the **Mean** times taken to complete the anagrams in the three conditions. It can be seen that when participants were not given any help to solve the anagrams (no letter), they took longer to generate the solution. When given the last letter, participants solved the anagrams quicker than when not given any letters, although not as quickly as when the first letter of the solution was given. These differences seem to be supporting our hypothesis, but to ascertain whether this result is significant or due to chance the **Tests of Between-Subjects Effects** table must be examined.

- The **Std. Deviation** shows that the spread of scores in the condition where no help was given is the largest (4.3970), with the most closely related scores being found in the condition where the first letter of the solution was given (2.9439).
- The table also displays the **Total** mean and standard deviations of all three conditions together.
- **N** is the number of participants.

The next table displays the results of **Levene's Test of Equality of Error Variances**, and tells us if we have met our homogeneity of variance assumption (the groups have approximately equal variances on the dependent variable).

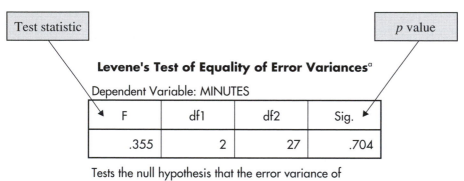

Test statistic

p value

Levene's Test of Equality of Error Variances[a]

Dependent Variable: MINUTES

F	df1	df2	Sig.
.355	2	27	.704

Tests the null hypothesis that the error variance of
the dependent variable is equal across groups.
  [a]. Design: Intercept+TYPE

SPSS essential

- If the Levene's test is not significant ($p > 0.05$), this indicates the variances are approximately equal.
- Here, we see that the probability is 0.704, which is greater than 0.05. We can therefore assume that the variances are approximately equal.
- If the Levene's test is significant ($p < 0.05$) then the variances are significantly different. You may then wish to have a closer look at your data to see if there are any

anomalous results causing this effect, or consider a transformation to make your variances more homogeneous.

The ANOVA summary table is labelled **Tests of Between-Subjects Effects**. This table contains the key information regarding our calculated F statistic.

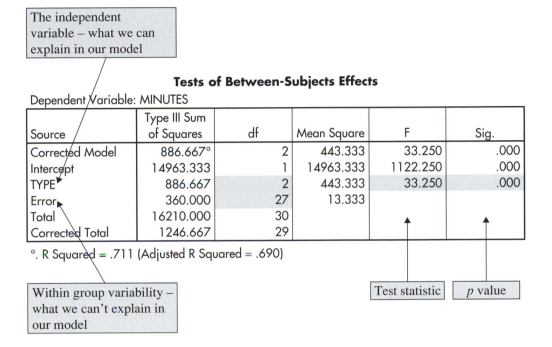

The independent variable – what we can explain in our model

Tests of Between-Subjects Effects

Dependent Variable: MINUTES

Source	Type III Sum of Squares	df	Mean Square	F	Sig.
Corrected Model	886.667ᵃ	2	443.333	33.250	.000
Intercept	14963.333	1	14963.333	1122.250	.000
TYPE	886.667	2	443.333	33.250	.000
Error	360.000	27	13.333		
Total	16210.000	30			
Corrected Total	1246.667	29			

ᵃ. R Squared = .711 (Adjusted R Squared = .690)

Within group variability – what we can't explain in our model

Test statistic p value

SPSS essential

- In the ANOVA table there are two rows we are interested in: our factor (**TYPE**) and **Error**. The F value on the **TYPE** row shows the 'significance' of our factor ($p = 0.000$).
- If SPSS states that the probability is 0.000, it means that SPSS has rounded up the amount to the nearest number at three decimal places. However, with 0.000 we always round the last 0, to a 1, so that $p < 0.001$.
- In an ANOVA there are two degrees of freedom values to report. One for the factor **TYPE**, which has 2 degrees of freedom, and the other for **Error**, which has 27 degrees of freedom.
- The conventional way of reporting the findings is to state the test statistic (F), degrees of freedom (df), and probability value (Sig.) as follows:

$F(2,27) = 33.250$; $p < 0.001$

- As $p < 0.001$, this indicates that there is a highly significant difference between the three groups. However, it does not state where the significance lies.

SPSS advanced

- The **Corrected Model** shows how much variability in the data we can explain by our independent variable. Note that these **Sums of Squares** are the same as the **Sums of Squares** of TYPE (886.667).
- The ANOVA works out the amount of variability in the data around the mean value. If this overall mean is zero then the intercept will also be zero. However, when the mean is not zero we are not interested in how the individual scores differ from zero, we are only interested in how they differ from the overall mean. In this case the **Intercept** sums of squares simply tells us how much variability is due to the overall mean being different from zero. We can remove this variability (as it is not relevant to our ANOVA calculation) to produce the **Corrected Total** sums of squares.
- In our example, the **Intercept** row shows us we can see that our overall mean is significantly different from zero.
- The **Sums of Squares** gives a measure of the variability in the scores due to a particular source of variability. The **Corrected Total** sums of squares (1246.667) is made up of the sums of squares of our factor **TYPE** (886.667) and the **Error** sums of squares (360.000). Note that there is a lot of variability due to our factor and much less due to error.
- The **Mean Square** is the amount of variance (sums of squares divided by degrees of freedom).
- The **R Squared** and **Adjusted R Squared** values give us an indication of the amount of variability in the scores that can be explained by our independent variable. This is calculated by dividing the **Sums of Squares** of the **Corrected Model** (886.667) by the **Corrected Total Sums of Squares** (1246.667), giving a value of 0.711. Therefore our model can explain 71.1 per cent of the variability.

We made a planned comparison through the **Contrasts** box, using the option **Difference**, and this is shown next.

The first table confirms which contrasts have been performed. We can see that two contrasts have been calculated, comparing level 2 with level 1, and comparing level 3 with both of these. The contrast that we are interested in for our specific hypothesis is the latter one, which compares the no letter group (level 3) with the other two groups who were given either the first or the last letter of the anagram.

Contrast Results (K Matrix)

TYPE Difference Contrast		Dependent Variable
		MINUTES
Level 2 vs. Level 1	Contrast Estimate	9.000
	Hypothesized Value	0
	Difference (Estimate – Hypothesized)	9.000
	Std. Error	1.633
	Sig.	.000
	95% Confidence Interval for Difference Lower Bound	5.649
	Upper Bound	12.351
Level 3 vs. Previous	Contrast Estimate	8.500
	Hypothesized Value	0
	Difference (Estimate – Hypothesized)	8.500
	Std. Error	1.414
	Sig.	.000
	95% Confidence Interval for Difference Lower Bound	5.598
	Upper Bound	11.402

SPSS advanced

- From the above table the figures which we are particularly interested in appear in the second block of the table headed '**Level 3 vs. Previous**' as this is the contrast which tests our specific hypothesis.
- The calculated **Contrast Estimate** is 8.500.
- By observing our **Sig.** value we can see that as $p < 0.001$ we have found a significant contrast.

In addition to this, SPSS also reports an ANOVA for the contrast comparisons made. This can be seen in the **Test Results** table below.

Test statistic

Test Results

Dependent Variable: MINUTES

Source	Sum of Squares	df	Mean Square	F	Sig.
Contrast	886.667	2	443.333	33.250	.000
Error	360.000	27	13.333		

p value

SPSS advanced

- The contrast ANOVA should be read in a similar fashion to other ANOVAs:

  $$F(2,27) = 33.250; \ p < 0.001$$

- The contrast performed is therefore found to be statistically significant.

The post hoc tests table (**Multiple Comparisons**) shows the Tukey HSD (Honestly Significant Difference); this compares each pair of conditions to see if their difference is significant. Multiple comparisons are undertaken when we have not planned a contrast.

Multiple Comparisons

Dependent Variable: MINUTES
Tukey HSD

(I) TYPE	(J) TYPE	Mean Difference (I-J)	Std. Error	Sig.	95% Confidence Interval Lower Bound	95% Confidence Interval Upper Bound
first letter	last letter	−9.0000*	1.6330	.000	−13.0489	−4.9511
	No letter	−13.0000*	1.6330	.000	−17.0489	−8.9511
last letter	first letter	9.0000*	1.6330	.000	4.9511	13.0489
	No letter	−4.0000	1.6330	.053	−8.0489	4.888E-02
No letter	first letter	13.0000*	1.6330	.000	8.9511	17.0489
	last letter	4.0000	1.6330	.053	−4.8880E-02	8.0489

Based on observed means.
 *. The mean difference is significant at the .05 level.

SPSS essential

- In the **Multiple Comparisons** table, the important columns have been shaded to highlight them.
- This table shows all the possible comparisons for our three groups of participants.
- In each comparison, one group is given the identifier 'I' and the second 'J'. This is evident in the **Mean Difference** column, which indicates the resulting figure when the mean of one group (J) has been subtracted from the mean of another group (I).
- In our example, the mean of group one (first letter) was shown to be 15.0000 minutes in our descriptive statistics calculations, and the mean of the second group (last letter) 24.0000 minutes.

  $$15.0000 \ (I) - 24.0000 \ (J) = -9.0000$$

- The **Sig.** column enables us to assess whether the mean differences between the groups are significant.
- We can see from our example that the difference between the first letter and last letter group is significant, as is the difference between the first letter and no letter group as the p values are small and less than 0.05.
- We have not found a significant difference between the last letter and no letter group as $p > 0.05$. However, this is only just outside the realm of claiming a significant difference, so examining the confidence intervals may give more information as to the strength of this difference.

SPSS advanced

- The **95% Confidence Interval** provides us with a different method for assessing the differences in our groups. From looking at the significance level we concluded that there was no significant difference between the no letter and the last letter groups. However, the confidence interval calculated suggests that there may be a difference.
- The upper and lower bounds of the confidence interval are 0.0488 to -8.0489. This is quite a large range, however it does include zero just at the top of the range, despite the mean being -4.
- Confidence intervals are therefore a good way of complementing significance levels, particularly if the figures are found to be on the edge of significance. See Chapter 6 for more details on confidence intervals and their uses.

The findings of the above are summarised in the homogeneous subsets (**MINUTES**) table shown below.

MINUTES

Tukey HSD[a,b]

		Subset	
TYPE	N	1	2
first letter	10	15.0000	
last letter	10		24.0000
No letter	10		28.0000
Sig.		1.000	.053

Means for groups in homogeneous subsets are displayed.
Based on Type III Sum of Squares
The error term is Mean Square(Error) = 13.333.
  [a]. Uses Harmonic Mean Sample Size = 10.000.
  [b]. Alpha = .05.

SPSS advanced

- The homogeneous subsets table combines together those pairwise comparisons which were not found to be significantly different from each other.
- As we found in the **Multiple Comparisons** table above, the group who were given the first letter of the anagram performed significantly differently from the other two groups (last letter and no letter groups). However, these last two groups did not perform significantly differently from each other.
- SPSS has therefore created two subsets from the data. Because the first letter group was found to perform differently from the other two, it appears in a subset on its own.
- The two remaining groups were found to be different from the first letter group, but not different from each other, and hence appear in the same subset.
- If all three groups were found to be significantly different from each other, three separate subsets would have been created, one for each group in our study.

In our ANOVA procedure we selected the option for SPSS to produce a plot of the means of our groups of participants. This will enable us to obtain a visual image of the performance of the three groups on the anagrams. This is shown below.

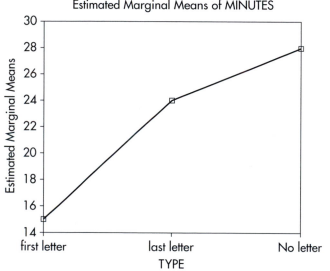

Estimated Marginal Means of MINUTES

SPSS essential

- We can see from the graphical display of the means the patterns previously discussed.
- Those participants in the group that was given the first letter of the anagram as a hint completed the tasks in the shortest amount of time.
- The group that performed the worst was the one whose members were not given any hints to help them complete the anagram.

One factor repeated measures analysis of variance

The repeated measures ANOVA is used when we have the same participants in each of the conditions of the independent variable, such as testing the same children on a comprehension test of three different stories to see if there is an effect of 'story' on their performance. (Clearly we would need to counterbalance the order of testing to control for 'carry-over' or practice effects.) There is an advantage of repeated measures over the independent measures ANOVA, but also a cost! The advantage is that when we use the same participant in all the conditions of the independent variable we are able to remove the 'individual differences' from the analysis before we calculate the statistic. This results in a smaller error term and a greater likelihood of finding a significant effect when it is there.

For example, if we test the same group of children on their comprehension of three stories to see if there is a difference in understanding between the stories, we might find that John understands all the stories very well and gets high marks in the comprehension test but scores lower on story 1. Even though Peter gets low marks on all the comprehension tests he too scores lowest on story 1. Even though John is scoring much higher than Peter the pattern of results across the stories is the same, with story 1 giving the lowest score for both (even though John's scores are all much higher than Peter's). The repeated measures ANOVA removes the individual differences of the participants, called 'within subjects variance', which in this case is that Peter generally scores much higher than John, and then analyses the differences between the conditions – both boys are scoring lower on story 1 than on stories 2 and 3.

The cost of this is that the analysis of repeated measures is more complicated to undertake and SPSS provides us with a lot more output. First, as well as the same assumptions as the independent measures ANOVA, requiring interval data in each condition, drawn from normal distributions of equal variance and unbiased samples, the repeated measures ANOVA has the additional assumption of 'sphericity'. This is often more complicated to explain than test! (See Chapter 9 for an account of how SPSS deals with this assumption.) Essentially, the ANOVA assumes that the differences between scores in each pair of conditions have equal variances. It needs to do this to undertake the

ANOVA properly, otherwise it would work out the variances inappropriately and the analysis would not be very meaningful. In a repeated measures design, with the same participants performing in each condition, we risk violating this assumption and causing an incorrect F value to be calculated.

SPSS adopts a belt and braces approach to sphericity. First, it provides us with checks (Mauchly's test and epsilon) to see if the sphericity is OK. If it is, then we can use the usual 'sphericity assumed' F value. However, if there is a problem SPSS provides us with a choice of F values corrected for the violation in sphericity (for example Greenhouse–Geisser). SPSS goes further and for those of us worried about sphericity it provides an alternative to the original 'univariate' test. This is the 'multivariate' analysis that does not require the assumption of sphericity at all (for example Wilks' lambda) which we can use instead. Our advice is that you should check the Mauchly test and epsilon, then use the 'sphericity assumed' F value if the Mauchly test is not significant and epsilon is close to 1. (However, it is sensible to have a quick glance at the Greenhouse–Geisser and Wilks' lambda to check they are giving the same result.) If the Mauchly test indicates a sphericity violation or you have concerns about the value of epsilon, you should choose a correction such as the Greenhouse–Geisser or the slightly less conservative Huynh–Feldt. Alternatively, with large samples you may choose a multivariate test, such as Wilks' lambda (the most popular) where sphericity is not an issue. However, the univariate test is often the more powerful test.

This may all sound very complicated, but like so many things in statistics it sounds worse than it is. For many analyses the sphericity will be all right – the Mauchly test will be non-significant – and the 'sphericity assumed' F value will be fine (with the other tests, such as Wilks' lambda or Greenhouse–Geisser indicating the same result). But it is simply good sense to look at the different tables to check this is so, and if it's not then take a little time to decide on the best statistic to use (see Chapter 9).

Scenario

A research programme was set up to develop user-friendly computer equipment for people with physical disabilities. Three new designs of computer keyboard for people with difficulties in hand and finger movement were developed and prototypes created. The research task was to decide which of these prototypes was the most successful. Four potential users of the new equipment agreed to take part in a test of the new keyboards. Each participant was asked to use the keyboard to input a piece of text and the number of errors was recorded. Three equally difficult pieces of text were used so that a participant did not improve performance by practice on the same piece of text. The choice of text and the order in which each subject tested the keyboards was controlled for, to account for possible confounding variables.

Data entry

Enter the dataset as shown in the example. (We are using such a small dataset for illustration purposes.)

> ✓ Remember when entering data without decimal places to change the decimal places to zero in the **Variable View**.
> ✓ See Chapter 2 for the full data entry procedure.

Untitled - SPSS Data Editor

File   Edit   View   Data   Transform   Analyze   Graphs

14 :

	key1	key2	key3
1	5	6	10
2	1	2	3
3	0	4	5
4	2	4	6
5			

Test procedure

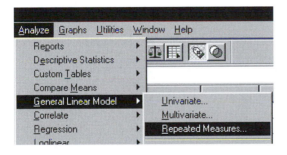

- All inferential statistics are found under the **Analyze** command.
- Select **General Linear Model** and then **Repeated Measures** as we have a repeated measures design.
- The repeated measures variable is called the Within Subjects Factor by SPSS.

- We then need to define which is the **Within-Subject Factor** by choosing a suitable name.
- Enter the number of levels this factor has and then click on **Add**.
- We only have one factor so no further factors need to be added. Click on **Define**.

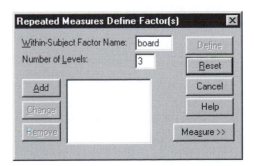

✓ Note that in version 12 this box will look slightly different and options under **Measure** will be visible.

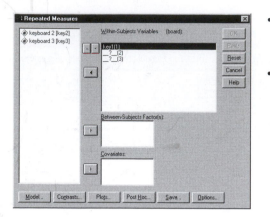

- All the conditions of the repeated measures variable need to be sent over to the **Within-Subjects Variables** box.
- Our dataset has only three conditions, so all of these are the within subjects variables. If the variables form part of a larger dataset, all the variables will appear in the left-hand column, and the within subject variables under current study should be selected and sent over to the conditions box.

✓ If you had chosen planned contrasts, you could click the **Contrasts** option to select the contrast you wanted as explained in Chapter 9.

- The appropriate graph for an ANOVA (a line graph) can be generated as part of the ANOVA procedure.
- Click on **Plots** and send the factor to the **Horizontal Axis** box and click on **Add**.
- This will produce a line chart with the three repeated measures conditions on the X-axis, and a line plotting the means of the three conditions.
- Click **Continue**.

✓ Graphs generated in this manner may need editing, as the labelling technique is not always clear. If you prefer, you can generate a line chart separately from the ANOVA procedure by going to the **Graphs** command. See Chapter 4 for further details.

- Click on the **Options** button. This is where we can instruct SPSS to generate descriptive statistics and calculate pairwise comparisons using the Bonferroni post hoc test.
- Click on our factor 'board' and send it across to the **Display Means for** box.
- Place a tick in **Compare main effects**, and change the **Confidence interval adjustment** to Bonferroni.
- Within the **Display** box, place a tick next to **Descriptive statistics**.
- Click on **Continue**, then **OK**.

SPSS output

The first table produced by SPSS (**Within-Subjects Factors**) gives a description of the factor entered into the ANOVA equation. This confirms that our within subjects factor (our repeated measures factor) has three conditions, KEY1, KEY2, and KEY3.

Within-Subjects Factors

Measure: MEASURE_1

BOARD	Dependent Variable
1	KEY1
2	KEY2
3	KEY3

The first table of importance is the table of **Descriptive Statistics**.

Descriptive Statistics

	Mean	Std. Deviation	N
keyboard 1	2.00	2.16	4
keyboard 2	4.00	1.63	4
keyboard 3	6.00	2.94	4

Essential

SPSS essential

- The table displays the **Mean** number of errors committed by the participants on the three keyboards.
- By observing the means we can see that the number of errors increased from keyboard 1, to keyboard 2 to keyboard 3, (2.00, 4.00, 6.00 respectively).
- The **Std. Deviations** indicate the spread of scores within the keyboard trials. By observing the standard deviations we can see that keyboard 3 led to the most variability in performance (2.94), while keyboard 2 produced the least variability in errors (1.63) among our participants.
- **N** represents the number of participants who took the trial on each keyboard.

The next table shows the **Multivariate Tests** results. This table is generated by default by SPSS during one factor repeated measures ANOVAs. We only use this if sphericity is shown to be a problem in our data.

Multivariate Tests[b]

Effect		Value	F	Hypothesis df	Error df	Sig.
BOARD	Pillai's Trace	.914	10.667[a]	2.000	2.000	.086
	Wilks' Lambda	.086	10.667[a]	2.000	2.000	.086
	Hotelling's Trace	10.667	10.667[a]	2.000	2.000	.086
	Roy's Largest Root	10.667	10.667[a]	2.000	2.000	.086

[a]. Exact statistic
[b]. Design: Intercept
   Within Subjects Design: BOARD

SPSS advanced

- The above tests make fewer assumptions about the data, and may therefore be appropriate if **Mauchly's Test of Sphericity** is significant, or the **Epsilon** value is not large enough (as displayed in the next table).
- The most popular test is **Wilks' Lambda**.
- From our example above, using **Wilks' Lambda** we can conclude that there is not a significant difference between the performances on our keyboards:

$F(2,2) = 10.667;\ p > 0.05$

- In this particular example, the multivariate tests produce non-significant results. This is in conflict with the univariate test shown later, which returns a significant result. This is because the multivariate tests are less powerful than the univariate tests with this small dataset.

The following table shows the sphericity checks. This is generated by default by SPSS during the one factor repeated measures ANOVA procedure.

Mauchly's Test of Sphericity[b]

Measure: MEASURE_1

Within Subjects Effect	Mauchly's W	Approx. Chi-Square	df	Sig.	Epsilon[a]		
					Greenhouse-Geisser	Huynh-Feldt	Lower-bound
BOARD	1.000	.000	2	1.000	1.000	1.000	.500

Tests the null hypothesis that the error covariance matrix of the orthonormalized transformed dependent variables is proportional to an identity matrix.

  [a]. May be used to adjust the degrees of freedom for the averaged tests of significance. Corrected tests are displayed in the Tests of Within-Subjects Effects table.

  [b]. Design: Intercept
    Within Subjects Design: BOARD

SPSS advanced

- When we have more than two conditions of the repeated measures variable we check the sphericity assumption before calculating the F value results.
- If the sphericity assumption is met then we proceed to report the F value from the **Sphericity Assumed** line of the **Tests of Within-Subjects Effects** table, which follows next.
- If the sphericity assumption is not met and **Mauchly's Test of Sphericity** is significant we cannot take the **Sphericity Assumed** line of the **Tests of Within-Subjects Effects** table and need to employ a correction. SPSS provides us with several correction models, the Greehouse–Geisser is the one usually reported.
- The **Mauchly's Test of Sphericity** table above gives a **Mauchly's W** test statistic of 1.000, $df = 2$; $p > 0.05$. We can therefore conclude that the sphericity assumption has been met and we can use the output from the univariate model without correction.
- There is, however, some debate as to the sensitivity of Mauchly's test in its ability to detect sphericity. There is therefore the alternative of consulting the **Epsilon** value quoted in the **Greenhouse-Geisser** column. This figure should be as close to 1.00 as

possible in order to indicate no sphericity problems. Our value is 1.00 so we can be confident that issues of sphericity do not affect our calculations (refer back to Chapter 9 if you need a more detailed explanation of these issues).

If the sphericity assumption is met, as it is in our example, we can take the values from the **Sphericity Assumed** rows in the **Tests of Within-Subjects Effects** table below.

Tests of Within-Subjects Effects

Measure: MEASURE_1

Source		Type III Sum of Squares	df	Mean Square	F	Sig.
BOARD	Sphericity Assumed	32.000	2	16.000	16.000	.004
	Greenhouse-Geisser	32.000	2.000	16.000	16.000	.004
	Huynh-Feldt	32.000	2.000	16.000	16.000	.004
	Lower-bound	32.000	1.000	32.000	16.000	.028
Error(BOARD)	Sphericity Assumed	6.000	6	1.000		
	Greenhouse-Geisser	6.000	6.000	1.000		
	Huynh-Feldt	6.000	6.000	1.000		
	Lower-bound	6.000	3.000	2.000		

SPSS essential

- The important rows in this table have been highlighted above and are the **Sphericity Assumed** rows.
- The degrees of freedom (**df**) for both the variable and error must be reported, $df = (2,6)$.
- The conventional way of reporting the findings is to state the test statistic (**F**), degrees of freedom (**df**), and probability value (**Sig.**):

$$F(2,6) = 16.000, \ p < 0.01$$

- As $p < 0.01$, this indicates that we have found a significant difference in the performance on our keyboards. We do not, however, know where the differences lie, and therefore must consult the post hoc test for this information.

The **Tests of Within-Subjects Contrasts** table is generated by default by SPSS during the one factor repeated measures ANOVA procedure and is a trend analysis.

Tests of Within-Subjects Contrasts

Measure: MEASURE_1

Source	BOARD	Type III Sum of Squares	df	Mean Square	F	Sig.
BOARD	Linear	32.000	1	32.000	32.000	.011
	Quadratic	.000	1	.000	.000	1.000
Error(BOARD)	Linear	3.000	3	1.000		
	Quadratic	3.000	3	1.000		

SPSS advanced

- The **Tests of Within-Subjects Contrasts** table examines the trends displayed in our data. This will give information as to the underlying model best fitting the data.
- As we have three keyboards that we are testing the number of errors on, the two possible trends are a linear or quadratic model (see Chapter 9 for more details of contrasts).
- In our example we can see that we have found a significant linear trend in our data $F(1,3) = 32.000$; $p < 0.05$. However, we have not identified a significant quadratic trend, $F(1,3) = 0.000$; $p > 0.05$.

The **Tests of Between-Subjects Effects** table is generated by default when calculating the one factor repeated measures ANOVA. As we are only calculating an ANOVA for a one factor model, and therefore do not have a between subjects factor, the information this table gives us is with reference to the intercept. If, however, we had a second variable, which was independent measure, as in a two factor mixed ANOVA, the effect of the independent factor would be shown here. Please see Chapter 11 for more details on this.

Tests of Between-Subjects Effects

Measure: MEASURE_1
Transformed Variable: Average

Source	Type III Sum of Squares	df	Mean Square	F	Sig.
Intercept	192.000	1	192.000	13.714	.034
Error	42.000	3	14.000		

SPSS advanced

- The **Tests of Between-Subjects Effects** table is produced. On this occasion, as we have no independent variables, there is only the intercept which tells us that our overall mean is significantly different from zero.

The following tables refer to the pairwise comparison analysis requested for our repeated measures factor, which was a comparison of the main effects with a Bonferroni adjustment.

Estimates

Measure: MEASURE_1

BOARD	Mean	Std. Error	95% Confidence Interval	
			Lower Bound	Upper Bound
1	2.000	1.080	−1.437	5.437
2	4.000	.816	1.402	6.598
3	6.000	1.472	1.316	10.684

SPSS advanced

- The **Mean** indicates the mean of each of the three keyboard error scores. This is a replication of the means discussed in the **Descriptive Statistics** table.
- The **Std. Error** is an estimate of the standard deviation of the sampling distribution of the mean. A small value tells us that we would expect a similar mean if we did the test again but a large value indicates a lot of variability predicted in the means.
- The **Std. Error** of the mean is a useful figure as it is used in the computation of significance tests comparing means and in the calculation of confidence intervals.
- The **95% Confidence Interval** indicates that we are 95 per cent confident that the true (population) mean will be between the upper and lower limits. The sample mean falls between these two values (see Chapter 6 for more detailed information).

The **Pairwise Comparisons** table gives us a multiple comparison for the means of all paired combinations of the three repeated measures conditions, which in our example is 'board'. All comparisons are adjusted using the Bonferroni method. This table should be inspected to ascertain where the significant differences that were evident from the calculation of our ANOVA are located.

Pairwise Comparisons

Measure: MEASURE_1

(I) BOARD	(J) BOARD	Mean Difference (I-J)	Std. Error	Sig.ᵃ	95% Confidence Interval for Differenceᵃ	
					Lower Bound	Upper Bound
1	2	−2.000	.707	.199	−5.434	1.434
	3	−4.000*	.707	.033	−7.434	−.566
2	1	2.000	.707	.199	−1.434	5.434
	3	−2.000	.707	.199	−5.434	1.434
3	1	4.000*	.707	.033	.566	7.434
	2	2.000	.707	.199	−1.434	5.434

Based on estimated marginal means

  *. The mean difference is significant at the .05 level.

  ᵃ. Adjustment for multiple comparisons: Bonferroni.

SPSS essential

- The **Pairwise Comparisons** table shows all the possible comparisons for the three levels of our repeated measures variable.
- In each comparison one level is given the identifier 'I' and the second 'J'. This is in the **Mean Difference** column, which indicates the resulting figure when the mean of one level of the variable (J) has been subtracted from a second level (I).
- In our example, the overall mean of our first keyboard (Board 1) was shown to be 2.000 in our descriptive statistics calculations, and the mean of the second keyboard (Board 2) was shown to be 4.000.

$$2.000 \text{ (I)} - 4.000 \text{ (J)} = -2.000$$

- The **Sig.** column enables us to assess whether the mean differences between the levels of the variable are significant.
- We can see from our example that the only possible pairwise comparison that is significantly different is the comparison of keyboard 1 with keyboard 3. The mean difference here is 4.000, and significant at $p < 0.05$. The other comparisons are not found to be significant as $p > 0.05$.

SPSS advanced

- The **Std. Error** values are all small, indicating low variability in the predicted mean differences.
- The **95% Confidence Interval** of the difference indicates that we are 95 per cent confident that the true population mean difference will be between the upper and lower limits (see Chapter 6 for more details).

As we produced pairwise comparisons via the Bonferroni method, the ANOVA also reproduces the **Multivariate Tests** table as well as the Bonferroni. This table is not of interest as we have followed the univariate method of analysis having first performed the suggested checks on our data (Mauchly and Epsilon).

Multivariate Tests

	Value	F	Hypothesis df	Error df	Sig.
Pillai's trace	.914	10.667[a]	2.000	2.000	.086
Wilks' lambda	.086	10.667[a]	2.000	2.000	.086
Hotelling's trace	10.667	10.667[a]	2.000	2.000	.086
Roy's largest root	10.667	10.667[a]	2.000	2.000	.086

Each F tests the multivariate effect of BOARD. These tests are based on the linearly independent pairwise comparisons among the estimated marginal means.

[a]. Exact statistic

The final part of the output is the graph plotting the means of the errors made while using the three keyboards.

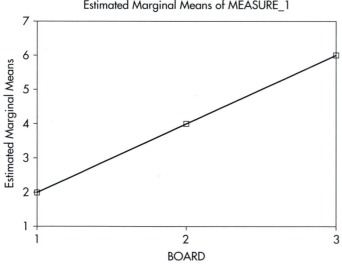

Estimated Marginal Means of MEASURE_1

SPSS essential

- We can see from the graphical display of our means the pattern previously discussed.
- The participants in our sample made more errors as they changed from keyboards 1 to 3, with fewest errors made on keyboard 1.

SPSS advanced

- It is clear from the graphical display above that the data shows a linear trend and not a quadratic trend.

✓ Graphs generated in this manner may need editing, as the labelling technique is not always clear. If you prefer, you can generate a line chart separately from the ANOVA procedure by going to the **Graphs** command (see Chapter 4 for further details).

FAQ

Why do I need to do contrasts or post hoc tests? Why doesn't a significant F value tell me all I need to know?

A significant F value allows us to reject the overall null hypothesis but does not tell us which conditions are producing it. If we have three conditions they might all be different or only one different to the other two. We can look at the graph of our means to try to work out which differences are causing the significant effect but only through contrasts or post hoc tests will we know which differences are significant.

I've read the chapter but I'm still confused about which F value I should be reporting in my repeated measures ANOVA. Are there any general rules that I can follow?

It can be a little confusing, but here is a brief list of things to help you decide.

1 *Check the table titled Mauchly's Test of Sphericity. You want Mauchly's W to be non-significant and the epsilon value to be as close to 1.000 as possible.*

2   If the above is true, take the sphericity assumed values of df, F, and
     p from the Tests of Within-Subjects Effects table.
3   If Mauchly's test is significant and the epsilon value is not close to 1.000,
     you need to use a correction on the Tests of Within-Subjects Effects table
     such as the Greenhouse–Geisser (only take the df, F, and p from the
     Multivariate Tests table if you know what you are doing).

I've got two independent factors, what do I do?

*Because you have got two independent factors, you need to be calculating a
two factor independent measures ANOVA rather than two one factor ANOVAS.
Details of this procedure can be seen in Chapter 11.*

**My ANOVA table only states the actual probability value and not the
significance level, what do I do?**

*You take the probability value from your ANOVA table (Sig.) and compare this
to the chosen level of significance. For example, from the table $p = 0.004$. This is
not only less than the conventional 0.05 level of significance but also less than
the more conservative 0.01 level. So as our value is less than the 0.01 level of
significance we report it as $p < 0.01$.*

In my output one of the values is shown as –4.8880E-02. What does this mean?

*The E in your result means 'exponential' and is used for expressing very large
or very small values. The number after the E tells you which direction to move
the decimal point and by how many places. For example 1000 is the same as
1.0E+03 and 0.0001 is the same as 1.0E-04. In your example the value is
really –0.048880.*

Details on how to calculate both a one factor independent and a one factor repeated
measures ANOVA test by hand can be found in Chapter 11 and Chapter 13 respectively of Hinton (2004).

Two factor analysis of variance

W̲E PERFORM A TWO FACTOR ANOVA when we wish to examine the effect of two independent variables on one dependent variable, and the assumptions of a parametric test are met. The two factor ANOVA is a very popular test, partly because it models an interaction. As well as looking at the effect of the independent variables separately (referred to as the main effects) we are able to analyse their effect in combination (referred to as the interaction). Imagine that we investigated the effect of location and product type on people's spending. We selected participants from either a rural or an urban location and examined their spending on household and luxury products. We might find a main effect of location, for example urban dwellers spend more overall than rural dwellers. We might also find a main effect of product type, say more money is spent on household products than on luxury goods. But we might also find an interaction, such as the urban dwellers spending more on luxury goods than the rural dwellers but less on household products. An interaction shows that the effect of one independent variable is not the same at each condition of the other independent variable. So when we perform a two factor ANOVA we obtain three F values: one for the main effect of each independent variable and one for the interaction.

There are three types of two factor ANOVA and we need to make sure that we select the correct one for our data. When both the independent variables are independent measures (there are different participants in each condition) we perform a two factor independent measures ANOVA. When both independent variables have repeated measures across the conditions (each participant contributes a score to each condition of the variable) we undertake a two factor repeated measures ANOVA. Finally, when one independent variable is independent measures and the other repeated measures we perform a two factor mixed design ANOVA. In the above example we have a mixed design as there are independent measures on 'location' (different people live in the different locations) and repeated measures on 'product type' (as we measure the spending of each person on both household products and luxury goods).

Two factor independent measures analysis of variance

The two factor independent measures ANOVA is the simplest form of the two factor ANOVA and produces the least amount of output from SPSS. This is because both independent variables are independent measures, that is the scores in each condition come from different participants. For example, if we are comparing the effects of gender (boys and girls) and birth position (first born, middle child, youngest child) on reading ability in 10-year-old children, both variables are independent measures.

The important aspect of the two factor independent measures ANOVA is that we examine the two factors together, so we produce an interaction as well as the main effects of gender and birth position. If, for example, first-born boys read better than boys in other birth positions, but the youngest girls read better than the other girls then we would have found an interaction of the two factors: gender and birth order.

There are assumptions that need to be met for an ANOVA, as we saw in the previous chapter, for it to correctly model our data:

- the data is randomly sampled
- the scores are measured on an interval scale and are from normally distributed populations
- the samples in each condition are drawn from populations with equal variances (the homogeneity of variance assumption).

Scenario

An expanding company wanted to know how to introduce a new type of machine into the factory. Should it transfer staff working on the old machine to operate it or employ new staff who had not worked on any machine before? A researcher selected 12 staff who had experience of the old machine and 12 staff who had no such experience. Half the participants from each group were allocated to the new machine and half to the old machine. The number of errors made by the participants over a set period was measured.

Data entry

	experien	machine	errors
1	novice	old	4.00
2	novice	old	5.00
3	novice	old	7.00
4	novice	old	6.00
5	novice	old	8.00
6	novice	old	5.00
7	novice	new	5.00
8	novice	new	6.00
9	novice	new	5.00
10	novice	new	6.00
11	novice	new	5.00
12	novice	new	6.00
13	experien	old	1.00
14	experien	old	2.00
15	experien	old	2.00
16	experien	old	3.00
17	experien	old	2.00
18	experien	old	3.00
19	experien	new	8.00
20	experien	new	9.00
21	experien	new	8.00
22	experien	new	8.00
23	experien	new	7.00
24	experien	new	9.00

2 way independent - SPSS Data Editor

File   Edit   View   Data   Transform   Analyze   Graphs

Enter the dataset as shown in the example.

✓   See Chapter 2 for the full data entry procedure.

Test procedure

- All inferential statistics are found under the **Analyze** command.
- Select **General Linear Model** and then **Univariate** as we have only one dependent variable.

Analyze   Graphs   Utilities   Window   Help

Reports
Descriptive Statistics
Custom Tables
Compare Means
General Linear Model ▶   Univariate...
Correlate   Multivariate...
Regression   Repeated Measures...
Loglinear
Classify   Variance Components...
Data Reduction
Scale
Nonparametric Tests
Time Series
Survival
Multiple Response

- The dependent variable 'errors' should be sent to the **Dependent Variable** box.
- Send the independent variables across to the **Fixed Factor(s)** box.

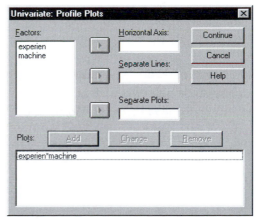

- Click on **Options** and place a tick in the **Descriptive statistics** box.
- Click on **Continue**.

> ✓ We can check the homogeneity of variance by selecting the **Homogeneity tests** option.

The interaction plot can be generated as part of the ANOVA procedure.

- Click on **Plots**.
- One factor should be sent to the **Horizontal Axis** and one to **Separate Lines**.
- Click on **Add** to send the interaction to the bottom box.
- Press **Continue** and then **OK**.

> ✓ Note in this example no post hoc tests were required as both independent factors only had two levels. For two factor independent measures ANOVAs, where one or both factors have three or more levels, click on the **Post Hoc** command and select the appropriate test. See Chapter 10 for details of this procedure in relation to a one factor independent ANOVA.

SPSS output

The first table that SPSS produces is the **Between-Subjects Factors** table that tells us how many participants were in each group, and how many conditions of each of our independent variables there are.

Between-Subjects Factors

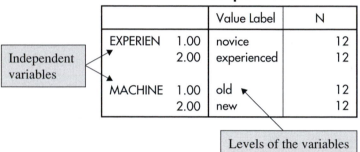

		Value Label	N
EXPERIEN	1.00	novice	12
	2.00	experienced	12
MACHINE	1.00	old	12
	2.00	new	12

Independent variables

Levels of the variables

The next table that SPSS produces is for **Descriptive Statistics**. This gives the mean, standard deviation and number of participants in each group.

Descriptive Statistics

Dependent Variable: ERRORS

EXPERIEN	MACHINE	Mean	Std. Deviation	N
novice	old	5.8333	1.4720	6
	new	5.5000	.5477	6
	Total	5.6667	1.0731	12
experienced	old	2.1667	.7528	6
	new	8.1667	.7528	6
	Total	5.1667	3.2146	12
Total	old	4.0000	2.2156	12
	new	6.8333	1.5275	12
	Total	5.4167	2.3575	24

Essential

SPSS essential

- The **Descriptive Statistics** table displays the **Mean** number of errors made by the novice and experienced workers on the old and new machines. It can be seen from the **Total** row that overall there does not appear to be a large difference in the number of errors made by novices and experienced workers (a mean of 5.6667 for novice workers compared to 5.1667 for experienced workers).
- However, when the factor of machine type is considered it can be clearly seen that differences do arise. The novice workers were making almost the same number of errors on the old machine type (5.8333) as on the new machine type (5.5000). The experienced workers, however, were making fewer errors on the old machine (2.1667) than on the new machine (8.1667).
- By observing the **Total** in the bottom row, it can be seen that the overall errors of machine type, irrespective of whether the participant is an experienced or a novice worker, do show some differences, with more errors being made when working with the new machine.
- The **Std. Deviation** (standard deviations) show that when comparing the overall scores of the two groups, the experienced group has the largest spread of scores (3.2146), with the most closely related scores being found in the novice group (1.0731). Even though the overall standard deviation is bigger for the experienced group, when we consider machine type it is the novices working with the old machines who show the greatest spread of scores (1.4720).

With our two factor independent measures ANOVA we are looking for significant main effects for our two factors, experience and machine, and a possible interaction between the two. All this information is contained in the **Tests of Between-Subjects Effects** table shown below. The important information has been highlighted.

Tests of Between-Subjects Effects

Dependent Variable: ERRORS

Source	Type III Sum of Squares	df	Mean Square	F	Sig.
Corrected Model	109.833[a]	3	36.611	40.679	.000
Intercept	704.167	1	704.167	782.407	.000
EXPERIEN	1.500	1	1.500	1.667	.211
MACHINE	48.167	1	48.167	53.519	.000
EXPERIEN * MACHINE	60.167	1	60.167	66.852	.000
Error	18.000	20	.900		
Total	832.000	24			
Corrected Total	127.833	23			

[a]. R Squared = .859 (Adjusted R Squared = .838)

SPSS essential

- We can see from the **Test of Between-Subjects Effects** table that for our factor 'experience' we have not found a significant main effect, $F(1,20) = 1.667$, $p > 0.05$. This was expected from previous discussions of the descriptive statistics.
- We have found a significant main effect for our factor 'machine', i.e. whether our participants were using old or new machinery, $F(1,20) = 53.519$, $p < 0.001$.

✓   Remember if SPSS states that the probability (**Sig.**) is 0.000, it means that SPSS has rounded up the amount to the nearest number at three decimal places. However, we would always round the last 0 to a 1, so that $p < 0.001$.

- Our results also indicate a significant interaction between our two factors, $F(1,20) = 66.852$, $p < 0.001$.

SPSS advanced

- The **Corrected Model** shows how much variability in the data we can explain by our independent variables. Note that these **Sums of Squares** are made up of the **Sums of Squares** of 'experience', 'machine' and their interaction.
- In our example, the **Intercept** row shows us that our overall mean is significantly different from zero.
- The **Sums of Squares** gives a measure of the variability in the scores due to a particular source of variability. The **Corrected Total** sums of squares (127.833) is made up of the sums of squares of our factor 'experience' (1.500), 'machine' (48.167) and the interaction between them (60.167) plus the **Error** sums of squares (18.000). Note that there is a lot of variability due to error for our factor 'experience'.
- The **Mean Square** is the variance (sums of squares divided by degrees of freedom).
- The **R Squared** and **Adjusted R Squared** values give us an indication of the amount of variability in the scores that can be explained by our independent variables. This is calculated by dividing the **Sums of Squares** of the **Corrected Model** (109.833) by the **Corrected Total Sums of Squares** (127.833), giving a value of 0.859.

The final part of the SPSS output is our interaction plot, which allows us to examine the patterns previously discussed.

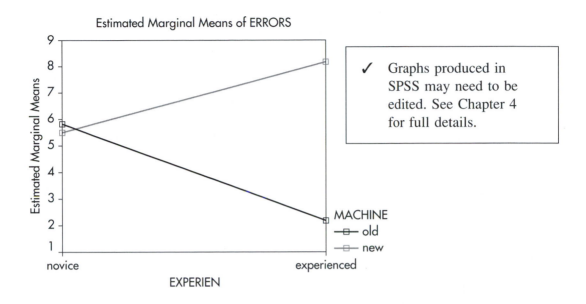

✓ Graphs produced in SPSS may need to be edited. See Chapter 4 for full details.

SPSS essential

• The chart plots the means and confirms our previously discussed findings of a significant interaction between the two variables.

✓ Remember, whenever the lines on an interaction plot are not parallel, this indicates that there is an interaction, although this may not be a statistically significant interaction.

• We can see from the interaction plot that the experienced workers, not surprisingly, made the fewest errors on the old machine, but made the most errors on the new machine. This looks like a case of negative transfer, where previously learnt skills can be a hindrance rather than a help. The novice workers appear to perform with equal accuracy on both machines.

SPSS advanced

- We may wish to carry out further tests with our data to enable us to more fully understand the patterns emerging in our analysis. For example, we can be quite confident that our experienced operators are making more errors on the new machinery compared to the old machinery, i.e. we have identified a simple main effect. However, we are less confident about the differences between the machines for the novice operators.

- A test for such simple main effects can therefore be calculated through the **Syntax** command within SPSS. An example of this is shown at the end of this chapter with reference to the two factor mixed design ANOVA.

Two factor repeated measures analysis of variance

We undertake a two factor repeated measures ANOVA when we have repeated measures on both variables. In a study on perception researchers were interested in the time it took a person to find a hidden shape (a diamond, a rectangle or a triangle) in visual patterns. They were also interested in whether there was difference in detection times for the dominant as opposed to the non-dominant eye, so each person saw half the patterns with one eye and half with the other. Counterbalancing was undertaken to control for any carry-over or practice effects. As each participant took part in each condition of both independent variables we have repeated measures on both factors. The times to detect the shapes with each eye were recorded for analysis. (Just out of interest you can find out which of your eyes is the dominant one by holding out a finger at arm's length. Line it up with an object on the other side of the room with both eyes open. Then, without moving your finger close one eye and then the other. With one eye the finger stays in front of the object and this is your dominant eye, with the other eye the finger shifts a little and this is the non-dominant eye.)

As we have two factors (two independent variables) there will be three F values produced by the ANOVA, one for the main effect of each of the two independent variables and one for the interaction. In the above example the main effect of 'eye' would tell us if there was a difference in the detection times between the dominant and non-dominant eye, and the main effect of 'shape' would tell us if there was a difference in the detection times for the different shapes. An interaction occurs when the effect of one factor is different at the different levels of the second factor. For example, if the dominant eye was better at detecting diamonds and the non-dominant eye was better at detecting triangles, with no difference for rectangles.

As for all two factor ANOVAs we need to make the assumptions that:

- the data is randomly chosen from the population
- the scores are measured on an interval scale and are from normally distributed populations
- the samples in each condition are drawn from populations with equal variances (the homogeneity of variance assumption)

However, as the factors are repeated measures we also have the assumption of 'sphericity' and therefore there will be more tables produced in the SPSS output than with an independent measures ANOVA, to allow us to examine the sphericity of the data and correct for any violation of the assumption if necessary. Readers are referred to Chapter 9 for a fuller account of the importance of sphericity to repeated measures designs in the ANOVA and how SPSS deals with it.

Scenario

In a factory a machine produces two kinds of product, one that requires the operator to follow a complex set of instructions and one that is very simple to make. There are two shifts in the factory, a day shift and a night shift. The factory manager wants the factory to make the products with the minimum of errors. A researcher decides to study the effect of 'shift' (day versus night) and 'product' (complex versus simple to make) on the errors made by the operators. All operators work both shifts on a rotation system. Six operators are randomly selected and their error performance is measured during a day shift and a night shift. Appropriate balancing is undertaken so that testing three operators on the day shift first and three on the night shift first controls for carry-over effects from one shift to another.

Data entry

	day_com	pm_com	day_simp	pm_simp
1	5	9	3	2
2	5	8	2	4
3	7	7	4	5
4	6	10	5	4
5	4	8	3	3
6	6	9	5	6
7				

Untitled - SPSS Data Editor
File Edit View Data Transform Analyze Graphs Utilities Win

The data should be entered as shown. As this is a two factor repeated measures design, each participant will have four scores. These are the labels:

- day shift complex
- night shift complex
- day shift simple
- night shift simple

✓ See Chapter 2 for full data entry procedure.
✓ Ensure that you set the decimal places to 0 in the **Variable View** screen.

Test procedure

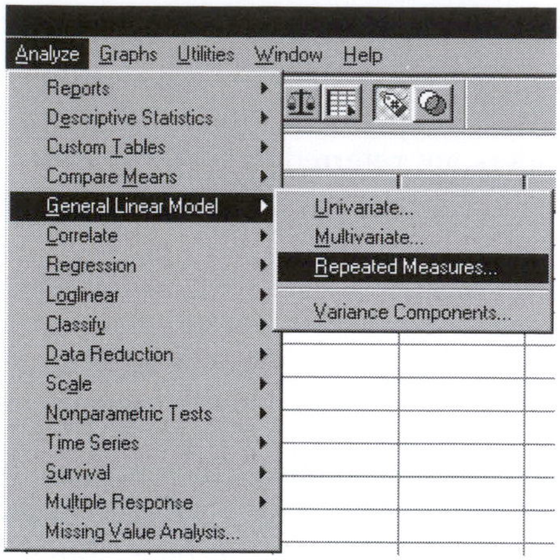

- All ANOVAs can be found under the **Analyze** and **General Linear Model** command.
- The type of ANOVA selected will depend on the design of the study.
- In our example both factors are repeated measures. We must therefore choose the **Repeated Measures** option.

- The **Within-Subject Factor Name** needs to be assigned for both factors.
- We will call our factors 'shift' and 'product'. Each of these has two levels.
- Click on **Add** after each factor, then **Define**.

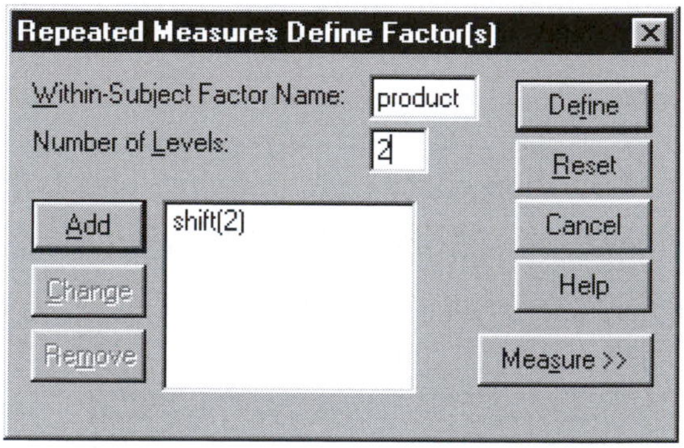

✓ Note that in version 12 this box will look slightly different and options under **Measure** will be visible.

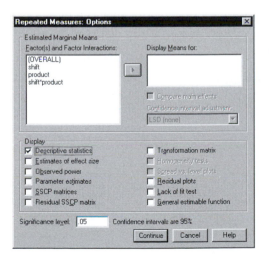

- Our variables need to be assigned in order to the **Within-Subjects Variables** box.
- This means that each variable needs to be sent over in accordance with the combination of levels it corresponds to on the factor.
- For example, the first level of our factor 'shift' is day, and the first level of our factor 'product' is complex (as set out in the dataset 'day_com') This corresponds to (1,1).

- The next variable to be sent across should correspond to the first level of the first factor (shift) and the second level of the second factor (product), indicated by (1,2). This combination will be our factor 'day_simp'.
- The other levels of factors should be sent across accordingly.

✓ It is important that the levels are assigned correctly in order for your output to be interpretable.

- Click on **Options** and place a tick in the **Descriptive statistics** box.
- Click on **Continue**.

> ✓ If we had more than two levels to our factors we would need to carry out a Bonferroni post hoc test in order to ascertain where any significant differences may lie. This would be done by sending our factors across to the **Display Means for** box, placing a tick in **Compare main effects**, and selecting the **Confidence interval adjustment** as Bonferroni. See Chapter 10 for an example of this on the one factor repeated measures ANOVA.

- The interaction plot can be generated as part of the ANOVA procedure.
- Click on **Plots**.
- One factor should be sent to the **Horizontal Axis** and one to **Separate Lines**.
- Click on **Add**, then **Continue**.
- Now that all our options for the ANOVA have been selected, click on **OK**.

SPSS output

The first table produced by SPSS gives a description of the two factors entered into the ANOVA calculation. The first column shows both variables, 'shift' and 'product'. The second column displays the variable name of the combination of the different levels of the factors.

Within-Subjects Factors

Measure: MEASURE_1

SHIFT	PRODUCT	Dependent Variable
1	1	DAY_COM
	2	DAY_SIMP
2	1	PM_COM
	2	PM_SIMP

SPSS essential

- We can see from the **Within-Subjects Factors** table that the combination of the first level of the variable 'shift' and the first level of the variable 'product' is labelled **DAY_COM**.
- Level 1 of 'shift', and level 2 of 'product' is **DAY_SIMP**.
- The other combinations of levels of the factors are assigned in similar ways.

The next table generated by SPSS is that of **Descriptive Statistics**. It is here that we can examine our dataset for potential differences in error rates.

Descriptive Statistics

	Mean	Std. Deviation	N
day shift complex	5.50	1.05	6
day shift simple	3.67	1.21	6
night shift complex	8.50	1.05	6
night shift simple	4.00	1.41	6

Essential

SPSS essential

- By observing the **Mean** errors from the **Descriptive Statistics** table we can see that making the complex product produces the greater number of errors (day shift complex 5.50, night shift complex 8.50, compared to day shift simple 3.67, night shift simple 4.00).
- When comparing the two combinations of simple products and the two combinations of complex products, we can see that in both cases the night shift made more errors.
- The combination that produced the most errors was the night shift, complex product condition.
- The **Std. Deviations** (standard deviations) do not indicate any large spreads of scores in any of the conditions.
- In summary, we seem to have found a possible difference between day shift and night shift, and between complex and simple, with possible interaction effects of our variables as indicated by the high number of errors made by complex product creation on the night shift.

The **Multivariate Tests** table is generated by default by SPSS during all repeated measures ANOVAs. We only use this table if sphericity is shown to be a problem in our data. However, as we only have two 'levels' to each repeated measures factor, sphericity won't be an issue here. The multivariate tests table is still produced though, as some people prefer to report these results. See Chapter 9 for further discussions on this.

Multivariate Tests[b]

Effect		Value	F	Hypothesis df	Error df	Sig.
SHIFT	Pillai's Trace	.877	35.714[a]	1.000	5.000	.002
	Wilks' Lambda	.123	35.714[a]	1.000	5.000	.002
	Hotelling's Trace	7.143	35.714[a]	1.000	5.000	.002
	Roy's Largest Root	7.143	35.714[a]	1.000	5.000	.002
PRODUCT	Pillai's Trace	.940	78.478[a]	1.000	5.000	.000
	Wilks' Lambda	.060	78.478[a]	1.000	5.000	.000
	Hotelling's Trace	15.696	78.478[a]	1.000	5.000	.000
	Roy's Largest Root	15.696	78.478[a]	1.000	5.000	.000
SHIFT * PRODUCT	Pillai's Trace	.593	7.273[a]	1.000	5.000	.043
	Wilks' Lambda	.407	7.273[a]	1.000	5.000	.043
	Hotelling's Trace	1.455	7.273[a]	1.000	5.000	.043
	Roy's Largest Root	1.455	7.273[a]	1.000	5.000	.043

[a]. Exact statistic
[b]. Design: Intercept
   Within Subjects Design: SHIFT + PRODUCT + SHIFT * PRODUCT

SPSS advanced

- As both our factors are repeated measures, three multivariate tests are generated; one for each factor, and one for the interaction between the two.
- The most popular test is the **Wilks' Lambda**. From this we can see that there is a significant main effect for our factor 'shift', $F(1,5) = 35.714$; $p < 0.01$. We have also found a significant main effect for our factor 'product', $F(1,5) = 78.478$; $p < 0.01$.
- When we examine the table for a possible interaction effect between the two variables, we can again report that this is significant, $F(1,5) = 7.273$; $p < 0.05$.

The following table shows the sphericity checks. Again this is generated by default by SPSS during repeated measures ANOVA calculations.

Mauchly's Test of Sphericity[b]

Measure: MEASURE_1

Within Subjects Effect	Mauchly's W	Approx. Chi-Square	df	Sig.	Epsilon[a]		
					Greenhouse-Geisser	Huynh-Feldt	Lower-bound
SHIFT	1.000	.000	0	.	1.000	1.000	1.000
PRODUCT	1.000	.000	0	.	1.000	1.000	1.000
SHIFT * PRODUCT	1.000	.000	0	.	1.000	1.000	1.000

Tests the null hypothesis that the error covariance matrix of the orthonormalized transformed dependent variables is proportional to an identity matrix.

[a]. May be used to adjust the degrees of freedom for the averaged tests of significance Corrected tests are displayed in the Tests of Within-Subjects Effects table.

[b]. Design: Intercept
Within Subjects Design: SHIFT + PRODUCT + SHIFT * PRODUCT

SPSS advanced

- You will notice from the **Mauchly's Test of Sphericity** table that the **Sig.** (probability) column is blank, and no degrees of freedom are reported. This is because sphericity is only a problem if you have more than two conditions on your repeated measures factors. Both of our factors have only two levels and therefore sphericity will not be a problem in our data.

- This table can therefore be ignored in this example. However, if one or more of your variables had more than two levels, you would need to check this in the same way as we discussed for the one factor repeated measures variable in Chapter 10.

As sphericity is not a problem in our data, we can take the values from the **Sphericity Assumed** rows in the **Tests of Within-Subjects Effects** table.

Tests of Within–Subjects Effects

Measure: MEASURE_1

Source		Type III Sum of Squares	df	Mean Square	F	Sig.
SHIFT	Sphericity Assumed	16.667	1	16.667	35.714	.002
	Greenhouse-Geisser	16.667	1.000	16.667	35.714	.002
	Huynh-Feldt	16.667	1.000	16.667	35.714	.002
	Lower-bound	16.667	1.000	16.667	35.714	.002
Error(SHIFT)	Sphericity Assumed	2.333	5	.467		
	Greenhouse-Geisser	2.333	5.000	.467		
	Huynh-Feldt	2.333	5.000	.467		
	Lower-bound	2.333	5.000	.467		
PRODUCT	Sphericity Assumed	60.167	1	60.167	78.478	.000
	Greenhouse-Geisser	60.167	1.000	60.167	78.478	.000
	Huynh-Feldt	60.167	1.000	60.167	78.478	.000
	Lower-bound	60.167	1.000	60.167	78.478	.000
Error(PRODUCT)	Sphericity Assumed	3.833	5	.767		
	Greenhouse-Geisser	3.833	5.000	.767		
	Huynh-Feldt	3.833	5.000	.767		
	Lower-bound	3.833	5.000	.767		
SHIFT * PRODUCT	Sphericity Assumed	10.667	1	10.667	7.273	.043
	Greenhouse-Geisser	10.667	1.000	10.667	7.273	.043
	Huynh-Feldt	10.667	1.000	10.667	7.273	.043
	Lower-bound	10.667	1.000	10.667	7.273	.043
Error(SHIFT*PRODUCT)	Sphericity Assumed	7.333	5	1.467		
	Greenhouse-Geisser	7.333	5.000	1.467		
	Huynh-Feldt	7.333	5.000	1.467		
	Lower-bound	7.333	5.000	1.467		

SPSS essential

- The important rows in **the Tests of Within-Subjects Effects** table have been shaded, and are the **Sphericity Assumed** rows.

- From this table we are looking for a significant main effect for our variable 'shift'; a significant main effect for our variable 'product'; and a possible interaction between the two.
- We have found a significant main effect for our factor 'shift', $F(1,5) = 35.714$, $p < 0.01$.
- We have also found a significant main effect for our factor 'product', $F(1,5) = 78.478$, $p < 0.01$.
- An interaction between the two variables is also evident, $F(1,5) = 7.273$, $p < 0.05$.
- We can therefore conclude that, as indicated by our descriptive results earlier, both 'shift' and 'product' have an effect on the number of errors made and this results in a significant interaction between the two factors.

The **Tests of Within-Subjects Contrasts** table is generated by default by SPSS during the calculation of repeated measures ANOVAs, and is a trend analysis.

Tests of Within-Subjects Contrasts

Measure: MEASURE_1

Source	SHIFT	PRODUCT	Type III Sum of Squares	df	Mean Square	F	Sig.
SHIFT	Linear		16.667	1	16.667	35.714	.002
Error(SHIFT)	Linear		2.333	5	.467		
PRODUCT		Linear	60.167	1	60.167	78.478	.000
Error(PRODUCT)		Linear	3.833	5	.767		
SHIFT * PRODUCT	Linear	Linear	10.667	1	10.667	7.273	.043
Error(SHIFT*PRODUCT)	Linear	Linear	7.333	5	1.467		

SPSS advanced

- The **Tests of Within-Subjects Contrasts** table examines the trends displayed in our data. This will give information as to the underlying model best fitting the data.
- As we only have two levels to each of our repeated measures factors, the only possible trends are those following a linear model. See Chapter 9 for more details of trends.
- In our example we can see that both our factors follow a significant linear trend, as does the interaction between the two factors. This is expected because each factor only has two levels.

The **Tests of Between-Subjects Effects** table is generated by default by SPSS when calculating repeated measures ANOVAs. As both our factors are repeated measures, we do not have a between subjects factor, and the information that this table provides is with reference to the intercept. If, however, we had an independent measures variable, as in the two factor mixed ANOVA, the effect of the independent factor would be shown here.

Tests of Between-Subjects Effects

Measure: MEASURE_1
Transformed Variable: Average

Source	Type III Sum of Squares	df	Mean Square	F	Sig.
Intercept	704.167	1	704.167	237.360	.000
Error	14.833	5	2.967		

SPSS advanced

• The **Tests of Between-Subjects Effects** table is produced. On this occasion, as we have no independent measures variables, there is only the **Intercept** which tells us that our overall mean is significantly different from zero.

The final part of the output is the interaction plot of the means of the four conditions. Notice that we have used the Chart Editor to add labels.

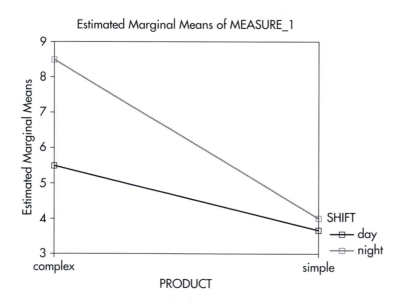

SPSS essential

- We can see from the interaction plot the pattern previously discussed.
- The participants made more errors on the night shift than on the day shift. This was particularly true when dealing with complex products, hence the significant interaction effect identified.

SPSS advanced

- We may wish to carry out further tests with our data to enable us to more fully understand the patterns emerging in our analysis. For example, we can be quite confident that our participants are making more errors on the complex product on the night shift than on the day shift, i.e. we have identified a simple main effect. However, we are less confident about the differences between the shifts when dealing with simple products.
- A test for such simple main effects can therefore be calculated through the **Syntax** command within SPSS. An example of this is shown at the end of this chapter with reference to the two factor mixed design ANOVA.

Two factor mixed design analysis of variance

The two factor mixed design ANOVA is undertaken when we have independent measures on one of our factors and repeated measures on the second of our factors. A researcher is interested in people's ability to remember world events and has devised a questionnaire on events from the past 4 years, with an equal number of questions (matched for difficulty) for each of the 4 years. The researcher is also interested in comparing young adults (20 to 25 years old) with an older group (40 to 45 years old) on the questionnaire. The two independent variables (factors) are 'year', with four conditions, which is a repeated measures factor, and 'age', with two conditions, which is an independent measures factor.

There will be two main effects of year and age as well as an interaction of the two. An interaction occurs when the effect of one factor is different at the different conditions of the second factor. In the example above, if the older adults knew more about some of the years than the younger adults but the younger adults knew more about other years then there would be an interaction.

As for all parametric tests we must assume that:

- the data is randomly chosen from the population
- the scores are measured on an interval scale and are from normally distributed populations
- the samples in each condition are drawn from populations with equal variances (the homogeneity of variance assumption).

As there is a repeated measures factor we must also make the assumption of sphericity (see Chapter 9). Even though we can have different numbers of participants in the independent measures factor (e.g. more older people than younger people) it is advisable to have equal numbers of participants in each condition for reasons of maintaining sphericity.

Scenario

A company has introduced a new machine on the factory floor and it wants to see how the workers gain skills on the machine. There is particular interest in comparing the performance of workers experienced on the old machine to that of novice operators who have not operated a machine on the factory floor before. A researcher randomly selects six experienced operators and six novices, and monitors the errors they make on the new machine over a 3-week period to see whether there are differences between the two groups in their performance on the machine.

Data entry

Enter the dataset as shown in the example.

✓ Remember when entering data without decimal places to change the decimal places to zero in the **Variable View**.
✓ See Chapter 2 for the full data entry procedure.

	workers	week1	week2	week3
1	novices	7	6	5
2	novices	4	4	3
3	novices	6	4	4
4	novices	7	6	5
5	novices	6	5	4
6	novices	4	2	2
7	experien	7	3	2
8	experien	8	4	2
9	experien	6	2	1
10	experien	9	6	3
11	experien	7	4	3
12	experien	10	6	3

Test procedure

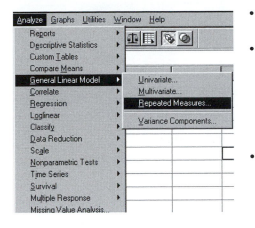

- All ANOVAs can be found under the **Analyze** and **General Linear Model** command.
- The type of ANOVA selected will depend on the design of the study. In the example above we have a two factor ANOVA of mixed design, with one factor, 'workers', being independent measures, and one factor, 'time', being repeated measures.
- Because there is a repeated measures factor, we must choose the **Repeated Measures** option.

- The first step is to define the repeated measures factor.
- The **Within-Subject Factor Name** should be entered. Our within subjects factor is the three time periods, hence the name entered is 'time' and this factor has three levels.
- Click on **Add**, then on **Define**.

✓ Note that in version 12 this box will look slightly different and options under **Measure** will be visible.

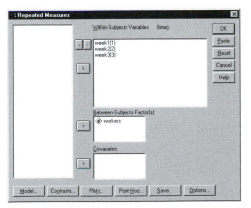

- The three levels of the **Within-Subjects Variables** need to be sent to the box opposite.
- The independent factor 'workers' should be sent to the **Between-Subjects Factor(s)** box.

- The interaction plot can be generated as part of the ANOVA procedure.
- Click on **Plots**.
- One factor should be sent to the **Horizontal Axis** and one to **Separate Lines**.
- Click on **Continue**.

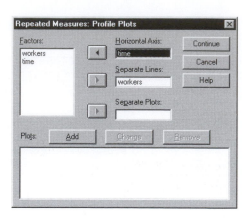

- Click on **Options** and place a tick in the **Descriptive Statistics** box.
- A pairwise comparison test for the repeated measures factor needs to be generated as this has more than two levels.
- Send the repeated measures factor 'time' across to the **Display Means for** box, and put a tick in the **Compare main effects** box.
- Change the **Confidence interval adjustment** from LSD (none) to Bonferroni.
- Click on **Continue** then OK.

✓ We can test the homogeneity of variance for our independent measures factor by selecting the **Homogeneity tests** box.

✓ In our example we only need a post hoc test for the repeated measures variable 'time'. Our independent measures variable 'workers' only has two levels so a post hoc test is not necessary. If our independent variable did have more than two levels we would click on the **Post Hoc** button and select the appropriate test. See Chapter 10 for details of this with reference to the one factor independent measures ANOVA.

SPSS output

The first two tables produced by SPSS give a description of the two factors entered into the ANOVA. This confirms that our **Within-Subjects Factor** (repeated measures factor) has three levels, and our **Between-Subjects Factor** (independent measures factor) has two levels.

Within-Subjects Factors

Measure: MEASURE_1

TIME	Dependent Variable
1	WEEK 1
2	WEEK 2
3	WEEK 3

Between-Subjects Factors

		Value Lable	N
WORKERS	1	novices	6
	2	experienced	6

The first table of importance is the table of **Descriptive Statistics**.

Descriptive Statistics

	WORKERS	Mean	Std. Deviation	N
WEEK 1	novices	5.67	1.37	6
	experienced	7.83	1.47	6
	Total	6.75	1.76	12
WEEK 2	novices	4.50	1.52	6
	experienced	4.17	1.60	6
	Total	4.33	1.50	12
WEEK 3	novices	3.83	1.17	6
	experienced	2.33	.82	6
	Total	3.08	1.24	12

Essential

SPSS essential

- The **Descriptive Statistics** table displays the **Mean** number of errors committed by the two groups at the three time periods. The **Total** mean is the overall mean for errors in the week, regardless of whether the participants were novices or experienced workers.
- By observing the means we can see that there appears to be a pattern in the number of errors produced by the two groups over time. In week 1 the experienced staff made more errors than the novices (7.83 compared to 5.67) but this difference was reduced by week 2 (4.17 compared to 4.50). In the final week the trend had reversed, with

novices now committing more errors than experienced staff members (2.33 compared to 3.83).

- The **Total** number of errors steadily reduces over time.
- The standard deviations show that the spread of scores between the groups within each time period is similar. Across the three weeks, the total standard deviation reduces, from 1.76 in week 1 to 1.24 in week 3. This indicates that at the end of the time period there is less variation in the work performance.
- **N** represents the number of participants in each group and time period.

The next table is the **Multivariate Tests** table. This is generated by default by SPSS during the mixed and repeated measures ANOVA calculations and is only normally consulted if the sphericity assumption is violated. See Chapter 9 for further details.

Multivariate Tests[b]

Effect		Value	F	Hypothesis df	Error df	Sig.
TIME	Pillai's Trace	.968	135.928[a]	2.000	9.000	.000
	Wilks' Lambda	.032	135.928[a]	2.000	9.000	.000
	Hotelling's Trace	30.206	135.928[a]	2.000	9.000	.000
	Roy's Largest Root	30.206	135.928[a]	2.000	9.000	.000
TIME * WORKERS	Pillai's Trace	.885	34.773[a]	2.000	9.000	.000
	Wilks' Lambda	.115	34.773[a]	2.000	9.000	.000
	Hotelling's Trace	7.727	34.773[a]	2.000	9.000	.000
	Roy's Largest Root	7.727	34.773[a]	2.000	9.000	.000

[a]. Exact statistic
[b]. Design: Intercept + WORKERS
Within Subjects Design: TIME

SPSS advanced

- SPSS produces a multivariate test output for the repeated measures factor and its interaction.
- We may choose the multivariate test results if we are concerned that the univariate test assumptions are not met. For example if **Mauchly's Test of Sphericity** is significant, or the **Epsilon** value is low.
- The most popular test is **Wilks' Lambda**. From this we can see that there is a significant main effect for our repeated measures factor 'time', $F(2,9) = 135.928$; $p < 0.01$. There is also a significant main effect for the interaction of our two factors, $F(2,9) = 34.773$; $p < 0.01$.

The following table shows the sphericity checks. This is generated by default by SPSS during the mixed and repeated measures ANOVA procedure.

Mauchly's Test of Sphericity[b]

Measure: MEASURE_1

Within Subjects Effect	Mauchly's W	Approx. Chi-Square	df	Sig.	Epsilon[a]		
					Greenhouse-Geisser	Huynh-Feldt	Lower-bound
TIME	.937	.584	2	.747	.941	1.000	.500

Tests the null hypothesis that the error covariance matrix of the orthonormalized transformed dependent variables is proportional to an identity matrix.

  [a]. May be used to adjust the degrees of freedom for the averaged tests of significance. Corrected tests are displayed in the Tests of Within-Subjects Effects table.

  [b]. Design: Intercept + WORKERS
     Within Subjects Design: TIME

SPSS advanced

- When there are more than two conditions of the repeated measures variable we can check the sphericity assumption before calculating the F value results.
- If the sphericity assumption is met then we proceed to inspect the **Sphericity Assumed** line of the **Tests of Within-Subjects Effects** table (univariate model).
- If the sphericity assumption is not met and **Mauchly's Test of Sphericity** is significant we do not take the **Sphericity Assumed** line of the **Tests of Within-Subjects Effects** table (univariate model) and need to employ a correction. SPSS provides us with several correction models, the Greehouse–Geisser is the one usually reported.
- The **Mauchly's Test of Sphericity** table above gives a **Mauchly's W** test statistic of 0.937, $df = 2$; $p > 0.05$. We can therefore conclude that the sphericity assumption is met and we can use the output from the univariate model without correction.
- There is however some debate as to the sensitivity of Mauchly's test in its ability to detect sphericity. There is therefore the alternative of consulting the **Epsilon** value quoted in the **Greenhouse-Geisser** column. This figure should be as close to 1.00 as possible in order to indicate no sphericity problems. Our value is 0.941 so we can be fairly confident that issues of sphericity do not affect our calculations.

If the sphericity assumption is met, as it is in our example, we can take the values from the **Sphericity Assumed** rows of the **Tests of Within-Subjects Effects** table. This table will enable us to decide whether we have found a significant main effect for our repeated measures factor 'time', and a significant interaction between our two factors 'time' and 'workers'.

Tests of Within-Subjects Effects

Measure: MEASURE_1

Source		Type III Sum of Squares	df	Mean Square	F	Sig.
TIME	Sphericity Assumed	83.389	2	41.694	150.100	.000
	Greenhouse-Geisser	83.389	1.882	44.313	150.100	.000
	Huynh-Feldt	83.389	2.000	41.694	150.100	.000
	Lower-bound	83.389	1.000	83.389	150.100	.000
TIME * WORKERS	Sphericity Assumed	21.056	2	10.528	37.900	.000
	Greenhouse-Geisser	21.056	1.882	11.189	37.900	.000
	Huynh-Feldt	21.056	2.000	10.528	37.900	.000
	Lower-bound	21.056	1.000	21.056	37.900	.000
Error(TIME)	Sphericity Assumed	5.556	20	.278		
	Greenhouse-Geisser	5.556	18.818	.295		
	Huynh-Feldt	5.556	20.000	.278		
	Lower-bound	5.556	10.000	.556		

SPSS essential

- The important rows in the **Tests of Within-Subjects Effects** table have been highlighted and are the **Sphericity Assumed** rows.

✓ Remember that because this is a two factor ANOVA the repeated measures factor and the interaction information will appear in this table. The figures for the possible main effect of our independent measures variable will appear later in the **Tests of Between-Subjects Effects** table.

- The main effect for our variable 'time' is $F(2,20) = 150.100$; $p < 0.001$.

✓ If SPSS states that the profitability is 0.000, it means that SPSS has rounded up the amount to the nearest number at three decimal places. However, we would always round the last 0 to a 1, so that $p < 0.001$.

- As $p < 0.001$, this indicates that we have found a significant main effect for our repeated measures factor 'time'. We do not however know where the differences lie, and therefore must consult the post hoc test for this information.
- We have also found a significant interaction between our two factors, $F(2,20) = 37.900$, $p < 0.001$.

SPSS advanced

- We can confidently take the figures given by the **Sphericity Assumed** model because when we observed **Mauchly's Test of Sphericity** this was found to be non-significant, and the **Epsilon** value was 0.941. If this is not the case then one of the suggested correction models should be used. SPSS provides us with several correction models, the Greehouse–Geisser is the one usually reported.
- The **Sums of Squares** gives a measure of the variability in the scores due to a particular source of variability. The **Mean Square** is the variance (sums of squares divided by the degrees of freedom). Note that there is a lot of variability due to our factors and much less due to error indicating a large effect.

The **Tests of Within-Subjects Contrasts** table is generated by default by SPSS during the mixed and repeated measures ANOVA procedure and is a trend analysis.

Tests of Within-Subjects Contrasts

Measure: MEASURE_1

Source	TIME	Type III Sum of Squares	df	Mean Square	F	Sig.
TIME	Linear	80.667	1	80.667	254.737	.000
	Quadratic	2.722	1	2.722	11.395	.007
TIME * WORKERS	Linear	20.167	1	20.167	63.684	.000
	Quadratic	.889	1	.889	3.721	.083
Error(TIME)	Linear	3.167	10	.317		
	Quadratic	2.389	10	.239		

SPSS advanced

- The **Tests of Within-Subjects Contrasts** table examines the trends displayed in our data. This will give information as to the underlying model best fitting the data.

- As we have three time periods, the two possible trends are those following a linear or quadratic trend.
- In our example we can see that we have found a significant linear trend in our data for our repeated measures factor 'time', $F(1,10) = 254.737$; $p < 0.001$. However, our data also shows evidence of a significant quadratic trend, $F(1,10) = 11.395$; $p < 0.01$.
- The interaction between our factors is found to have a significant linear model underlying it, $F(1,10) = 63.684$; $p < 0.001$. The quadratic trend underpinning this interaction is not significant, $F(1,10) = 3.721$; $p > 0.05$.

The **Tests of Between-Subjects Effects** table enables us to decide whether we have a significant main effect for our independent measures factor 'workers' (novices or experienced workers).

Tests of Between-Subjects Effects

Measure: MEASURE_1
Transformed Variable: Average

Source	Type III Sum of Squares	df	Mean Square	F	Sig.
Intercept	802.778	1	802.778	163.462	.000
WORKERS	.111	1	.111	.023	.883
Error	49.111	10	4.911		

SPSS essential

- The effect of our independent measures factor 'workers' is not statistically significant: $F(1,10) = 0.023$, $p > 0.05$.
- As p is greater than 0.05 we can conclude that we have not found a significant main effect for 'workers', i.e. there are no significant differences *overall* between novice and experienced workers on the number of errors they committed in the three time periods.

SPSS advanced

- The **Intercept** row shows that our overall mean is significantly different from zero.

The following table refer to the pairwise comparison analysis requested for the repeated measures factor, which was a Bonferroni.

Estimates

Measure: MEASURE_1

TIME	Mean	Std. Error	95% Confidence Interval	
			Lower Bound	Upper Bound
1	6.750	.410	5.837	7.663
2	4.333	.450	3.330	5.337
3	3.083	.291	2.435	3.732

SPSS advanced

- The **Mean** indicates the mean number of errors made across the three weeks. This is a replication of the means discussed in the **Descriptive Statistics** table.
- The **Std. Error** column gives an estimate of the standard deviation of the sampling distribution of the mean. This is a useful figure as it is used in the computation of significance tests comparing means and in the calculation of confidence intervals (see Chapter 6 for more detailed information).
- The **95% Confidence Interval** of the difference provides an estimate of the population mean. For example at TIME 1 we are 95 per cent confident that the population mean lies between 5.837 and 7.663.

The **Pairwise Comparisons** table gives us a comparison of the means for all paired combinations of the levels of our repeated measures factor, which in our example is 'time'. All comparisons are adjusted using the Bonferroni method. This table should be inspected to ascertain where the significant differences that were evident from the calculation of our main effect for 'time' are located.

Pairwise Comparisons

Measure: MEASURE_1

(I) TIME	(J) TIME	Mean Difference (I-J)	Std. Error	Sig.[a]	95% Confidence Interval for Difference[a]	
					Lower Bound	Upper Bound
1	2	2.417*	.186	.000	1.882	2.951
	3	3.667*	.230	.000	3.007	4.326
2	1	−2.417*	.186	.000	−2.951	−1.882
	3	1.250*	.227	.001	.599	1.901
3	1	−3.667*	.230	.000	−4.326	−3.007
	2	−1.250*	.227	.001	−1.901	−.599

Based on estimated marginal means

*. The mean difference is significant at the .05 level.

[a]. Adjustment for multiple comparisons: Bonferroni.

SPSS essential

- In the **Pairwise Comparisons** table above, the important columns have been shaded.
- This table shows all the possible comparisons for the three levels of our repeated measures variable.
- In each comparison one level is given the identifier 'I' and the second 'J'. This is evident in the **Mean Difference** column, which indicates the resulting figure when the mean of one level of the variable (J) has been subtracted from a second level (I).
- In our example, the overall mean of our first level (week 1) was shown to be 6.750 in our descriptive statistics calculations, and the mean of level 2 (week 2) was shown to be 4.333.

$$6.750 \text{ (I)} - 4.333 \text{ (J)} = 2.417$$

- The **Sig.** column enables us to assess whether the mean differences between the levels of the variable are significant. We can see from our example that all the possible pairwise comparisons are significant, as all the values in the **Sig.** column are less than 0.01.

SPSS advanced

- The **Std. Error** values are all small, indicating low variability in the predicted mean differences.
- The **95% Confidence Interval for Difference** gives us an estimate of the mean difference in the populations. For example we are 95 per cent confident that the mean difference between TIME 1 and TIME 2 lies between 1.1882 and 2.951.

As we produced pairwise comparisons via the Bonferroni method, the ANOVA also produces the following **Multivariate Tests** table as well as the Bonferroni. This table is not of interest as we have followed the univariate method of analysis, having first performed the suggested checks on our data (Mauchly and Epsilon).

Multivariate Tests

	Value	F	Hypothesis df	Error df	Sig.
Pillai's trace	.968	135.928[a]	2.000	9.000	.000
Wilks' lambda	.032	135.928[a]	2.000	9.000	.000
Hotelling's trace	30.206	135.928[a]	2.000	9.000	.000
Roy's largest root	30.206	135.928[a]	2.000	9.000	.000

Each F tests the multivariate effect of TIME. These tests are based on the linearly independent pairwise comparisons among the estimated marginal means.

[a]. Exact statistic.

The final part of the SPSS output is our interaction plot, which allows us to examine the patterns previously discussed.

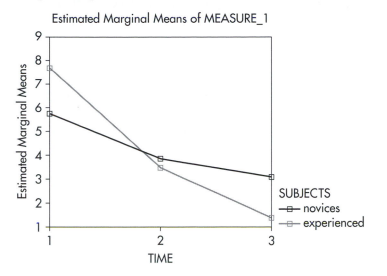

SPSS essential

- The graph above shows the main effects and interactions that have been identified as part of the ANOVA analysis.
- The significant main effect for our repeated measures variable can be seen by examining the trend across the three weeks. It can be seen from the plot that both groups of operators made fewer errors over the testing period.
- The plot indicates that there were some differences between our groups of workers, particularly at times 1 and 3. However, we found a non-significant main effect between our two groups of operators. There is therefore no evidence of significant differences between the two groups of operators overall when using the new machinery.
- A significant interaction between our variables was found, and this can be clearly seen in the interaction plot.
- In week 1 the experienced operators were making more errors than the novice operators on the new machinery. However, this trend was reversed by week 3 when the experienced operators made fewer errors than the novice operators.

> ✓ Graphs generated in this manner may need editing as the labelling technique is not always clear. If you prefer, you can generate a line chart separately from the ANOVA procedure by going to the **Graphs** command. See Chapter 4 for further details.

SPSS advanced

- We may wish to carry out further tests with our data to enable us to more fully understand the patterns emerging in our analysis. For example, we can be quite confident that our experienced operators are making more errors than the novice operators in week 1, i.e. we have identified a simple main effect. However, we are less confident about the differences between the operators in week 2.
- A test for such simple main effects can therefore be calculated through the **Syntax** command within SPSS. This is shown next.

Calculation of simple main effects – two factor mixed design analysis of variance

Sometimes when carrying out a two factor ANOVA we need to assess the *simple main effects* as well as the overall main effects for a factor. This examines the effect of one factor, 'workers', at each level of our second factor, 'time', *separately*. This advanced procedure is possible using the SPSS syntax function.

The interaction plot from our current example is shown below. Looking at the graph we can be reasonably confident that there is a significant difference between our two groups of workers in week 1 and week 3, with the direction being reversed across these times. However, we may be unsure as to the effect of 'workers' week 2.

In this case we may wish to carry out further statistical analysis examining the simple main effects at this time. The period of interest is circled on the chart below.

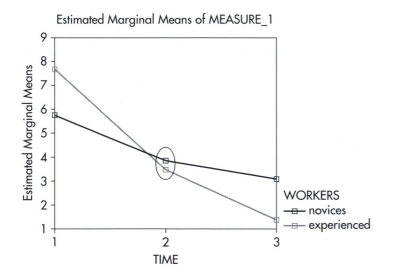

Testing such simple main effects can be achieved by using the **Syntax** option within the two factor ANOVA procedures. The following example will remain focused on the two factor mixed ANOVA, although the procedure for calculating the simple main effects for both two factor repeated and two factor independent ANOVAs is similar.

We follow the procedure for the two factor mixed design ANOVA as described earlier. However, when we get to the **Options** command we undertake the following procedure.

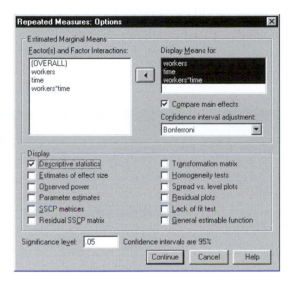

✓ It is important that before carrying out this command both the factors and the interaction have been sent to the **Display Means for** box within the **Options** screen. Failure to do this will make the calculation of your simple main effects more difficult as more commands will need to be typed.

- Once the desired options have been selected as part of the two factor ANOVA procedure, click on **Paste**.
- A syntax screen will then appear, as shown below.

```
Syntax3 - SPSS Syntax Editor
File  Edit  View  Analyze  Graphs  Utilities  Run  Window  Help

GLM
  week1 week2 week3 BY workers
  /WSFACTOR = time 3 Polynomial
  /METHOD = SSTYPE(3)
  /EMMEANS = TABLES(workers) COMPARE ADJ(BONFERRONI)
  /EMMEANS = TABLES(time) COMPARE ADJ(BONFERRONI)
  /EMMEANS = TABLES(workers*time)
  /PRINT = DESCRIPTIVE
  /CRITERIA = ALPHA(.05)
  /WSDESIGN = time
  /DESIGN = workers.
```

- The lines of syntax confirm the analysis that will take place.
- As we can see, the main effects of the two factors are to be compared using a Bonferroni test.
- We need to change the syntax to ensure that, in addition to this, a Bonferroni is conducted on the interaction at /EMMEANS = TABLES(workers*time).
- This will ensure that our simple main effects will be produced.

- The following instruction should be typed on the interaction command line.
  This has been highlighted in the example on the right:

COMPARE(workers) ADJ(BONFERRONI)

- We want to compare the two groups of workers within each time measurement, hence we choose the variable 'workers' for the COMPARE command.
- Once this has been added, place the cursor at the top of the screen before the letters GLM.

```
Syntax3 - SPSS Syntax Editor
File  Edit  View  Analyze  Graphs  Utilities  Run  Window  Help

GLM
  week1 week2 week3 BY workers
  /WSFACTOR = time 3 Polynomial
  /METHOD = SSTYPE(3)
  /EMMEANS = TABLES(workers) COMPARE ADJ(BONFERRONI)
  /EMMEANS = TABLES(time) COMPARE ADJ(BONFERRONI)
  /EMMEANS = TABLES(workers*time) COMPARE(workers) ADJ(BONFERRONI)
  /PRINT = DESCRIPTIVE
  /CRITERIA = ALPHA(.05)
  /WSDESIGN = time
  /DESIGN = workers.
```

- Go to the **Run** drop down menu and select **To End**.
- The two factor mixed ANOVA will now run in the same manner as before, but this time will produce additional tables which will assess the significance of simple main effects.

The output from this procedure will be identical to that previously discussed, with the exception of two additional tables, a more detailed **Pairwise Comparisons** table and a **Univariate Tests** table. The tables will be found following the original **Pairwise Comparisons** table in the output.

As can be seen from the table below a comparison is made within each time measurement between the two groups of workers. It should be read in a similar manner to the other **Pairwise Comparisons** tables.

Pairwise Comparisons

Measure: MEASURE_1

TIME	(I) WORKERS	(J) WORKERS	Mean Difference (I-J)	Std. Error	Sig.ᵃ	95% Confidence Interval for Differenceᵃ	
						Lower Bound	Upper Bound
1	novices	experienced	−2.167*	.820	.025	−3.993	−.340
	experienced	novices	2.167*	.820	.025	.340	3.993
2	novices	experienced	.333	.901	.719	−1.673	2.340
	experienced	novices	−.333	.901	.719	−2.340	1.673
3	novices	experienced	1.500*	.582	.028	.203	2.797
	experienced	novices	−1.500*	.582	.028	−2.797	−.203

Based on estimated marginal means
  *. The mean difference is significant at the .05 level.
  ᵃ. Adjustment for multiple comparisons: Bonferroni.

SPSS advanced

- Taking the first block of the table, TIME 1, we can see that the two groups of workers are performing differently, and from the **Sig.** column we can see that this difference is significant ($p < 0.05$). The experienced workers are making more errors in week 1.
- In TIME 3 the differences are also significant as $p < 0.05$. The novice workers are making more errors in week 3.
- The period of measurement we are interested in is week 2. We can see that at this time period, TIME 2, the difference between the two groups is not significant as $p > 0.05$.
- We can therefore conclude that there is no simple main effect at week 2.

The second extra table generated by this command is shown below.

Univariate Tests

Measure: MEASURE_1

TIME		Sum of Squares	df	Mean Square	F	Sig.
1	Contrast	14.083	1	14.083	6.983	.025
	Error	20.167	10	2.017		
2	Contrast	.333	1	.333	.137	.719
	Error	24.333	10	2.433		
3	Contrast	6.750	1	6.750	6.639	.028
	Error	10.167	10	1.017		

Each F tests the simple effects of WORKERS within each level combination of the other effects shown. These tests are based on the linearly independent pairwise comparisons among the estimated marginal means.

SPSS advanced

- This produces an ANOVA table showing the effect of the contrasts we are interested in. This tells us whether there are any effects within the time period we are studying.
- We can see that the significant differences between the workers occur at week 1 and week 3, the details of which were shown in the **Pairwise Comparisons** table.

FAQ

All your examples have two factors covering the different design possibilities, however, what happens if there are more than two factors?

If you do have more than two factors, whatever the design, the same procedures apply, adding in extra factors as necessary. However, be aware that with more factors the output becomes more complicated to interpret, particularly the interactions.

I've entered my data for a two factor repeated measures ANOVA and have started to follow the procedure. When I get to send my variables across to the 'Within Subjects Variable' box I don't seem to have the correct number of variables for the number of spaces stated.

The first thing that you should check is that you have entered the data correctly for a two factor repeated measures ANOVA. Remember that each person is going to have a score on each of the possible combinations of each factor. For example, say we were measuring alertness among a group of office workers and have two factors 'time of day' (am and pm) and 'caffeine' (with caffeine or without caffeine). As this is a repeated measures analysis every participant will have four scores, one for each level of each factor. Before entering the data, let's think about how our factors should appear.

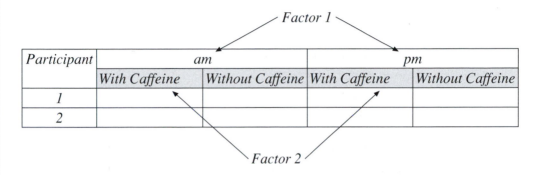

As we can see from the table above, Factor 1 has two levels and Factor 2 has two levels, and the combination of these factors produces four measurement points for each person.

I have collected three dependent measures of data from my participants and have two independent factors as well. I'm trying to get SPSS to calculate a two factor independent ANOVA on my data, but it will only let me send across one dependent variable, what am I doing wrong?

That's because two factor ANOVAs only use one dependent variable. You have the option of carrying out three two factor independent ANOVAs or one MANOVA.

Details on how to calculate a two factor ANOVA by hand can be found in Chapter 15 of Hinton (2004). An explanation of the meaning of an interaction in a two factor ANOVA is given in Chapter 14 of Hinton (2004).

Chapter 12

Introduction to multivariate analysis of variance

$\mathbf{T}$HE ANOVA IS REFERRED TO as a univariate test as the analysis involves only one dependent variable despite allowing more than one independent variable. However, there are cases where we wish to analyse data with more than one dependent variable. In this case we perform a multivariate analysis of variance or MANOVA. For example, we may have collected information on individuals' satisfaction with their home life and their working life using a satisfaction index. We might be interested in comparing four age groups (as an independent variable) on both home satisfaction and work satisfaction (two dependent variables). Rather than undertaking two separate one factor independent measures ANOVAs we can undertake a single MANOVA on the data.

The key point to note about a MANOVA is that it is essentially examining the effect of the independent variable(s) on the composite dependent variable. In our example the MANOVA will tell us if there is an effect of age on the combined dependent variables of home satisfaction and work satisfaction.

The advantage of the MANOVA over a number of separate ANOVAs is that we can keep the overall probability of a Type I error fixed at a chosen level (for example 0.05). The more tests we undertake on the same data the greater the risk of making a Type I error. Furthermore, the MANOVA allows us to examine the relationship between the dependent variables.

SPSS prints out four statistics for the results of the MANOVA: Pillai's Trace, Hotelling's T^2, Wilks' Lambda and Roy's Largest Root. The reason for this is that each is a different formula – although they all attempt to show the proportion of the variability in the dependent variables explained by the independent variable(s). Choosing the appropriate statistic does require quite an advanced knowledge of the purpose of the MANOVA but in general terms we recommend two things. First, look to see if all four statistics agree on the significance of the effect and if they do then we can be confident that it is genuine. Second, the statistics do differ in their power depending on the type of data and the sample sizes and so choosing the appropriate one will be dependent on the differences being examined. However, Wilks' lambda is more or less a good 'middle' value to take – neither the most powerful nor the least powerful of the tests, regardless of the data.

With an ANOVA we often need to undertake comparisons to discover the specific location of the differences causing the overall significant F value. The MANOVA is similiar in that a significant Wilks' lambda tells us that there is an effect of the independent variable(s) on the dependent variables, but not exactly where the effect lies.

SPSS gives us additional information, providing the univariate ANOVA calculations for the effect of the independent variable(s) on each dependent variable separately. We can use these tables when we have a significant finding in the MANOVA, to see where the independent variable(s) is/are having the greatest effect. However, we do need to remember that these are straightforward univariate ANOVAs (identical to having undertaken them without the MANOVA) so it is advisable to correct for the increased risk of Type I errors given that the MANOVA was calculated first (i.e. make a Bonferroni correction on the significance level).

The MANOVA, being a more complex version of the ANOVA, requires the same assumptions as a repeated measures ANOVA.

Independent measures multivariate analysis of variance

An independent measures MANOVA is one where there are independent measures on the independent variable(s). For example, we may be examining the difference between a group of extraverts and a group of introverts on the performance of a number of different problem-solving tasks involving working with other people and working on one's own. In this case introversion–extraversion is an independent measures variable. The hypothesis for the analysis would be that there is an effect of introversion–extraversion on the problem-solving tasks (as a composite dependent variable).

Usually the univariate ANOVAs will provide enough information to show to what extent the dependent variables are contributing to a significant MANOVA. So we could examine the effect of introversion–extraversion on each of the tasks separately. However, if you were interested in the underlying relationship between the dependent variables in combination, with respect to an independent variable, then a discriminant function analysis could be performed to investigate this relationship. In this case the analysis would produce a function of the dependent variables that would be able to classify a person as either an introvert or an extravert.

Scenario

A researcher wanted to evaluate a new teaching method, to improve students' performance on English and mathematics. Two schools were selected to participate in this study: a traditional school and a newly built school. The newly built school offered to pilot the new teaching method, while the traditional school continued with existing teaching methods. Maths scores are measured on a scale out of 100 and English on a scale out of 60.

Data entry

Enter the dataset as shown in the example.

	school	english	maths
1	new sch	54.00	53.00
2	new sch	50.00	52.00
3	new sch	56.00	59.00
4	new sch	54.00	77.00
5	new sch	52.00	56.00
6	new sch	58.00	53.00
7	new sch	50.00	56.00
8	new sch	49.00	78.00
9	new sch	59.00	58.00
10	new sch	57.00	54.00
11	tradition	48.00	65.00
12	tradition	52.00	77.00
13	tradition	58.00	65.00
14	tradition	46.00	46.00
15	tradition	48.00	69.00
16	tradition	52.00	68.00
17	tradition	42.00	63.00
18	tradition	49.00	54.00
19	tradition	43.00	58.00
20	tradition	39.00	60.00

✓ See Chapter 2 for the full data entry procedure.

Test procedure

- All inferential statistics are found under the **Analyze** command.
- Select **General Linear Model** and then **Multivariate** as we have more than one dependent variable.

- The dependent variables 'English scores' and 'Maths scores' should be sent to the **Dependent Variables** box.
- Send the independent variable 'school' across to the **Fixed Factor(s)** box.

- Click on **Options** and place a tick in the **Descriptive statistics** box.
- We can test for homogeneity by selecting the option **Homogeneity tests**.
- Click on **Continue**.

✓ Note in this example no post hoc test was required as the independent factor only had two levels. For two factor independent measures MANOVAs, where one or both factors have three or more levels, click on the **Post Hoc** command and select the appropriate test. See Chapter 10 for details of this procedure in relation to a one factor independent ANOVA.

SPSS output

The first table that SPSS produces is the **Between-Subjects Factors** table that tells us how many participants were in each group and how many levels our independent factor has.

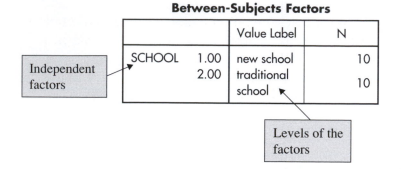

Between-Subjects Factors

		Value Label	N
SCHOOL	1.00	new school	10
	2.00	traditional school	10

Independent factors

Levels of the factors

The next table that SPSS produces is for **Descriptive Statistics**. This table gives the mean, standard deviation and number of participants in each group.

Descriptive Statistics

	SCHOOL	Mean	Std. Deviation	N
English scores	new school	53.9000	3.5730	10
	traditional school	47.7000	5.5588	10
	Total	50.8000	5.5498	20
Maths scores	new school	59.6000	9.6977	10
	traditional school	62.5000	8.6056	10
	Total	61.0500	9.0465	20

Essential

SPSS essential

- The **Descriptive Statistics** table displays the **Mean** test scores for each school for their English and maths results. As we are not interested in comparing the scores of English and maths (i.e. the two dependent variables), both appear in separate rows. However, we are interested in comparing the scores from the two schools on each of the dependent variables. For example, by observing the English results we can see that the new school has a higher mean (53.9000) than the traditional school (47.7000).

* The **Total** mean tells us the overall mean score on the tests across both groups.
* The **Std. Deviation** shows the spread of scores found in both tests.

The next table that is generated is the **Box's Test of Equality of Covariance Matrices** table, this shows whether our data violates the assumption of equality of covariance.

One of the assumptions of the MANOVA is that there is not a difference in the covariance of the dependent variables across the independent groups. The **Box's Test of Equality of Covariance Matrices** indicates if we have a problem with covariance.

Box's Test of Equality of Covariance Matrices[a]

Box's M	4.023
F	1.180
df1	3
df2	58320.000
Sig.	.316

Tests the null hypothesis that the observed covariance
matrices of the dependent variables are equal across groups.
 [a]. Design: Intercept + SCHOOL

SPSS essential

* Remember, as with the repeated measures ANOVA, it is always important to check for the homogeneity of variances assumption as well as the homogeneity of covariance assumption (see Chapter 9). Within the MANOVA these assumptions are checked by **Levene's Test of Equality of Variances** and **Box's Test**. If we found a significant result this would suggest that the assumption had been violated. As we can see we have met this assumption as **Box's Test** is not significant ($p > 0.05$).

With our independent measures MANOVA we are examining whether our two dependent variables, English and maths scores, are together being influenced by the new teaching strategy. This information is contained in the **Multivariate Tests** table shown below. The important information has been highlighted.

Multivariate Tests[b]

Effect		Value	F	Hypothesis df	Error df	Sig.
Intercept	Pillai's Trace	.994	1409.663[a]	2.000	17.000	.000
	Wilks' Lambda	.006	1409.663[a]	2.000	17.000	.000
	Hotelling's Trace	165.843	1409.663[a]	2.000	17.000	.000
	Roy's Largest Root	165.843	1409.663[a]	2.000	17.000	.000
SCHOOL	Pillai's Trace	.353	4.645[a]	2.000	17.000	.025
	Wilks' Lambda	.647	4.645[a]	2.000	17.000	.025
	Hotelling's Trace	.547	4.645[a]	2.000	17.000	.025
	Roy's Largest Root	.547	4.645[a]	2.000	17.000	.025

[a]. Exact statistic
[b]. Design: Intercept + SCHOOL

SPSS essential

- Within the **Multivariate Tests** table we are looking to see if the **Wilks' Lambda** test statistic is significant, which would indicate that overall there is a significant effect of the new teaching strategy on both dependent variables.
- We can see in our example above that overall there is a significant effect of the new teaching strategy on the combination of both dependent variables:

$$F(2,17) = 4.645, p < 0.05; \text{ Wilks' lambda} = 0.647$$

The **Levene's Test of Equality of Error Variances** table tests for the homogeneity of variances for each dependent variable.

Levene's Test of Equality of Error Variances[a]

	F	df1	df2	Sig.
English scores	1.028	1	18	.324
Maths scores	.088	1	18	.770

Tests the null hypothesis that the error variance of the dependent variable is equal across groups
[a]. Design: Intercept + SCHOOL

SPSS essential

- The **Levene's Test of Equality of Variance** allows us to look at the homogeneity assumption for each dependent variable. A significant result indicates that the assumption has been violated.
- As we can see in our example, non-significant results were obtained from both dependent variables, $p > 0.05$.

The next table is the more familiar **Tests of Between-Subjects Effects** table, which allows us to examine each of the dependent variables individually.

Tests of Between-Subjects Effects

Source	Dependent Variable	Type III Sum of Squares	df	Mean Square	F	Sig.
Corrected Model	English scores	192.200[a]	1	192.200	8.803	.008
	Maths scores	42.050[b]	1	42.050	.500	.488
Intercept	English scores	51612.800	1	51612.800	2363.945	.000
	Maths scores	74542.050	1	74542.050	886.877	.000
SCHOOL	English scores	192.200	1	192.200	8.803	.008
	Maths scores	42.050	1	42.050	.500	.488
Error	English scores	393.000	18	21.833		
	Maths scores	1512.900	18	84.050		
Total	English scores	52198.000	20			
	Maths scores	76097.000	20			
Corrected Total	English scores	585.200	19			
	Maths scores	1554.950	19			

[a]. R Squared = .328 (Adjusted R Squared = .291)
[b]. R Squared = .027 (Adjusted R Squared = −.027)

SPSS essential

- We can see from the table above that for our dependent variable 'English scores' we have found a significant effect of teaching method, $F(1,18) = 8.803$; $p < 0.01$.
- We have not found a significant effect of teaching method for our dependent variable 'Maths scores', $F(1,18) = .500$; $p > 0.05$.

SPSS advanced

- The **Sums of Squares** give a measure of the variability in the scores due to a particular source of variability. The **Mean Square** is the amount of variance produced as a result of that source.
- The **R Squared** values under the table indicate the amount of variation in each dependent variable that can be accounted for by the independent factor. For example we can see that the **R Square** for English is 0.328, which shows that the new teaching method can account for 32.8 per cent of the variation in English scores.
- Due to the possible Type 1 error it may be worth performing a Bonferroni correction on the ANOVA results.

Repeated measures multivariate analysis of variance

In a repeated measures MANOVA we have repeated measures on the independent variable(s) (so we have no grouping variable). For example, a researcher is investigating the effect of tiredness on three different monitoring tasks. A group of participants have to sit in a pretend control room monitoring three different types of visual displays, and make adjustments when the displays move into the unsafe zones. The same set of participants are measured on their responses on the three different tasks at two time periods: at the beginning of a 10-hour shift and at the end of the shift.

The MANOVA will show whether there is an effect of tiredness on the composite dependent variable consisting of the responses to the three tasks. If we find a significant effect in the MANOVA, we can examine the outcome of three one factor repeated measures ANOVAs, which will show the effect of the independent variable on each of the dependent variables separately (we would not perform a discriminant function analysis as there is no grouping variable in this repeated measures analysis).

Scenario

A researcher wanted to evaluate a new teaching method over time to see if it improved students' performance on English and maths. Maths scores out of 100 were tested before the new method (maths1) and then after the implementation of the teaching strategy two months later (maths2). Similarly, English scores were tested before the new teaching method (eng1) and two months later (eng2), scores out of 100 were noted.

Data entry

<table>
<tr><td colspan="5">▦ RM MANOVA 17.10.03.sav - SPSS Data Editor</td></tr>
<tr><td colspan="5">File Edit View Data Transform Analyze Graphs Utilities Wi</td></tr>
<tr><td colspan="5">1 : eng1   41</td></tr>
<tr><td></td><td>eng1</td><td>eng2</td><td>maths1</td><td>maths2</td></tr>
<tr><td>1</td><td>41.00</td><td>42.00</td><td>53.00</td><td>65.00</td></tr>
<tr><td>2</td><td>50.00</td><td>55.00</td><td>49.00</td><td>70.00</td></tr>
<tr><td>3</td><td>57.00</td><td>58.00</td><td>59.00</td><td>66.00</td></tr>
<tr><td>4</td><td>66.00</td><td>68.00</td><td>70.00</td><td>82.00</td></tr>
<tr><td>5</td><td>51.00</td><td>48.00</td><td>56.00</td><td>72.00</td></tr>
<tr><td>6</td><td>53.00</td><td>55.00</td><td>52.00</td><td>73.00</td></tr>
<tr><td>7</td><td>51.00</td><td>52.00</td><td>56.00</td><td>63.00</td></tr>
<tr><td>8</td><td>50.00</td><td>49.00</td><td>73.00</td><td>82.00</td></tr>
<tr><td>9</td><td>48.00</td><td>51.00</td><td>58.00</td><td>78.00</td></tr>
<tr><td>10</td><td>50.00</td><td>50.00</td><td>52.00</td><td>60.00</td></tr>
<tr><td>11</td><td></td><td></td><td></td><td></td></tr>
</table>

- The data should be entered in a similar fashion to a two factor repeated measures design ANOVA.
- In our example we have two dependent variables 'English' and 'maths' scores and a repeated measures factor, pre- and post-measurement.

✓ See Chapter 2 for full data entry procedure.

Test procedure

Analyze Graphs Utilities Window Help

- Reports ▶
- Descriptive Statistics ▶
- Custom Tables ▶
- Compare Means ▶
- General Linear Model ▶ — Univariate...
- Correlate ▶ — Multivariate...
- Regression ▶ — Repeated Measures...
- Loglinear ▶ — Variance Components...
- Classify ▶
- Data Reduction ▶
- Scale ▶
- Nonparametric Tests ▶
- Time Series ▶
- Survival ▶
- Multiple Response ▶
- Missing Value Analysis...

- All MANOVAs can be found under the **Analyze** and **General Linear Model** command.
- The type of MANOVA selected will depend on the design of the study.
- In our example our factor is of a repeated measures design. We must therefore choose the **Repeated Measures** option.

- The **Within-Subject Factor Name** needs to be assigned for the factor.
- We will call our factor 'prepost'. This has two levels.
- Click on **Add** and then **Measure**, this will open up an additional part to the window.
- This is where the dependent variables should be named and then added.
- Once both dependent variables appear in the bottom white box, click on **Define**.

✓ Note that in SPSS version 12 the bottom half of the box will already be visible and therefore there will be no need to click on **Measure**.

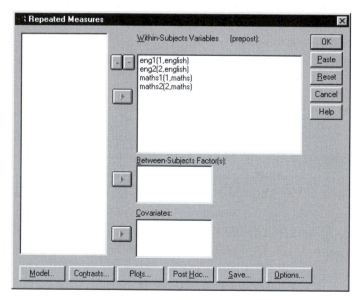

- Our variables need to be assigned (in order) to the **Within-Subjects Variables** box.
- This means that each variable needs to be sent over in accordance with the combination of levels it corresponds to on the factor and the dependent variable.

✓ It is important that the levels are assigned correctly in order for your output to be interpretable.

- Click on **Options** and place a tick in the **Descriptive statistics** box.
- Click on **Continue**.

SPSS output

The **Within-Subjects Factors** table produced first by SPSS gives a description of the two dependent variables entered into the MANOVA calculation. The first column shows both dependent variables, 'English' and 'Maths'. The second column displays the levels of the repeated measures factor.

Within-Subjects Factors

Measure	PREPOST	Dependent Variable
ENGLISH	1	ENG1
	2	ENG2
MATHS	1	MATHS1
	2	MATHS2

SPSS essential

- We can see from the **Within-Subjects Factors** table that **ENG1** is the label for the 'English' scores at the beginning of the study.
- We have labelled the 'English' scores at the end of the study **ENG2**.
- The other combinations of levels of the factors are assigned in similar ways.

The next table generated by SPSS is that of **Descriptive Statistics**. It is here that we can examine our dataset for potential differences in test scores.

Descriptive Statistics

	Mean	Std. Deviation	N
English scores 1	51.7000	6.4300	10
English scores 2	52.8000	6.9410	10
Maths scores 1	57.8000	7.8571	10
Maths scores 2	71.1000	7.7667	10

Essential

SPSS essential

• We can see from the table above that the mean for the English scores at the end of the study after the teaching strategy has been applied is greater (52.8000) than at the beginning of the study (51.7000).

• Similarly, the initial mean for the maths scores (57.8000) has increased to 71.1000 at the end of the study.

• As the two sets of scores were measured on different scales it is not appropriate to compare maths and English scores.

• The standard deviations indicate that there was a larger spread of scores within the maths scores than within the English scores.

The next table shows the **Multivariate Tests** results. This table is generated by default by SPSS during all repeated measures general linear model (GLM) procedures. This table shows our main findings. The important information has been highlighted.

Multivariate Tests[b]

Effect			Value	F	Hypothesis df	Error df	Sig.
Between Subjects	Intercept	Pillai's Trace	.991	437.154[a]	2.000	8.000	.000
		Wilks' Lambda	.009	437.154[a]	2.000	8.000	.000
		Hotelling's Trace	109.289	437.154[a]	2.000	8.000	.000
		Roy's Largest Root	109.289	437.154[a]	2.000	8.000	.000
Within Subjects	PREPOST	Pillai's Trace	.865	25.546[a]	2.000	8.000	.000
		Wilks' Lambda	.135	25.546[a]	2.000	8.000	.000
		Hotelling's Trace	6.386	25.546[a]	2.000	8.000	.000
		Roy's Largest Root	6.386	25.546[a]	2.000	8.000	.000

[a]. Exact statistic

[b]. Design: Intercept
Within Subjects Design: PREPOST

SPSS essential

• Within the **Multivariate Tests** table we look to see if the **Wilks' Lambda** test statistic is significant, which would indicate that overall there is a significant effect of the new teaching strategy on both dependent variables.

• We can see in our example that there is a significant effect of the new teaching strategy on the dependent variables 'English' and 'maths'.

$$F(2,8) = 25.546, \ p < 0.001; \ \text{Wilks' lambda} = 0.135$$

The **Mauchly's Test of Sphericity** table shows the sphericity checks.

Mauchly's Test of Sphericity[b]

Within Subjects Effect	Measure	Mauchly's W	Approx. Chi-Square	df	Sig.	Epsilon[a]		
						Greenhouse-Geisser	Huynh-Feldt	Lower-bound
PREPOST	ENG	1.000	.000	0	.	1.000	1.000	1.000
	MATHS	1.000	.000	0	.	1.000	1.000	1.000

Tests the null hypothesis that the error covariance matrix of the orthonormalized transformed dependent variables is proportional to an identity matrix.

[a]. May be used to adjust the degrees of freedom for the averaged tests of significance. Corrected tests are displayed in the Tests of Within-Subjects Effects table.

[b]. Design: Intercept
Within Subjects Design: PREPOST

You will notice from the above table that the **Sig.** column is blank, and no degrees of freedom are reported. This is because sphericity is only a problem if you have two or more conditions on your repeated measures factors. Our repeated measures factor 'PREPOST' has only two 'levels' and therefore sphericity will not be a problem in our data.

A second **Multivariate** table is produced, which details the **Within Subjects Effects**. In our example these values are the same as in the previous multivariate tests table.

Multivariate[b,c]

Within Subjects Effect		Value	F	Hypothesis df	Error df	Sig.
PREPOST	Pillai's Trace	.865	25.546[a]	2.000	8.000	.000
	Wilks' Lambda	.135	25.546[a]	2.000	8.000	.000
	Hotelling's Trace	6.386	25.546[a]	2.000	8.000	.000
	Roy's Largest Root	6.386	25.546[a]	2.000	8.000	.000

[a]. Exact statistic
[b]. Design: Intercept
   Within Subjects Design: PREPOST
[c]. Test are based on averaged variables.

The next table is the **Univariate Tests** table, which allows us to examine each of the dependent variables individually.

Univariate Tests

Source	Measure		Type III Sum of Squares	df	Mean Square	F	Sig.
PREPOST	ENG	Sphericity Assumed	6.050	1	6.050	2.538	.146
		Greenhouse-Geisser	6.050	1.000	6.050	2.538	.146
		Huynh-Feldt	6.050	1.000	6.050	2.538	.146
		Lower-bound	6.050	1.000	6.050	2.538	.146
	MATHS	Sphericity Assumed	884.450	1	884.450	53.049	.000
		Greenhouse-Geisser	884.450	1.000	884.450	53.049	.000
		Huynh-Feldt	884.450	1.000	884.450	53.049	.000
		Lower-bound	884.450	1.000	884.450	53.049	.000
Error(PREPOST)	ENG	Sphericity Assumed	21.450	9	2.383		
		Greenhouse-Geisser	21.450	9.000	2.383		
		Huynh-Feldt	21.450	9.000	2.383		
		Lower-bound	21.450	9.000	2.383		
	MATHS	Sphericity Assumed	150.050	9	16.672		
		Greenhouse-Geisser	150.050	9.000	16.672		
		Huynh-Feldt	150.050	9.000	16.672		
		Lower-bound	150.050	9.000	16.672		

SPSS essential

- The important rows in this table are the **Sphericity Assumed** rows.
- From the above table we are looking for a significant effect for our variable 'prepost' on the two dependent variables 'English' and 'maths'.

- We have not found a significant main effect for our factor 'prepost' on the dependent variable 'English', $F(1,9) = 2.538$; $p > 0.05$.
- We have found a significant main effect for our factor 'prepost' on the dependent variable 'maths', $F(1,9) = 53.049$; $p < 0.001$.

The **Tests of Within-Subjects Contrasts** table is generated by default by SPSS during the calculation of repeated measures GLM procedures, and is a trend analysis.

Tests of Within–Subjects Contrasts

Source	Measure	PREPOST	Type III Sum of Squares	df	Mean Square	F	Sig.
PREPOST	ENG	Linear	6.050	1	6.050	2.538	.146
	MATHS	Linear	884.450	1	884.450	53.049	.000
Error(PREPOST)	ENG	Linear	21.450	9	2.383		
	MATHS	Linear	150.050	9	16.672		

SPSS advanced

- The **Tests of Within-Subjects Contrasts** table examines the trends displayed in our data. This will give information as to the underlying model best fitting the data.
- As we only have two levels to our repeated measures factor, the only possible trends are those following a linear model.
- In our example we can see that our variable 'maths' follows a significant linear trend. This is expected due to the factor only having two levels.

The **Tests of Between-Subjects Effects** table is generated by default by SPSS when calculating repeated measures MANOVAs. As our factor is repeated measures, we do not have a between subjects factor, and the information that this table provides refers to the intercept.

Tests of Between-Subjects Effects

Transformed Variable: Average

Source	Measure	Type III Sum of Squares	df	Mean Square	F	Sig.
Intercept	ENG	54601.250	1	54601.250	626.600	.000
	MATHS	83076.050	1	83076.050	788.322	.000
Error	ENG	784.250	9	87.139		
	MATHS	948.450	9	105.383		

SPSS advanced

- On this occasion, as we have no independent measures variables there is only the **Intercept**, which tells us that our overall mean for both dependent variables is significantly different from zero.

FAQ

I am interested in comparing the effect of three different times of day (morning, afternoon and evening) on the performance of two cognitive tasks. Should I carry out an independent measures MANOVA or two separate independent measures ANOVAS?

If you are interested in looking at the effects on the two cognitive tasks separately, then perform two ANOVAs. However, if you are interested in the dependent variables in combination then perform a MANOVA.

You said that we could perform a discriminant function analysis after an independent measures MANOVA. How do I do this and what does it mean?

You select the Analyze drop-down menu and then Classify and Discriminant from the SPSS menu to select the Discriminant function analysis. You will be asked for a grouping variable. This is an independent measures variable (such as 'school' in our independent measures MANOVA example). You can only do this analysis when you have a grouping variable so we would not perform it after a repeated measures MANOVA. In our example 'school' is the grouping variable with 'new school' as group 1 and 'traditional school' as group 2.

In this analysis the dependent variables from the MANOVA (for example English scores, mathematics scores) are now the INDEPENDENT variables. The analysis seeks to find a combination of them (a function or functions) that discriminates between the groups of the grouping variable, and can predict which group a participant belongs to from their results on the English and maths scores.

In our example we only have two groups so there will only be one function produced, therefore this is the simplest case of discriminant function analysis and the function will be the multiple regression equation. If we put the values of the maths and English scores for a new participant into the function we can then predict which school that person belongs to.

Chapter 13

One factor analysis of variance for nonparametric data

RESEARCHERS OFTEN PREFER to use a parametric test rather than a non-parametric test. This is partly because a parametric test is more powerful (it is better for finding an effect when it really is there). Second, we are able to calculate means and standard deviations, which provide a nice clear summary of the data. In fact, even when we have ratings (such as people's judgement of how happy they are) some researchers will perform a parametric test, arguing that they will treat the data as being from an interval scale. This is only advisable for researchers who are confident in their understanding of their data and the analyses they are undertaking, as we do risk producing erroneous results. So it is only worth doing if you are able to weigh up the risk (the advantages and disadvantages) correctly.

There are a number of reasons for deciding that it is not appropriate to use a parametric test, particularly when one or more of the assumptions of a parametric test is violated. If you know that the population from which you drew the data is not normally distributed or you know that the data is not from a continuous variable then you would undertake a nonparametric test. For example, if a teacher was rating students on effort on a 100-point scale and only rated the children between either 0 and 40 or 60 and 100 we can see that the variable is not continuous as the middle range is not being used and certainly doesn't look to be normally distributed.

There are two nonparametric tests we can use instead of the one factor ANOVA. The Friedman test is a nonparametric equivalent of the one factor repeated measures ANOVA and the Kruskal–Wallis test is the nonparametric test used instead of the one factor independent measures ANOVA.

Kruskal–Wallis test for independent samples

When we wish to undertake a nonparametric analysis and have a single independent measures factor (independent variable) with more than two samples we choose the Kruskal–Wallis test. For example, a researcher chooses four towns of different sizes and inhabitants are asked to rate their overall happiness on a 100-point scale. The researcher is interested in seeing whether there is an effect of town size on the ratings of happiness.

The key feature of many nonparamatric tests is that the data is treated as ordinal and the first part of the analysis involves ranking the data. The Kruskal–Wallis test is no different. All the scores (from all the conditions) are ranked from lowest to highest. After that an analysis similar to the ANOVA is undertaken on the ranks. The statistic *H* (rather than F in the ANOVA) gives a measure of the relative strength of the variability in the ranks between the conditions compared to a standard value for this number of participants.

Within the Kruskal–Wallis formula are calculations based on the ranks and the squares of the ranks. When we have tied values and hence tied ranks it can cause us a problem. For example, with only three scores we have the ranks 1, 2 and 3. If we square these ranks we get 1, 4 and 9 which gives a total of 14. If the first two values were tied we would have to give the ranks 1.5, 1.5 and 3. When these are squared we get 2.25, 2.25 and 9, giving a total of 13.5. If there are only a few ties we normally do not worry. However, with a lot of ties the Kruskal–Wallis test can be inappropriate.

Scenario

A group of 18 people who found it hard to relax agreed to take part in a test of three relaxation techniques, a pill to aid restfulness, hypnosis and exercise. After a week of employing the technique the participants were asked to rate their ability to relax on a 50-point scale (ranging from 0, much worse, to 25, no change, through to 50, much better than before). Six people tried the pill method, five used hypnosis and seven exercise. Is there an effect of relaxation method on their ratings?

Data entry

	group	relax
1	pill	14
2	pill	10
3	pill	18
4	pill	22
5	pill	14
6	pill	20
7	hypnosis	29
8	hypnosis	38
9	hypnosis	27
10	hypnosis	25
11	hypnosis	26
12	exercise	44
13	exercise	30
14	exercise	40
15	exercise	28
16	exercise	33
17	exercise	35
18	exercise	42

Kruskal-Wallis - SPSS Data Editor
File Edit View Data Transform Anal

✓ The data should be entered into SPSS in a similar manner to the independent ANOVA. Due to the design being independent groups, one column will be the grouping variable and the other the rating score for each person.

✓ See Chapter 2 for the full data entry procedure.

Test procedure

- The command for the Kruskal–Wallis test is found under the drop-down menu **Analyze**, followed by **Nonparametric Tests**.
- SPSS refers to Kruskal–Wallis as **K Independent Samples**.

- Send the dependent variable to the **Test Variable List** box – in our case this is the variable 'relax'.
- Send the independent variable to the **Grouping Variable** box.
- SPSS will then require you to define the range of your groups by clicking on the **Define Range** option and entering the minimum and maximum values assigned to your groups. In the current example, the values 1, 2 and 3 were used and therefore are entered as below.

Several Independent Samples: Define Range ☒

Range for Grouping Variable

Minimum: 1

Maximum: 3

[Continue]
[Cancel]
[Help]

- Click on **Continue**.
- Ensure that the test type **Kruskal–Wallis H** is selected.
- Click on **OK**.

SPSS advanced

- The Kruskal–Wallis H test statistic should be adequate for most statistical testing of this nature. SPSS provides us with two alternatives, the less powerful **Median** test and the more powerful **Jonckheere–Terpstra** test. You would choose the latter if you were looking for ordered differences between your groups (an upward or downward trend).
- The default calculation performed for the p value is the **Asymptotic** p, which is an estimate of the true p value. This is generally an adequate method for calculating the p value but it is possible to calculate it exactly. This can be achieved through the **Exact** button.
- The **Monte Carlo** method for p calculation is preferred if it is not possible to calculate the exact p value because the sample size is too large (it would simply take too long to work out). The Monte Carlo method gives an unbiased estimate of the exact p.

✓ Under **Options** is the selection for means and standard deviations. While these descriptive statistics can be performed on ordinal datasets we recommend a degree of caution when calculating and interpreting them.

SPSS output

The first table generated by SPSS is the **Ranks** table, which is a description of the data giving the number of participants and the **Mean Rank** for each group.

Ranks

	GROUP	N	Mean Rank
relaxation	pill	6	3.50
	hypnosis	5	10.00
	exercise	7	14.29
	Total	18	

SPSS essential

> ✓ It may be worth consulting a statistics book to refresh your memory on how to work out a Kruskal–Wallis calculation by hand to enable a fuller understanding of this table, for example Hinton (2004).

- **N** is the number of participants in each group and the total number of participants.
- The **Mean Rank** indicates the mean rank of scores within each group.
- If there were no differences between the groups' ratings, i.e. the null hypothesis was true, we would expect the mean ranks to be roughly equal across the three groups.
- We can see from our example above that the three groups do not appear to be equal in their ratings of the relaxation method.

In order to determine whether the difference in the rankings is significant we must look at the **Test Statistics** table.

Test Statistics[a,b]

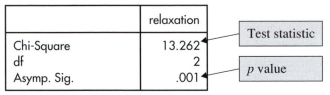

	relaxation
Chi-Square	13.262
df	2
Asymp. Sig.	.001

[a]. Kruskal Wallis Test
[b]. Grouping Variable: GROUP

SPSS essential

- The test statistic to report is the Kruskal–Wallis **Chi-Square**, which in the above example has a value of 13.262.
- The **Asymp. Sig.** gives the probability value.
- In the above example $\chi^2 = 13.262$, $df = 2$, $p < 0.01$.
- We can conclude that the difference between the ratings of the three groups is significant.

SPSS advanced

- SPSS always presents the results as a chi-square rather than the Kruskal–Wallis H. This is because the distribution of H closely approximates that of the chi-square.

✓ The Kruskal–Wallis procedure in SPSS does not offer the opportunity to perform post hoc multiple comparison tests. There are a number of tests that could be employed, but these would have to be calculated without the aid of SPSS.

Friedman test for related samples

We use the Friedman test as a nonparametric equivalent of a one-factor repeated measures ANOVA in cases where the assumptions for the ANOVA are not met. For example, if we have ratings and therefore believe that the data are not interval or ratio we would use the Friedman test. As an example, a researcher is interested in television viewers' preferences for different types of programmes and asks 20 people to rate the following four categories of programme in terms of their interest on a 1 to 10 scale: soap opera, documentary, action/adventure, current affairs. One person might rate the programmes as follows: soap opera 8, documentary 3, action/adventure 9, current affairs 1. A second person might produce the following ratings: soap opera 6, documentary 5, action/adventure 7, current affairs 4. Even though the ratings are very different both participants have given the same order for the four types of programme. It is the order of participants' results that the Friedman test analyses.

The first part of a Friedman test is to rank order the results from each participant separately. So both participants described above would have the following ranks: 3, 2, 4, 1. These ranks are then analysed in a similar way to an ANOVA. It is not exactly the same because, as we are dealing with ranks, certain values are fixed and it makes our analysis somewhat easier. The Friedman test produces a chi-square statistic, with a large value indicating that there is a difference between the rankings of one or more of the conditions.

While there are not the assumptions that we require for a one factor repeated measures ANOVA, we should examine how many tied ranks we have in the Friedman test. The fewer tied ranks the more appropriate the analysis. As you can imagine, in the above example a person's scores of 5, 7, 7, 7 would give ranks of 1, 3, 3, 3, and this is not very informative data for this type of analysis. Fortunately, as we are ranking within each participant rather than across all participants, we do not normally have a lot of tied ranks in a Friedman test.

Scenario

Ten people stay at a hotel where they eat all their meals. On one day they are asked to rate the quality of food for the three meals, breakfast, lunch and dinner, on a scale of 0 to 100 (from bad to good). Is there a significant difference between the three meals in their rated quality?

Data entry

✓ The dataset is set up like the repeated measures ANOVA. Each person will have three ratings and hence three variable columns are required.

Test procedure

- The command for the Friedman test is found under the drop-down menu **Analyze**, followed by **Nonparametric Tests**.
- SPSS refers to Friedman as **K Related Samples**.

- Send the variables to the **Test Variables** box.
- Ensure that **Friedman** is selected in the **Test Type** box.
- Click on **OK**.

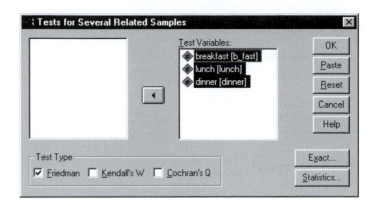

SPSS advanced

The **Friedman** test will be suitable for most statistical analyses, although further testing opportunities are available in SPSS.

- **Kendall's W** test produces a coefficient of agreement among raters. Coefficients range from 0 to 1, with 1 being complete agreement and 0 being no agreement.
- **Cochran's Q** test is an extension of the McNemar tests (see page 132). This is used when there are more than two variables which are categorical or dichotomous in nature.

SPSS advanced

- The default calculation performed for the p value is the **Asymptotic** p, which is an estimate of the true p value. This is generally an adequate method for calculating the p value but it is possible to calculate it exactly. This can be achieved through the **Exact** button.
- The **Monte Carlo** method for p calculation is preferred if it is not possible to calculate the exact p value because the sample size is too large (it would simply take too long to work out). The Monte Carlo method gives an unbiased estimate of the exact p.
- Under **Options** is the selection for means and standard deviations. While these descriptive statistics can be performed on ordinal datasets, we recommend a degree of caution when examining and interpreting them.

SPSS output

The first table generated by SPSS is the **Ranks** table, which is a description of the data giving the number of participants and the **Mean Rank** for each condition.

Ranks

	Mean Rank
breakfast	1.50
lunch	2.70
dinner	1.80

SPSS essential

✓ It may be worth consulting a statistics book to refresh your memory on how to work out a Friedman calculation by hand to enable a fuller understanding of this table, for example Hinton (2004).

- The **Mean Rank** indicates the mean rank of scores within each condition.
- If there were no difference between the ratings of the quality of food in the three meals, i.e. the null hypothesis was true, we would expect the mean ranks to be roughly equal across the three meals.
- We can see from our example above that the three meals do not appear to be equally rated, with lunch receiving a higher rating than the other two meals.

In order to determine whether the difference in these rankings is significant we must look at the Test Statistics table.

Test Statistics[a]

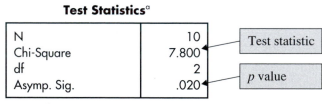

N	10
Chi-Square	7.800
df	2
Asymp. Sig.	.020

Test statistic

p value

[a]. Friedman Test

SPSS essential

- The test statistic to report is the Friedman **Chi-Square**, which in the above example has a value of 7.800.
- The significance of the result is checked by examining the *p* value (**Asymp. Sig.**).

- In our example $\chi^2 = 7.800$, $df = 2$; $p < 0.05$.
- We can therefore conclude that the enjoyment of the food is affected by the time of day, with lunch having the highest rating.

✓ The Friedman procedure in SPSS does not offer the opportunity to perform post hoc multiple comparison tests. There are a number of tests that could be employed, for example the Nemenyi test, but these would have to be calculated without the aid of SPSS.

FAQ

You advise that I should be careful of calculating means and standard deviations on my ordinal data, why is this?

When calculating descriptive statistics on ordinal data care should be taken as we cannot be confident that the whole of the scale is being used when making the judgements, or that the scale is being employed with equal intervals.

For example, a football manager judging the ability of his players on a 20-point scale might put a very high value on one player (18), a lower value on a second (10) and an even lower value on a third player (8). The information that we can confidently draw from his judgement is the order he puts his players in rather than the value he assigns to each player. The calculation of a mean on this data would not be appropriate, as we don't trust this to be an interval scale.

I've just worked out a Kruskal–Wallis and I'm looking for the H value, why can't I find it in my output?

You will not find H in your output as SPSS always presents the results as a chi-square rather than the Kruskal–Wallis H. This is because the distribution of H closely approximates the chi-square distribution. Therefore, in your results it is fine to report the chi-square statistic instead of H.

Details on the logic of the Kruskal–Wallis and Friedman tests, along with how to calculate them by hand, can be found in Chapter 18 of Hinton (2004).

Crosstabulation and chi-square

A RESEARCHER PRODUCES a questionnaire to find out about teenagers' leisure activities. There will be a lot of data produced, particularly if there are a lot of questions, and it is given out to teenagers who are 13 to 18 years old. Once the data has been put into the computer the researcher can print out a range of descriptive statistics, such as how many respondents there were of each age, how many males and females, how many people (or what percentage of them) participated in a particular leisure activity. However, the researcher will want to go further than simply summarising the findings of each question and this is where crosstabulation comes in.

We can combine the results of different questions in a table with the results of one question as the rows and the results of another question as the columns. The most common crosstabulation is when the data are frequency counts, so in our example the researcher can crosstabulate the question 'are you male or female?' with the question 'what is your age in years?' This will provide us with a table showing how many males and females there are of each age. We can create a table with more than two variables (questions). We might add the results of another question ('do you have a boy/girl-friend?') to the table. Now this is quite hard to picture as a piece of paper only has two dimensions and, after putting down the first two variables as the rows and columns, the third variable needs a third dimension. There are ways to draw the graph (as we can draw a three-dimensional object like a cube on a piece of paper). One way is to draw one table of age and gender for those who have a boy/girlfriend and a second table of age and gender for those who do not. We can refer to these two tables as 'layers' produced by the third variable. We are producing a crosstabulation with three variables by adding the third variable as a layer after using up the rows and columns. We can add more variables, if we wish, as additional layers. So even though we are creating a table with many variables it is not a problem for SPSS because it adds variables as layers to the table.

Now, why do we go to this trouble to produce a crosstabulation? The answer is that it will allow us to examine the association between the variables. We might have pre-planned predictions or we might simply be examining whether there is evidence of an association. Let us take some different variables from the research questionnaire. One question is 'what is your favourite film?' We want to see if this differs according to age, and to simplify things we might decide that we would add together the results of the 13- to 15-year-olds as younger teenagers and the 16- to 18-year-olds as older teenagers. Imagine that most choices were either the *Harry Potter* films or the *Lord of the Rings* films. So we choose columns as 'Harry Potter', 'Lord of the Rings' and 'other' and rows as 'younger' and 'older'. The data in the table will be the number of people in each group choosing the film. We might have a prediction that *Harry Potter* will be chosen by a larger proportion of the younger group and *Lord of the Rings* by the older group, but we do not have to.

When we test the association between age and favourite film we are examining the null hypothesis that there is no difference between the age groups in their film choice. So when the null hypothesis is true we should see roughly the same proportion of each age group choosing each of the films. The chi-square test examines these proportions and presents the probability of obtaining this pattern when there is no difference in the choices. A large value of chi-square indicates a large difference between the groups. If the probability is very small ($p < 0.05$) then we can conclude that there is a difference in the choice of film for the different age groups. If we had made a specific prediction that more of the younger group would choose *Harry Potter* then we are making a one-sided (one-tailed or directional) prediction and we would need to check the results to make sure that the predicted pattern is the one that emerged rather than some other difference.

The key assumption of the chi-square test is that there is independence of the observations, i.e. the results in each section (or 'cell') of the table are independent of each other. So if 45 younger teenagers choose *Harry Potter* and 28 choose *Lord of the Rings*, the 45 and 28 are unrelated. We could not allow a respondent to say they liked both films equally and score them in both cells.

There is a second assumption that the calculated chi-square is 'continuous' as the chi-square distribution is continuous. In order to satisfy this assumption it is better to have large numbers in each cell rather than small numbers. When the 'expected frequency' of a cell is lower than five we are concerned that this assumption is violated. Also, when we have a table with only two columns and two rows (2×2) there is a real risk that we will violate this assumption. To compensate for this a 'continuity correction' value is generated in SPSS, so you need to be careful when analysing a 2×2 table. On the positive side, with such a small table, the Fisher's Exact test (also produced by SPSS) can be used for an accurate calculation.

Usually, with tables larger than 2×2 and cell frequencies larger than five (and preferably over ten) we use the 'standard' chi-square value. If the cells have small numbers (expected frequency below five) but the table is large then it might be worth collecting more data or, if this is not possible, combining cells (see Chapter 5 for details on recoding data). If we were looking at favourite films, rather than looking at each film individually, we might group them into 'fantasy', 'romance', etc. to make the numbers in each cell larger. If we don't want to do this we should take the 'continuity correction' value. If we have a 2×2 table we take the Fisher's Exact value, as it is just that, an exact value for our table.

Finally, we have seen that chi-square compares patterns of results to see if they are similar or different. We can also use the chi-square test as a 'goodness of fit test'. This means 'does the pattern of results match (or fit) a predicted pattern?' For example, if we believe that younger teenagers will prefer *Harry Potter* over *Lord of the Rings* by 2 to 1, then we have a model where we expect there to be two people choosing *Harry Potter* for each one choosing *Lord of the Rings*. We would put the predictions of the model in our SPSS data table. We can then compare the actual findings (the frequencies) to the model to see if it 'fits' the data. In this case a significant chi-square value would tell us that the data is significantly different to the pattern predicted by the model. A non-significant chi-square would indicate that the data does not significantly differ from the model's predicted pattern.

Crosstabulation and chi-square

Scenario

A researcher wanted to test the difference of opinion between conservatives and liberals on some new taxation legislation. In a survey 120 people were identified as conservatives and 80 as liberals. A question on the survey asked whether the respondent agreed with new taxation legislation ('for'), disagreed with it ('against'), or had no opinion or did not know about it ('don't know'). The researcher believed that the respondent's party affiliation would influence their view of the new tax legislation.

Data entry

There are two methods for entering data for a crosstabulation and chi-square.

Data entry procedure: method 1

Each person can be entered separately, using the procedure outlined in Chapter 2, remembering to code the categories appropriately as we will be using nominal data.

People are entered into the dataset separately, coding their individual preferences for both political party and taxation legislation

✓ Remember selecting **View** and **Value labels** can show the value labels given in the data entry procedure.

Data entry procedure: method 2

Total frequency counts can be entered by **Weight Cases**. This procedure is particularly useful if you have a large dataset. Each combination of scores is entered along with the total frequency count for that group, as seen in the example below.

In order for SPSS to associate the frequency counts with the variables, the following procedure should be used.

* Go to **Data** and **Weight Cases** to bring up the following window.

* The variable we want to weight the categories by is frequency, therefore select the **Weight Cases by** option and send the variable 'freq' over to the **Frequency Variable box**.
* Click on **OK**.

You can be sure that the procedure has been carried out successfully as in the bottom right-hand corner of the screen a message saying '**Weight On**' will be displayed.

Test procedure

To produce the crosstabulation table and chi-square the following procedure should be adopted.

- All inferential statistics are found under the **Analyze** command.
- A crosstabulation is the appropriate descriptive statistic for nominal or category data, so choose **Descriptive Statistics** then **Crosstabs**.
- The **Crosstabs** box will then appear.

- At this point you need to decide which variable is to be considered your influencing variable and which is the one to be influenced.
- Our influencing variable is 'Political Party'.

> ✓ There are no strict rules as to which one goes where, although a general rule of thumb is that the influencing variable should go to the **Column(s)**, because when the output appears the convention is to read across the table rather than down a column.

- A clustered bar chart is the most appropriate way to display the findings of your crosstabulation, and this can be generated as an integral part of the procedure. If you would like to create this chart, place a tick against **Display clustered bar charts** in the **Crosstabs** box.

✓ If you have set up your dataset by weighting cases, a third variable will appear in the column (frequency). You need to ignore this variable and select the two variables under investigation, the frequency count will automatically be taken into account if the '**Weight On**' display is in the bottom right-hand corner of the screen.

- Click on **Statistics** to bring up the box to the left.
- The inferential statistic we want is the **Chi-square**. Place a tick next to this then click on **Continue**.

- Remember that when carrying out a crosstabulation and chi-square we are comparing how many people we have in a category with how many people we would expect to have in that category if the null hypothesis was true.
- In order to generate these we need to click on **Cells** to reveal the following box.

- Place a tick in both the **Observed** and **Expected** counts boxes so the two can be compared.
- A tick also needs to be placed in the **Percentages** box next to where you sent your influencing variable (generally the columns). Percentages give the best descriptor for nominal or category data as we often have unequal numbers in each group and therefore actual counts do not always give a representative picture. Percentages will give a proportion of each group total in each category.
- Click on **Continue** and finally on **OK** to complete the procedure.

SPSS output (2 × 3 crosstabulation and chi-square)

The following list of tables will be produced by SPSS when the above procedure has been completed.

The first table is the **Case Processing Summary**. This gives us a description of our dataset.

Case Processing Summary

	Cases					
	Valid		Missing		Total	
	N	Percent	N	Percent	N	Percent
Tax Law * Political Party	200	100.0%	0	.0%	200	100.0%

It also gives us an indication of the number and percentage of missing scores in our dataset. As we can see, no scores in our dataset are missing and therefore we are considering all 200 participants when making judgements about the association between the two variables.

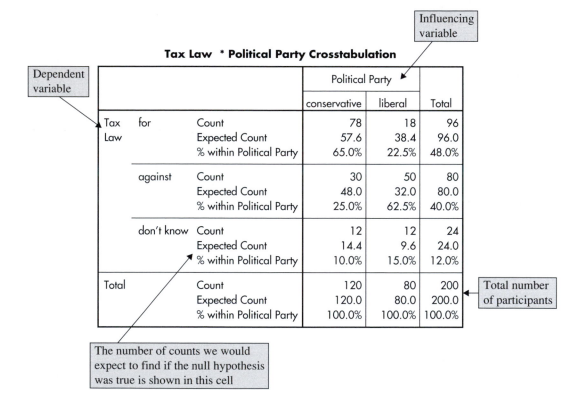

Tax Law * Political Party Crosstabulation

Influencing variable

Dependent variable

			Political Party		
			conservative	liberal	Total
Tax Law	for	Count	78	18	96
		Expected Count	57.6	38.4	96.0
		% within Political Party	65.0%	22.5%	48.0%
	against	Count	30	50	80
		Expected Count	48.0	32.0	80.0
		% within Political Party	25.0%	62.5%	40.0%
	don't know	Count	12	12	24
		Expected Count	14.4	9.6	24.0
		% within Political Party	10.0%	15.0%	12.0%
Total		Count	120	80	200
		Expected Count	120.0	80.0	200.0
		% within Political Party	100.0%	100.0%	100.0%

Total number of participants

The number of counts we would expect to find if the null hypothesis was true is shown in this cell

SPSS essential

- The **Count** represents the actual frequency counts obtained in the survey.
- The **Expected Count** represents how many we would expect to find in this combination if the null hypothesis was true, i.e. if the distribution of frequencies was completely random.
- The percentages are a better representation of the data because of the uneven numbers in the categories. All columns add up to a total of 100 per cent as we asked for percentages for the columns, which is where we sent the influencing variable 'political party'.
- The percentages represent what the count is as a proportion of the total number for that column, for example 18 liberal voters who are in favour of the tax law account for 22.5 per cent of the total number of liberal voters, which is 80.
- The total percentages, which appear in the **Total** column, represent the percentage of the population that fell into each category of preference, for example 48.0 per cent of the total population were for the tax law irrespective of voting preference.
- As we have totalled our percentages in the columns because of the placement here of our influencing variable, we read the table across in order to ascertain if there is a difference between the percentages. If there does appear to be a difference, then there may be an association between the variables. The significance of this is assessed by the **chi-square** test statistic.
- In the above example we can see that within the group of people who were in favour of the tax law, 65.0 per cent of them were conservative compared to 22.5 per cent who were liberal. This trend is reversed within the group who are against the tax law, with 25.0 per cent being conservative and 62.5 per cent being liberal. The group who are unsure as to their opinions of the new tax law are reasonably evenly split in their voting preferences (10.0 per cent conservative and 15.0 per cent liberal).

An examination of the **Chi-Square Tests** table will enable us to ascertain whether the patterns identified above are significant.

| Test statistic | | | p value |

Chi-Square Tests

	Value	df	Asymp. Sig. (2-sided)
Pearson Chi-Square	35.938ᵃ	2	.000
Likelihood Ratio	37.429	2	.000
Linear-by-Linear Association	22.908	1	.000
N of Valid Cases	200		

ᵃ. 0 cells (.0%) have expected count less than 5. The minimum expected count is 9.60.

SPSS essential

- The test statistic usually chosen to determine whether the association described by the crosstabulation is a significant one, is the **Pearson Chi-Square**. In our example above it can be seen that the value for Pearson chi-square is 35.938, with 2 degrees of freedom, which is significant at the $p < 0.001$ level.
- Results of chi-square are typically reported as follows:

$$\chi^2 = 35.938, \ df = 2, \ p < 0.001$$

SPSS advanced

- From the above table it can be noted that the chi-square statistic assumes a non-directional hypothesis, which is indicated by the **Asymp. Sig. (2-sided)**. More details of the meaning of the asymptotic significance level can be found in Chapter 6. This refers to the approximations made in our p value calculations.
- The **Likelihood Ratio** is an alternative test to the chi-square employing a different method. Normally we use the chi-square result but this statistic is sometimes preferred when the sample size is small.
- The **Linear-by-Linear Association** is used when the categories are ordinal and we are interested in looking for a trend.
- The note at the bottom of the **Chi-Square Tests** table indicates if any individual cells in the crosstabulation table have expected counts less than five. For a 2×2 table SPSS will automatically perform a continuity correction. For a larger table if you have a

number of values less than five you may wish to combine cells to increase the individual cell size.

The final part of the SPSS output is a summary of the frequency counts in the form of a clustered bar chart. This gives a helpful representation of the data. We can see how the frequencies of the different choices are linked to the political parties.

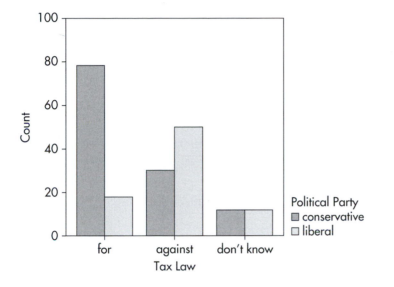

SPSS output (2 × 2 crosstabulation and chi-square)

> ✓ The data entry and procedure for a 2 × 2 crosstabulation are identical to those
>   for the 2 × 3 crosstabulation detailed earlier so will not be shown.

A survey was carried out to investigate television viewing habits in different parts of the country. The researchers were particularly interested in the viewing figures for the two most popular television soaps at the time *Country Life* and *City Limits*, and whether there was an association between people's preferences and the part of the country the person lived in: in the north or the south.

The first two tables have the same layout as for the 2 × 3 crosstabulation, indicating the number of responses and any possible missing data, along with the crosstabulation frequencies of the two variables.

Case Processing Summary

	Cases					
	Valid		Missing		Total	
	N	Percent	N	Percent	N	Percent
REGION * TV	26	100.0%	0	.0%	26	100.0%

REGION * TV Crosstabulation

			TV		
			country life	city limits	Total
REGION	north	Count	10	3	13
		Expected Count	7.5	5.5	13.0
		% within TV	66.7%	27.3%	50.0%
	south	Count	5	8	13
		Expected Count	7.5	5.5	13.0
		% within TV	33.3%	72.7%	50.0%
Total		Count	15	11	26
		Expected Count	15.0	11.0	26.0
		% within TV	100.0%	100.0%	100.0%

SPSS essential

- It can be seen from the above **Crosstabulation** that there does appear to be an association between what region a person lives in and their preference for television soaps.
- People who live in the north are more likely to watch *Country Life* (66.7 per cent) than *City Limits* (27.3 per cent), with the reverse being true for people from the south.

The table that produces the test statistics is the **Chi-Square Tests** table. The information given in this table will enable us to judge whether the viewing pattern is significantly different from the pattern we would expect by chance.

Test statistic

p value

Chi-Square Tests

	Value	df	Asymp. Sig. (2-sided)	Exact Sig. (2-sided)	Exact Sig. (1-sided)
Pearson Chi-Square	3.939[b]	1	.047		
Continuity Correction[a]	4.521	1	.112		
Likelihood Ratio	4.057	1	.044		
Fisher's Exact Test				.111	.055
Linear-by-Linear Association	3.788	1	.052		
N of Valid Cases	26				

[a]. Computed only for a 2×2 table

[b]. 0 cells (.0%) have expected count less than 5. The minimum expected count is 5.50.

SPSS essential

- The test statistic usually chosen to determine whether the association described by the crosstabulation is a significant one is the **Pearson Chi-Square**. In our example above it can be seen that the test statistic value for Pearson chi-square is 3.939, with 1 degree of freedom, and as the p value is smaller than 0.05, we can conclude that there is a significantly different viewing patterns in the two regions ($p < 0.05$).

- Results of chi-square are typically reported as follows:

$$\chi^2 = 3.939, df = 1, p < 0.05$$

- We have a 2×2 table with fairly small values, plus the probability of our value is close to the significance level, so you may wish to interpret the result with caution (and read the *SPSS advanced* section below).

SPSS advanced

- The **Continuity Correction** is produced automatically by SPSS for a 2×2 table, which performs a Yates' correction. This is a conservative adjustment and the use of this correction is controversial and often not recommended. We advise the use of **Fisher's Exact Test** in analysing a 2×2 table with a cell frequency less than five (see below).

- The **Likelihood Ratio** is an alternative test to the chi-square employing a different method. Normally we use the chi-square result but the likelihood ratio is sometimes preferred when the sample size is small.
- **Fisher's Exact Test** calculates the exact probability based on a calculation of all the possible combinations of frequency distributions in the crosstabulation table. This is only calculated for a 2×2 table because of the increase in possible combinations of frequency distributions afforded by a bigger crosstabulation. As the actual probability is calculated, it is often more conservative. As can be seen in the above example, the **Pearson Chi-Square** value = 3.939, which gives a probability of $p = 0.047$. However, when calculations are based on **Fisher's Exact Test** we find $p = 0.111$.
- The **Linear-by-Linear Association** is used when the categories are ordinal. This is also interpreted in the same way as the chi-square test statistic.
- The **Asymp. Sig.** is calculated as the default probability by SPSS. This is an approximation that is calculated for a dataset which is large and adequately distributed.

Test procedure: layered 2 × 3 crosstabulation and chi-square

Sometimes we may want to add a third variable to the crosstabulation calculation in order to obtain a more accurate picture of an association and investigate any possible influences of a third variable. The procedure for setting up the dataset and initial steps of analysis are identical to those previously described. An extra column needs to be added to the dataset for the extra variable and the possible combinations of the groups created.

	If you are entering data as shown, with the total number of male conservatives who were in favour of the tax law etc., then remember to weight the cases.

	sex	party	tax	freq
1	male	conserva	for	200
2	male	conserva	against	40
3	male	conserva	don't kno	24
4	female	conserva	for	112
5	female	conserva	against	80
6	female	conserva	don't kno	24
7	male	liberal	for	40
8	male	liberal	against	60
9	male	liberal	don't kno	24
10	female	liberal	for	32
11	female	liberal	against	140
12	female	liberal	don't kno	24

- The differences in the procedural element arise when creating layers for our crosstabulation, which are formed by the addition of a third variable.
- In our example we are still examining voting preferences and their relationship to opinions on a tax law. However, we wish to further investigate this relationship by examining the influence that sex may have.
- 'Party' and 'Tax' are entered into the crosstabulation as previously described, and 'Sex' is entered as the first layer.

SPSS output (layered 2 × 3 crosstabulation and chi-square)

The **Case Processing Summary** table again indicates the number of valid and missing cases in our dataset. As before we have no cases missing and are therefore considering all 800 cases when making our judgements about the relationship between the three variables.

Case Processing Summary

	Cases					
	Valid		Missing		Total	
	N	Percent	N	Percent	N	Percent
Tax Law * Political Party * Sex	800	100.0%	0	.0%	800	100.0%

The **Crosstabulation** table indicates any patterns in our data. As we can see this is layered into our third variable 'sex'.

Tax Law * Political Party * Sex Crosstabulation

sex				Political Party conservative	Political Party liberal	Total
male	Tax Law	for	Count	200	40	240
			Expected Count	163.3	76.7	240.0
			% within Political Party	75.8%	32.3%	61.9%
		against	Count	40	60	100
			Expected Count	68.0	32.0	100.0
			% within Political Party	15.2%	48.4%	25.8%
		don't know	Count	24	24	48
			Expected Count	32.7	15.3	48.0
			% within Political Party	9.1%	19.4%	12.4%
	Total		Count	264	124	388
			Expected Count	264.0	124.0	388.0
			% within Political Party	100.0%	100.0%	100.0%
female	Tax Law	for	Count	112	32	144
			Expected Count	75.5	68.5	144.0
			% within Political Party	51.9%	16.3%	35.0%
		against	Count	80	140	220
			Expected Count	115.3	104.7	220.0
			% within Political Party	37.0%	71.4%	53.4%
		don't know	Count	24	24	48
			Expected Count	25.2	22.8	28.0
			% within Political Party	11.1%	12.2%	11.7%
	Total		Count	216	196	412
			Expected Count	216.0	196.0	412.0
			% within Political Party	100.0%	100.0%	100.0%

SPSS essential

- The **Crosstabulation** table is split between the sexes in order to gain a fuller under-standing of the possible relationships between the variables.
- By examining the table above we can see that the relationships between voting preferences and tax law opinions are not the same when sex has been taken into consideration.

- The relationship between voting preferences and tax law identified previously suggested that most of the people who were in favour of the tax law were conservative, while most of those against the law were liberal. Of the group who were unsure of their opinions, there was a reasonably even split in voting preferences.
- When examining the male voters we can see that most male respondents were in favour of the tax law, regardless of their voting preferences (61.9 per cent in favour compared to 25.8 per cent against, and 12.4 per cent of no opinion).
- When examining the female voters we can see that this trend is reversed, with most females being against the tax law regardless of their voting preferences (35.0 per cent in favour, 53.4 per cent against, and 11.7 per cent of no opinion).
- Within the group in favour of the tax law, the majority were conservative in their voting preferences; this was true for both males and females.
- Within the group against the tax law, the majority were liberal in their voting preferences; this was true for both males and females.
- From the **Crosstabulation** we may summarise that the relationship between voting preferences and tax law opinions identified in the 2×3 crosstabulation holds across the sexes. However, the sexes in this sample do differ in their overall opinion about the tax law once voting preferences are separated, with the majority of males being in favour of the new law, and the majority of females being against the new law. This leads to a more complicated relationship between political party affiliation and opinions.

An examination of the **Chi-Square Tests** table will enable us to ascertain whether the patterns identified above are significant.

Chi-Square Tests

Sex		Value	df	Asymp. Sig. (2-sided)
male	Pearson Chi-Square	69.155[a]	2	.000
	Likelihood Ratio	68.795	2	.000
	Linear-by-Linear Association	48.904	1	.000
	N of Valid Cases	388		
female	Pearson Chi-Square	59.979[b]	2	.000
	Likelihood Ratio	62.673	2	.000
	Linear-by-Linear Association	33.459	1	.000
	N of Valid Cases	412		

Test statistic

p value

[a]. 0 cells (.0%) have expected count less than 5. The minimum expected count is 15.34.
[b]. 0 cells (.0%) have expected count less than 5. The minimum expected count is 22.83.

SPSS essential

- The test statistic usually chosen to determine whether the association described by the crosstabulation is a significant one is the **Pearson Chi-Square**.
- In the example above we have two values for this as we are examining the relationship across two groups of people, males and females, which creates a layer to our crosstabulation. For the male participants it can be seen that the test statistic value for Pearson chi-square is 69.155, with 2 degrees of freedom and as, the p value is smaller than 0.001, we can conclude that this pattern of scores is significant.
- Results of chi-square are typically reported as follows:

$$\chi^2 = 69.155,\ df = 2,\ p < 0.001$$

- For the female participants the relationship is also significant, with a Pearson chi-square value of 59.979, 2 degrees of freedom and, as the p value is smaller than 0.001, we can conclude that this pattern of scores is significant.
- Results of chi-square are typically reported as follows:

$$\chi^2 = 59.979,\ df = 2,\ p < 0.001$$

SPSS advanced

- From the above table it can be noted that the chi-square statistic assumes a non-directional hypothesis, which is indicated by the **Asymp. Sig. (2-sided)**.
- The **Likelihood Ratio** is an alternative test to the chi-square employing a different method. Normally we use the chi-square result but the likelihood ratio is sometimes preferred when the sample size is small.
- The **Linear-by-Linear Association** is used when the categories are ordinal and we are interested in looking for a trend.
- The note at the bottom of the **Chi-Square Tests** table indicates if any individual cells in the crosstabulation table have expected counts less than five. For both sexes none of the expected counts are less than five (0 per cent).

Chi-square as a 'goodness of fit' test

As mentioned in the introduction, chi-square can also be used as a 'goodness of fit' test. This assesses whether the pattern of results matches (or fits) a predicted pattern.

Scenario

An experimenter set out to test whether there is a difference in people's colour preference for cars. One hundred participants were given four pictures of cars, identical but for the colour, and asked to state their preference. The colours presented were red, blue, black and white.

If there was no preference then we would expect each colour to be chosen equally, so we would expect the probability of each category chosen to be a quarter or $p = 0.25$ when the null hypothesis is true. With a total (N) of 100 participants we would expect each category to be chosen by $N \times p$ participants, 100×0.25, which is 25 participants.

On performing the experiment, the researcher finds 48 participants choose the red car, 15 the blue, 10 the black, and 27 the white. Do these observed frequencies differ significantly from the expected frequencies?

Test procedure

File	Edit	View	Data	Transform	Analyze

1:

	colour	freq	va
1	red	48	
2	blue	15	
3	black	10	
4	white	27	
5			

✓ The data can be entered as frequency counts if the **Weight Cases** command is used. See data entry method 2 earlier in this chapter

• From the drop-down menu, choose **Analyze**, **Nonparametric Tests**, then **Chi-Square**.

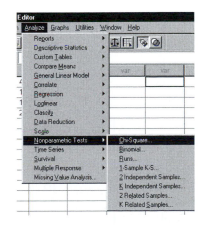

- The test variable 'colour' should be sent to the **Test Variable List**. The variable 'freq' can be left because if the data has been entered via the weight cases method, this is no longer necessary.
- As we are testing our null hypothesis that the numbers in each colour category will be equal, we can leave the **Expected Values** box set to the default as **All categories equal**.

✓ If we were testing an assumption that certain proportions were not equal but followed a specific pattern, for example 40 per cent of participants would prefer black cars, with the other preferences being equal, then we would enter the respective values by selecting the **Values** option, entering the frequencies, then clicking **Add**.

SPSS output

The first table produced by SPSS shows the observed and expected counts for the four car colours.

COLOUR

	Observed N	Expected N	Residual
red	48	25.0	23.0
blue	15	25.0	−10.0
black	10	25.0	−15.0
white	27	25.0	2.0
Total	100		

SPSS essential

- The **Observed** counts show us how many people preferred each colour car.
- The **Expected** counts confirm how many people we would expect to choose each colour if the null hypothesis was true. We can see from the table that the observed and expected counts are quite different from each other. This is confirmed by inspection of the **Residual** column. The residual values indicate that only the observed count of preferences for white cars approximates to the expected count. Both blue and black cars fall short of the expected count as indicated by the minus figure, while red cars exceed the expected count by 23.0.

   In order to assess whether the distribution found through data collection differs from the expected pattern, the **Test Statistics** table needs to be examined.

Test Statistics

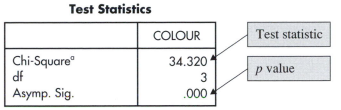

	COLOUR
Chi-Square^a	34.320
df	3
Asymp. Sig.	.000

^{a}. 0 cells (.0%) have expected frequencies less than 5. The minimum expected cell frequency is 25.0.

SPSS essential

- As can be seen from the table above $\chi^2 = 34.320$, $df = 3$, $p < 0.001$.

✓   Remember to change the last zero to a 1 if the *p* value given is 0.000.

- We can therefore conclude that there is a significant difference between the observed and expected counts, and we can therefore reject the null hypothesis; the four colours are not equally preferred.
- The findings can be expressed as follows:

   $$\chi^2 = 34.320, \ df = 3, \ p < 0.01$$

FAQ

In my dataset one variable is measured on an interval scale and one has dichotomous categories. If I want to look for associations can I use this data in chi-square?

Yes, all you need to do is to convert your interval scale into groups/categories. See Chapter 5 for details on how to recode your data.

I have calculated my chi-square using SPSS, but I think I may have done something wrong in the procedure. The associations that I am describing do not seem to make sense in light of my hypothesis.

Check that you are reading the rows and columns the right way round. Remember that, as a common rule, the influencing variable should be sent to the columns. This will mean that the Crosstabulation table produced by SPSS can be read across the rows. It does not matter however if you have sent your influencing variable to the rows, it just means that your Crosstabulation table should be read down the columns.

Details on how to calculate a chi-square test by hand can be found in Chapter 19 of Hinton (2004).

Linear correlation and regression

SOMETIMES WE WISH TO COLLECT a score on two variables from a set of participants to see whether there is a relationship between the variables. For example, we might measure a person's experience in a job (number of weeks) and the number of items they produce each day to ask if there is a relationship between experience and productivity. Where we have two variables like this, produced by the same or related participants, we are able to examine the association between the variables by a correlation. A correlation is performed to test the degree to which the scores on the two variables co-relate. That is, the extent to which the variation in the scores on one variable results in a corresponding variation in the scores on the second variable.

We shall only be considering linear correlations in this book. The simplest relationship between two variables is a *linear* relationship and a linear relationship is the underlying model we propose for our data. Chapter 9 explains the reasons for this. In this case, with two variables, we are arguing that if they are correlated then if we plot the points on a graph they will follow a straight line. We refer to this line as the *regression* line. However, we are unlikely to find that our data points lie exactly on a straight line. We explain this by claiming that it arises from random factors referred to as 'error'. Given that the equation of a straight line is defined mathematically as $Y = a + bX$, where X and Y are the variables, with 'a' the intercept (or 'constant') and 'b' the slope of line, then our observed values are defined as follows:

$Y = a + bX +$ error

We can work out the regression line by finding the equation that gives us the smallest amount of error.

A strong correlation indicates that there is only a small amount of error and most of the points lie close to the regression line; a weak correlation indicates that there is a lot of error and the points are more scattered. In the second case we are likely to conclude that a linear relationship is not a good model for our data.

High values of one variable associated with high values of the second variable indicate that the correlation is positive. For example, we might find a positive correlation between height and foot size, with taller people having larger feet and shorter people having smaller feet. When high values of the first variable are associated with low values of the second variable then we refer to this as a negative correlation. So, for a car travelling at a constant speed along a track, we will find that the distance travelled is negatively correlated with the amount of petrol left in the tank.

The statistical measures of correlation in this chapter (Pearson, Spearman, Kendall tau-b) all produce a statistic that ranges from −1, indicating a perfect negative correlation, to +1 indicating a perfect positive correlation. A value of zero indicates no correlation at all.

Introduction to the Pearson correlation

The Pearson correlation coefficient (r) is often referred to as Pearson's product moment correlation. Essentially, it works out a measure of how much the scores of the two variables vary together (their 'product') and then contrasts this with how much they vary on their own. The joint variability is referred to as the *sums of products* and will be largest when high values of one variable are matched with high values of the second variable. It will be a negative value when the correlation is negative. If the joint variability matches the individual variation in the scores then these values will be equal, so one divided by the other will result in $r = 1$ (or −1 if the sums of products is negative). If there is no joint variability the scores do not correlate at all and r will be zero.

Like other methods of parametric analysis Pearson's correlation relies on a number of assumptions.

* The relationship between the variables is linear.
* The points are evenly distributed along the straight line. This is the assumption of homoscedasticity. If the data has the points unevenly spread along the proposed straight line (or there is an outlying point or two) then the Pearson correlation is not an accurate measure of the association.
* The data are drawn from normally distributed populations.
* The data collected must be interval or ratio, from continuous distributions.

The important point to remember is that we are considering a *linear* correlation here, so our key assumption is that the points follow a straight line if they are correlated. If we believe the relationship between the variables is not linear then we do not use the Pearson statistic but instead use the Spearman or Kendall tau-b explained later in the chapter.

Scenario

A researcher postulated that students who spent the most time studying would achieve the highest marks in science examinations, whereas those that did the least studying would achieve lower marks. The researcher noted the results of ten first-year university students, showing how much time (in hours) they spent studying (on average per week throughout the year) along with their end-of-year examination marks (out of 100).

> ✓ As our prediction states that we are expecting a positive correlation this indicates a direction. Our prediction is therefore one-tailed. If we did not know which direction our relationship between the two variables would be, we would have a two-tailed prediction, and we would be looking for either a positive or a negative correlation.

Data entry

Enter the dataset as shown in the example.

	studytim	science
1	40	58
2	43	73
3	18	56
4	10	47
5	25	58
6	33	54
7	27	45
8	17	32
9	30	68
10	47	69

> ✓ Remember when entering data without decimal places to change the decimal places to zero in the **Variable View**.
> ✓ See Chapter 2 for the full data entry procedure.

Test procedure

- All inferential statistics are found under the **Analyze** command.
- Select **Correlate** and then **Bivariate** (meaning having two variables).

- Highlight both the study time and the science exam variables and send them to the **Variables** box.
- You can see that SPSS selects the **Pearson** correlation coefficient as a default.
- Select whether your prediction is **One-tailed** or **Two-tailed**. Ours is one-tailed as we stated there would be a positive correlation.
- Click on **OK**.

✓ The **Flag significant correlations** box is selected as default. Significant correlations are highlighted underneath the output table with a * for a significance of $p < 0.05$ and ** for $p < 0.01$.

✓ If you require the means and standard deviations for each variable click on the **Options** button and tick **means** and **standard deviations**, then **Continue** and **OK**.

SPSS output

SPSS produces one output table, the **Correlations** table, unless descriptive statistics have been selected.

Correlations

		Study time for exams	Science Exam
Study time for exams	Pearson Correlation	1.000	.721**
	Sig. (1-tailed)	.	.009
	N	10	10
Science Exam	Pearson Correlation	.721**	1.000
	Sig. (1-tailed)	.009	.
	N	10	10

**. Correlation is significant at the 0.01 level (1-tailed).

299

SPSS essential

- The **Pearson Correlation** test statistic $= 0.721$. SPSS indicates with ** that it is significant at the 0.01 level for a one-tailed prediction. The actual p value is shown to be 0.009. These figures are duplicated in the matrix.
- A conventional way of reporting these figures would be as follows:

$$r = 0.721, N = 10, p < 0.01$$

- These results indicate that as study time increases, science exam performance also increases, which is a positive correlation.
- As the r value reported is positive and $p < 0.01$, we can state that we have a positive correlation between our two variables and our null hypothesis can be rejected. If the r value was negative this would indicate a negative correlation, and be counter to our hypothesis.
- The **Pearson Correlation** output matrix also shows the r value when 'Study time' is correlated with itself, and there is a perfect correlation coefficient of 1.000. Similarly, 'Science Exam' has a perfect correlation with itself, $r = 1.000$. These values are therefore not required.

✓ The appropriate illustrative statistic to support a correlation is a scatterplot, see later in this chapter for more details.

Introduction to the Spearman correlation

There are times when we wish to correlate data when it is ordinal (one or both variables are not measured on an interval scale), when data is not normally distributed, or when other assumptions of the Pearson correlation are violated. On these occasions we use the Spearman correlation coefficient, which is the nonparametric equivalent of the Pearson correlation. The Spearman correlation uses exactly the same calculations as the Pearson but performs the analysis on the ranks of the scores instead of on the actual data values. The Spearman correlation coefficient is known as r_s. As we are using the ranks rather than the actual scores the Spearman correlation can still be used even when the relationship between the two variables is non-linear.

The Spearman correlation can cope with a few tied ranks in the data without needing to worry about the effect on r_s. However, when there are a lot of tied values the result is that it will make r_s larger than it should be. In this case, the Kendall tau-b can be used instead.

Scenario

Two teachers were asked to rate the same eight teenagers on the variable 'how well they are likely to do academically at university' on a 0 to 20 scale, from unlikely (0) to highly likely (20). It was thought that there would be a significant correlation between the teachers' ranking.

✓ Our prediction does not state whether we expect a positive or negative correlation, therefore we have a two-tailed prediction. If we predicted that our correlation would be either positive or negative then we would have a one-tailed prediction.

Data entry

	teacher1	teacher2
1	15	8
2	13	12
3	18	4
4	11	9
5	14	16
6	16	7
7	8	16
8	12	9

Enter the dataset as shown in the example.

✓ Remember when entering data without decimal places to change the decimal places to zero in the **Variable View**.
✓ See Chapter 2 for the full data entry procedure.

Test procedure

- All inferential statistics are found under the **Analyze** command.
- Select **Correlate** and then **Bivariate** (meaning having two variables).

Analyze	Graphs	Utilities	Window	Help
Reports	▶			
Descriptive Statistics	▶			
Custom Tables	▶		var	v
Compare Means	▶			
General Linear Model	▶			
Correlate	▶		Bivariate...	
Regression	▶		Partial...	
Loglinear	▶		Distances...	
Classify	▶			
Data Reduction	▶			
Scale	▶			
Nonparametric Tests	▶			
Time Series	▶			
Survival	▶			
Multiple Response	▶			
Missing Value Analysis...				

Bivariate Correlations

Variables:
- teacher1
- teacher2

Buttons: OK, Paste, Reset, Cancel, Help

Correlation Coefficients:
- ☐ Pearson
- ☐ Kendall's tau-b
- ☑ Spearman

Test of Significance:
- ● Two-tailed
- ○ One-tailed

☑ Flag significant correlations

Options...

- Highlight both teacher variables and send them to the **Variables** box.
- As SPSS selects the **Pearson** correlation coefficient as a default, deselect that box and put a tick in the **Spearman** box.
- Select whether your prediction is **One-tailed** or **Two-tailed**.
- Click on **OK**.

✓ The **Flag significant correlations** box is selected as default. Significant correlations are highlighted underneath the output table with a * for a significance of $p < 0.05$ and ** for $p < 0.01$.

SPSS output

In order to check if there is a significant correlation between the two teachers' ratings the **Correlations** table must be observed.

Correlations

			TEACHER1	TEACHER2
Spearman's rho	TEACHER1	Correlation Coefficient	1.000	-.735*
		Sig. (2-tailed)	.	.038
		N	8	8
	TEACHER2	Correlation Coefficient	-.735*	1.000
		Sig. (2-tailed)	.038	.
		N	8	8

Test statistic

Essential

p value

*. Correlation is significant at the .05 level (2-tailed).

SPSS essential

- The **Spearman's rho** correlation test statistic $= -0.735$. The negative sign indicates a negative correlation. SPSS also illustrates with * that it is significant at the 0.05 level for a two-tailed prediction. The actual p value is shown to be 0.038. These figures are duplicated in the matrix.
- By observing the Spearman correlation output matrix it can be seen that teacher 1 is (of course) perfectly correlated with teacher 1, hence the Spearman's rho correlation coefficient of 1.000. Similarly, teacher 2 is perfectly correlated with teacher 2, with a Spearman's rho correlation coefficient of 1.000.
- A conventional way of reporting these figures is as follows:

    $r_s = -0.735, N = 8, p < 0.05$

- These results indicate that as one teacher's ratings increase the other teacher's ratings decrease. Therefore, as each teacher's perceptions of the teenagers' academic perform- ance is different, these ratings may not be a good indicator of the actual performance.

✓ While a scatterplot is generally the most appropriate illustrative statistic to support a correlation, when conducting a Spearman's test it should be used with caution. The Spearman rho correlation coefficient is produced by using the rank of scores rather than the actual raw data, whereas the scatterplot displays the raw scores. The procedure for this is shown at the end of this chapter.

Introduction to the Kendall tau-b correlation

The Kendall tau-b correlation is another nonparametric correlation coefficient and is an alternative to the Spearman correlation. It is a measure of association between two ordinal variables and takes tied ranks into account, so can be used for small data sets with a large number of tied ranks (unlike the Spearman test, the presence of tied ranks does not artificially inflate the value of the statistic).

Like the Spearman test, in the Kendall tau-b all the scores are ranked on each variable. However, it operates on a different principle to the Pearson or Spearman correlations. The Kendall tau-b assesses how well the rank ordering on the second variable matches the rank ordering on the first variable. If we put the ranks of the first variable in order we can place the matched ranks of the second variable alongside. We can then look at how this orders the ranks of the second variable. In Kendall's tau-b, each and every pair of ranks on the second variable is examined. When these pairs match the order of the ranks of the first variable, then the pair is concordant and when the order is reversed the pair is discordant. The difference in the number of concordant and discordant pairs is calculated. This value is compared to the value when every single pair is concordant to produce tau-b.

Like other correlation coefficients tau-b ranges from −1 to +1. However, because the methods used are different the Kendall tau-b will produce a different value to that of Spearman, but the probabilities will be very similar.

Scenario

A consumer testing company wanted to pilot a new breakfast cereal. They decided to ask people if the new brand was as tasty as a current leading brand. They gave 20 people the current leading brand (brand A) and also gave them the new breakfast cereal (brand B). The order in which the participants tasted each brand differed to counterbalance order effects. Each participant was then asked to rate their enjoyment of the cereal on a 1 to 10 scale (1 they didn't enjoy it and 10 it was very tasty).

✓ As our prediction states that we are expecting a positive correlation this indicates a direction. Our prediction is therefore one-tailed. If we did not know which direction the relationship between our two variables would have, we would have a two-tailed prediction. In that case we would be looking for either a positive or a negative correlation.

Data entry

	branda	brandb
1	6.00	6.00
2	8.00	9.00
3	8.00	8.00
4	7.00	10.00
5	6.00	8.00
6	8.00	8.00
7	6.00	9.00
8	5.00	6.00
9	4.00	8.00
10	6.00	6.00
11	8.00	7.00
12	6.00	6.00
13	6.00	6.00
14	5.00	8.00
15	7.00	8.00
16	5.00	5.00
17	7.00	8.00
18	4.00	4.00
19	4.00	8.00
20	5.00	5.00

Enter the dataset as shown in the example.

> ✓ Remember when entering data without decimal places to change the decimal places to zero in the **Variable View**.
> ✓ See Chapter 2 for the full data entry procedure.
> ✓ As we are worried about the number of tied ranks in our dataset, we are going to carry out a Kendall tau-b rather than a Spearman correlation.

Test procedure

- The test procedure for the Kendal tau-b is found under the **Analyze**, **Correlate**, **Bivariate** commands.
- Deselect the default **Pearson** command and select **Kendall's tau-b**.
- Select whether your prediction is **One-tailed** or **Two-tailed**. As our prediction stated a direction, we select the one-tailed option.
- Press **OK**.

> ✓ The **Flag significant correlations** box is selected as default. Significant correlations are highlighted underneath the output table with a * for a significance of $p < 0.05$ and ** for $p < 0.01$.

SPSS output

The Kendall tau-b output is displayed in the **Correlations** table.

Correlations

			Brand A Breakfast Cereal	Brand B Breakfast Cereal
Kendall's tau_b	Brand A Breakfast Cereal	Correlation Coefficient	1.000	.397*
		Sig. (1-tailed)	.	.017
		N	20	20
	Brand A Breakfast Cereal	Correlation Coefficient	.397*	1.000
		Sig. (1-tailed)	.017	.
		N	20	20

Test statistic

Essential

p value

*. Correlation is significant at the .05 level (1-tailed).

SPSS essential

- The **Kendall tau-b** correlation output matrix shows a correlation coefficient of 0.397. As this value is a positive number it shows that our data is positively correlated. SPSS also indicates with * that it is significant at the 0.05 level for a one-tailed prediction. The actual p value is shown to be 0.017.
- A conventional way of reporting these figures is as follows:

  Kendall tau-b $= 0.397$, $N = 20$, $p < 0.05$

- These results indicate that as the ratings for breakfast cereal brand A increase so do the ratings for breakfast cereal brand B. Therefore, as there are similar ratings of enjoyment for both cereals, the consumer testing company are happy to recommend the tasty new breakfast cereal.

✓ While a scatterplot is generally the most appropriate illustrative statistic to support a correlation, when conducting a Kendall tau-b test it should be used with caution. The Kendall tau-b correlation coefficient is produced by using the rank of scores rather than the actual raw data, whereas the scatterplot displays the raw scores. The procedure for producing a scatterplot is shown next.

Introduction to scatterplots

A scatterplot or scattergram illustrates the scores or data that we wish to correlate, where the axes are the two variables. If the scores on one variable increase and so do the scores on the second variable, this is known as a positive correlation. If scores on one variable increase while the scores on the other variable decrease this is known as a negative correlation. When the points are randomly scattered there is generally no correlation between the two variables. Though a scatterplot is recommended as an illustration supporting correlation, it must be used with caution in conjunction with Spearman and Kendall tau-b correlations because nonparametric analyses use the rank scores rather than the actual raw data, whereas the scatterplot displays the raw scores.

When producing a scatterplot you can ask SPSS to produce the regression line – the line of best fit. This particular line minimizes the distance of the points to the straight line.

Scatterplot procedure (SPSS versions 11 and earlier)

- Select the **Graphs** drop-down menu and select **Scatter**, then the following **Scatterplot** window appears.

- SPSS selects the **Simple** scatterplot as default. Click on **Define**.

- Send one of the variables to the **X Axis** box (in this example 'Study Time').
- Click on the other variable, 'Science Exam' and send it to the **Y Axis** box.

✓ If you have a predictor variable it is recommended that you send that to the **X Axis**.

The following chart is produced by SPSS.

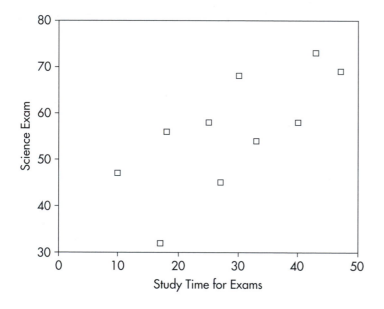

Although the positive linear relationship can be seen from the above chart, adding a regression line will enable a more accurate judgement to be made.

To insert the regression line, double click inside the scatterplot and the **SPSS Chart Editor** window will appear.

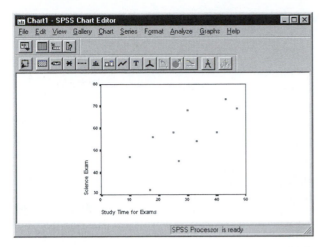

- Select the **Chart** drop-down menu and select **Options**.

- The **Scatterplot Options** box should now be visible.
- Place a tick in the **Fit Line Total** box.
- Click on **OK**.
- You will now see the regression line on your scatterplot.

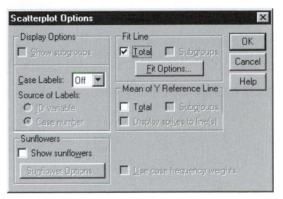

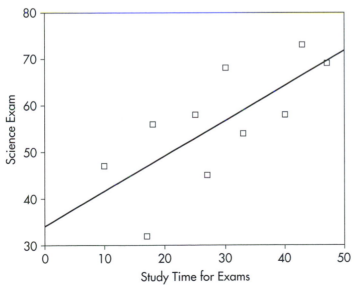

- Close the small **Chart** window and SPSS will return to your output screen.
- The scatterplot now clearly illustrates that there is a positive correlation between 'study time' and the 'science exam' marks.

Scatterplot procedure (SPSS version 12)

The procedure for creating scatterplots in version 12 of SPSS is similar to that for versions 11 and earlier. The chart is also initially created using the same procedure as that described above. In order to fit a regression line to this, the following procedure should be adopted.

- Create the scatterplot as above. Double click on this to enter the **Chart Editor** window.
- Select the points on the chart and right click on the mouse to select the **Add Fit Line at Total** option.
- The **Properties** window will then become active.

- Ensure the **Linear** fit method has been selected.
- Click on **Close**, then close the **Chart Editor** window.
- Your scatterplot now displays a regression line showing a positive correlation between study time for exams and science exam marks as shown below.

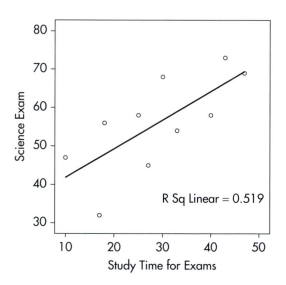

Partial correlation

Previously we have analysed some example data to show a significant correlation between study time and science examination performance. However, we might decide a third variable, *intelligence*, could be influencing the correlation. If intelligence positively correlates with study time, that is, the more intelligent students spend the most time studying; and if it also positively correlates with examination performance, that is, the more intelligent students get the higher marks in the examination, then the correlation of study time and examination performance might simply be due to the third factor 'intelligence'. If this is the case then the relationship between study time and examination performance is not genuine, in that the reason they correlate is because they are both an outcome of *intelligence*. That is, the more intelligent students both study more and get higher marks in the examination. If we take out the effect of intelligence the relationship of study time to examination performance could disappear.

To answer the question of the influence of intelligence on the study time/examination performance correlation we need to examine the correlation of study time and examination performance after removing the effects of intelligence. If the correlation disappears then we know it was due to the third factor. To do this we calculate a *partial correlation*.

Data entry

	studytim	science	intellig
1	40	58	118
2	43	73	128
3	18	56	110
4	10	47	114
5	25	58	138
6	33	54	120
7	27	45	106
8	17	32	124
9	30	68	132
10	47	69	130

Enter the dataset as shown in the example.

✓ See Chapter 2 for the full data entry procedure.

✓ We could add labels to our variables as in the earlier example.

Procedure for partial correlation

- From the **Analyze** drop-down menu select **Correlate** and then **Partial**.

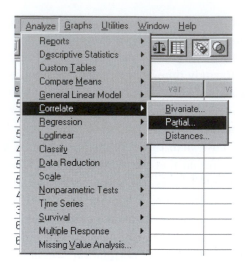

- In the **Partial Correlations** window highlight the two variables that we want to correlate and then send them across to the **Variables** box.
- The third factor that we want to control for needs to be sent to the **Controlling for** box.
- Change the **Test of Significance** to **One-tailed**.

✓ If you require the correlation coefficients for all three variables without controlling for intelligence scores click on the **Options** button and tick **Zero-Order** correlations.

Output for partial correlation

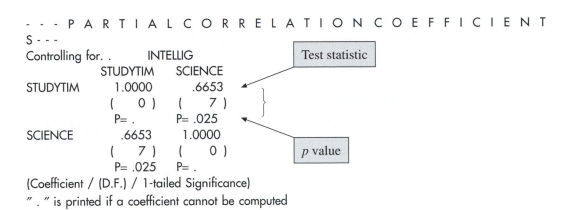

- - - P A R T I A L C O R R E L A T I O N C O E F F I C I E N T
S - - -

Controlling for. .   INTELLIG
                STUDYTIM   SCIENCE
STUDYTIM   1.0000   .6653
              (0)   (7)
                P= .   P= .025
SCIENCE   .6653   1.0000
              (7)   (0)
                P= .025   P= .

(Coefficient / (D.F.) / 1-tailed Significance)
" . " is printed if a coefficient cannot be computed

SPSS essential

- The correlation test statistic = 0.6653. The p value is shown to be 0.025. As this value is under 0.05 there is a significant correlation. These figures are duplicated in the matrix.
- A conventional way of reporting these figures would be $r = 0.6653$, $df = 7$, $p < 0.05$.
- These results indicate that as study time increases science exam performance also increases, when the effects of intelligence have been controlled for. This is a positive correlation. So the relationship between study time and science exam performance is not a result of intelligence.
- The output matrix also shows that study time is perfectly correlated with itself, $r = 1.000$. Similarly, science exam results have a perfect correlation with science exam, $r = 1.000$. These values are therefore not required.

Linear regression

We have previously identified a positive correlation between the two variables 'study time' and 'science exam' mark. We may wish to further investigate this relationship by examining whether study time reliably *predicts* the science exam mark. To do this we use a linear regression.

Test procedure

- All inferential statistics are found under the **Analyze** command.
- Select **Regression** and then **Linear**.

- Highlight 'science' and send it across to the **Dependent** box as we shall be predicting science score from the study time.
- Highlight 'studytim' and then send it to the **Independent(s)** box.
- We will leave all the other choices as their default.
- Click on **OK**.

SPSS output

The first table reminds us that we are predicting science scores (the dependent variable) from the study time (the independent variable).

Variables Entered/Removed[b]

Model	Variables Entered	Variables Removed	Method
1	STUDYTIM[a]	.	Enter

[a]. All requested variables entered
[b]. Dependent Variable: SCIENCE

The next table is the **Model Summary**, which provides us with the correlation coefficient. We can compare this table with the output from the Pearson correlation on the same data, shown earlier.

Model Summary

Model	R	R Square	Adjusted R Square	Std. Error of the Estimate
1	.721[a]	.519	.459	9.1444

[a]. Predictors: (Constant), STUDYTIM

Advanced   *Essential*   *Advanced*

SPSS essential

- The **R Square** value in the **Model Summary** table shows the amount of variance in the dependent variable that can be explained by the independent variable.
- In our example the independent variable of study time accounts for 51.9 per cent of the variance in the scores of the science exam.

SPSS advanced

- The **R** value (0.721[a]) indicates that as study time increases the science score also increases, and this is a positive correlation, with $r = 0.721$. We know this to be statistically significant from the Pearson correlation output.
- The **Adjusted R Square** adjusts for a bias in **R Square**. R^2 is sensitive to the number of variables and scores there are, and adjusted R^2 corrects for this.
- The **Std. Error of the Estimate** is a measure of the variability of the multiple correlation.

The ANOVA summary table that follows shows details of the significance of the regression.

ANOVA[b]

Test statistic

Model		Sum of Squares	df	Mean Square	F	Sig.
1	Regression	723.038	1	723.038	8.647	.019[a]
	Residual	668.962	8	83.620		
	Total	1392.000	9			

[a]. Predictors: (Constant), STUDYTIM
[b]. Dependent Variable: SCIENCE

p value

SPSS essential

- The ANOVA tests the significance of the regression model. In our example does the independent variable, study time, explain a significant amount of the variance in the dependent variable: science exam result?
- As with any ANOVA the essential pieces of information needed are the *df*, the *F* value and the probability value. We can see from the above table that $F(1,8) = 8.647$, $p < 0.05$, and therefore can conclude that the regression is statistically significant.

Now we have the **Coefficients** output table, which gives us the regression equation.

Coefficients[a]

Model		Unstandardized Coefficients		Standardized Coefficients		
		B	Std. Error	Beta	t	Sig.
1	(Constant)	34.406	7.893		4.359	.002
	STUDYTIM	.745	.253	.721	2.941	.019

[a]. Dependent Variable: SCIENCE

SPSS essential

- The **Unstandardized Coefficients** B column gives us the value of the intercept (for the Constant row) and the slope of the regression line (from the STUDYTIM row). This gives us the following regression equation:

  Science exam score = 34.406 + 0.745 Study time

- The **Standardized Beta Coefficient** column informs us of the contribution that an individual variable makes to the model. From the above table we can see that study time 'contributes' 0.721 to science exam performance, which is our Pearson's r value.

SPSS advanced

- The t value ($t = 4.539$, $p < 0.01$) for Constant tells us that the intercept is significantly different from zero.
- The t value for study time ($t = 2.941$, $p < 0.05$) shows that the regression is significant.

Introduction to scatterplots through the Interactive command

A scatterplot can be produced using the procedure described earlier or, alternatively, the **Graphs** and **Interactive** commands can be used. This has an advantage when plotting scatterplots for regressions, as the regression equation can be displayed on the chart. The procedure is shown below.

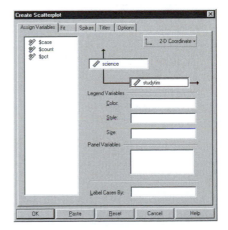

- Click on the **Graphs** drop-down menu and select **Interactive**.
- From the list choose **Scatterplot**.

- The **Create Scatterplot** box should now appear.
- Click on the variable 'science' and *drag* it to the Y-axis box. Similarly drag 'studytim' to the X-axis box.
- Click on the label **Fit**, and the following options should be shown.

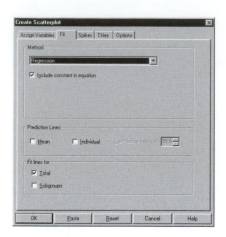

- Change the **Method** to **Regression** and ensure that the option to **Include constant in equation** is selected.
- Click on **OK**.

The following chart is produced in the output window, displaying both the regression equation and the regression line.

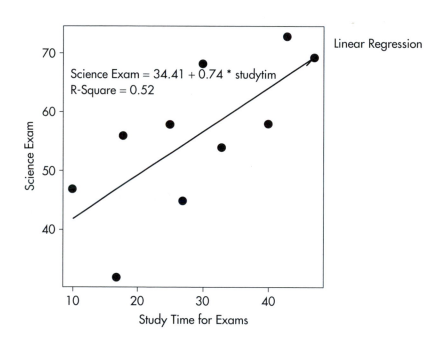

Other interactive charts can be produced through a similar procedure and these may be customised to display your data in the best way.

FAQ

I've carried out a correlation and my output states the significance for a two-tailed test. However, my prediction is one-tailed. What have I done wrong?

When carrying out correlations in SPSS you need to specify whether you require the test to be one- or two-tailed in the Bivariate Correlations window. To obtain a one-tailed significance value after selecting a two-tailed calculation, divide the p value by 2, or redo the correlation but this time select the one-tailed option.

I have predicted a positive correlation in my study (one-tailed). My result has come as r = −0.7, which is highly significant (p < 0.01). Have I found support for my hypothesis?

No, you have predicted a positive correlation, which is that r would be between 0 and +1. However your results show a negative correlation with r = −0.7, so the result has gone in the opposite direction to that which you predicted.

I have got two variables but am unsure whether to calculate a correlation or regression.

This will depend on what exactly you want to find out from your analysis. If you are interested in the strength of the linear relationship between the two variables, then a correlation will be the most appropriate. However, if you wish to predict values of one variable by the values of the other variable, you should be calculating a linear regression.

Details on the logic of linear correlation and linear regression and how to calculate them by hand can be found in Chapter 20 of Hinton (2004).

Chapter 16

Introduction to multiple regression and multiple correlation

I N CHAPTER 15 on linear correlation and regression we looked at the relationship between two variables, such as the amount of time spent studying and examination performance. We collected a score from a set of participants on both variables to see if the two sets of scores were linearly correlated: that is, the extent to which variation in one set of scores resulted in a corresponding variation in the other set of scores. The value of the correlation coefficient showed us the strength of the correlation, and the regression provided us with a linear model that we could use to predict values of the dependent variable using values of the independent variable.

When we examine more than two variables we can extend our correlation and regression analysis to take account of these variables but we still assume that the relationship between the variables is linear. For example, we can collect data from a group of students on their study time, examination performance and intelligence (as measured by an IQ test). We can look at the pairwise correlations by taking each pair of variables in turn and examine the correlation between them. If we look at the *correlation matrix* of all these pairwise correlations we may see combinations of variables that vary together. We might wish to examine whether there are underlying factors that could explain these combinations. If that were the case we would undertake a factor analysis (explained in Chapter 17). However, in this chapter we are interested in producing a multiple regression equation.

For the multiple regression we must decide which variable is to be the dependent variable (also called the *criterion* variable) and which variables are to be the independent variables (also called the *predictor* variables). SPSS cannot choose the dependent variable for you as this decision needs a conceptual justification. You need to have an academic reason for choosing this variable.

As we are testing for a linear relationship, we are able to work out the linear model that is the best fit of the data, called the multiple regression. We can represent this model by the following equation:

$$Y = a + b_1X_1 + b_2X_2 + b_3X_3 + \ldots + \text{error}$$

where Y is the dependent variable, a is the intercept, X_1, X_2, X_3, etc. are the independent variables, and b_1, b_2, b_3, etc. are the coefficients of the independent variables.

The multiple regression can be seen as a more complex model as it employs more than one independent variable as a predictor of the dependent variable, and also we can examine the contribution of each independent variable to the prediction. While it is still a linear model we can no longer represent it as a simple straight line.

In our example we take examination performance as the dependent variable, as we are interested in looking at the prediction of this variable, and wish to see to what extent the variation in the scores on study time *and* intelligence are able to predict the variation in the scores on examination performance. The multiple correlation coefficient (R) gives us a value of the strength of the relationship. But with multiple correlation we are less interested in R than in R^2, as this value tell us how much of the variation in the dependent variable can be accounted for by the predictor variables. For example, if $R = 0.60$, then $R^2 = 0.36$, indicating that 36 per cent of the variation in the dependent variable can be explained by variation in the independent variables. Please note that we use R to distinguish it from r, which is used when we are only correlating two variables.

The interesting thing about multiple regression is that with a lot of variables some will be more important than others in predicting variation in the dependent variable and some will have almost no influence at all. In SPSS we can choose to include all the independent variables in our regression calculation (by the *enter* method). We can use a variety of other methods for the regression equation, with the appropriate number of variables. We can decide which variables to include (*forward* method) or exclude (*backward* method) in the regression calculations or both (by the *stepwise* method). Thus, we can end up with a model that includes the variables we believe are important in the prediction and excludes the ones that have only a trivial effect on the dependent variable.

As we are producing this model we need to be aware of certain features of the analysis. We shall consider the assumptions in a moment. But first we should consider *multicollinearity*. When two or more independent predictors are highly correlated with each other this is known as multicollinearity. You might think this a good thing but consider the following. If you are comparing variables you believe to be related, such as intelligence and academic performance, you expect a correlation even though the variables are measuring different things. However, if you have two similar tests of intelligence you expect the results to correlate because they are measuring the same thing. Multicollinearity indicates that two variables may be measuring the same thing, rather than being related. One solution may be to eliminate one of the variables, another solution is to combine them. As a general rule of thumb, predictor variables can be correlated with each other as much as 0.8 before there is cause for concern about multicollinearity.

The assumptions underlying multiple correlation and regression are the same as those for the simple case looked at in Chapter 15. The key one is that we assume the relationship between variables to be linear, and the usual parametric assumptions are made for our model to be appropriate (see Chapter 9 for further details).

Scenario

A science teacher wanted to investigate what was the best predictor of her students' science exam score. Data was collected for ten students; this included their study time for the exam (mean hours per week, over 3 weeks), intelligence (measured using a standard test), hours attended in class over the last year and their examination marks for other core subjects, maths and literacy.

Data entry

Data for the ten students is shown below.

	studytim	science	intellig	maths	attend	literacy
1	40	58	118	44	51	30
2	43	73	128	61	57	21
3	18	56	110	58	55	42
4	10	47	114	55	66	27
5	25	58	138	54	67	49
6	33	54	120	50	72	23
7	27	45	106	56	66	50
8	17	32	124	39	63	21
9	30	68	132	71	70	38
10	47	69	130	65	71	17

✓ See Chapter 2 for the full data entry procedure.

✓ We have chosen a small dataset for our example, but the more data points per variable the better the prediction.

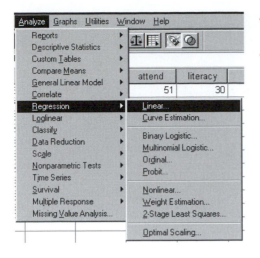

- From the **Analyze** drop-down menu select **Regression**.
- Then select **Linear**.

Enter method

The default method for multiple regression is the **Enter** method. This is also known as direct regression or simultaneous regression. It simply means that all the predictor variables are tested at once. This method is useful if you do not have any theoretical basis for deciding which variables to enter into the analysis.

- Select the variable to be predicted and send it to the **Dependent** variable box. We choose the science exam results ('science') as our dependent variable.
- Highlight all the other variables and send them to the **Independent(s)** box.
- Click on the **Statistics** button.

✓ We have entered all our predictor variables in one block. You can put groups of variables in different blocks, then, rather than including or excluding a single variable, it will include or exclude all those in the block.

- SPSS selects **Estimates** and **Model fit** as default.
- For a basic output we suggest ticking the **Descriptives** box as well.
- Click on **Continue** and then **OK**.

```
Linear Regression: Statistics                              ☒

┌─Regression Coefficients─┐   ☑ Model fit             ┌──────────┐
│ ☑ Estimates             │   ☐ R squared change      │ Continue │
│ ☐ Confidence intervals  │   ☑ Descriptives          ├──────────┤
│ ☐ Covariance matrix     │   ☐ Part and partial      │  Cancel  │
└─────────────────────────┘       correlations        ├──────────┤
                              ☐ Collinearity           │   Help   │
                                  diagnostics          └──────────┘
┌─Residuals────────────────────────────────────────┐
│ ☐ Durbin-Watson                                   │
│ ☐ Casewise diagnostics                            │
│    ○ Outliers outside   [3]  standard deviations  │
│    ○ All cases                                    │
└───────────────────────────────────────────────────┘
```

SPSS output

The first table that SPSS produces is for **Descriptive Statistics**.

Descriptive Statistics

	Mean	Std. Deviation	N
Science Exam	56.00	12.44	10
Study time for exams	29.00	12.04	10
Intelligence Score	122.00	10.24	10
Maths Exam	55.30	9.45	10
Hours Attended	63.80	7.19	10
Literacy Exam	31.80	12.14	10

Essential

SPSS essential

- The **Descriptive Statistics** table enables us to observe the variations in the scores.
- The **Mean** scores for each variable are displayed.
- The **Std. Deviation** shows the spread of scores for each variable.
- **N** represents the number of participants.

The second table SPSS produces is a correlation matrix of all of the variables. Each pair of variables is correlated and the results placed in the table, presenting details of the Pearson correlation r value, probability value and number of participants.

Correlations

		Science Exam	Study time for exams	Intelligence Score	Maths Exam	Hours Attended	Literacy Exam
Pearson Correlation	Science Exam	1.000	.721	.483	.740	−.010	−.111
	Study time for exams	.721	1.000	.373	.293	−.026	−.352
	Intelligence Score	.483	.373	1.000	.264	.326	−.195
	Maths Exam	.740	.293	.264	1.000	.352	.150
	Hours Attended	−.010	−.026	.326	.352	1.000	−.051
	Literacy Exam	−.111	−.352	−.195	.150	−.051	1.000
Sig. (1-tailed)	Science Exam	.	.009	.079	.007	.489	.380
	Study time for exams	.009	.	.144	.206	.472	.159
	Intelligence Score	.079	.144	.	.231	.179	.295
	Maths Exam	.007	.206	.231	.	.159	.340
	Hours Attended	.489	.472	.179	.159	.	.444
	Literacy Exam	.380	.159	.295	.340	.444	.
N	Science Exam	10	10	10	10	10	10
	Study time for exams	10	10	10	10	10	10
	Intelligence Score	10	10	10	10	10	10
	Maths Exam	10	10	10	10	10	10
	Hours Attended	10	10	10	10	10	10
	Literacy Exam	10	10	10	10	10	10

SPSS essential

- From this table we can get an idea of the variables that show a significant correlation (shown as shaded values). We can see that in our study the 'Science Exam' scores are positively correlated with both 'Maths Exam' scores ($p < 0.01$) and 'Study time' ($p < 0.01$).

SPSS advanced

- The correlation matrix is useful to 'eyeball' for patterns and to check for multicollinearity.

✓ For more details on pairwise correlations see Chapter 15.

By applying the **Enter** method, SPSS enters all the variables we have chosen to enter into the multiple regression equation.

Variables Entered/Removed[b]

Model	Variables Entered	Variables Removed	Method
1	Literacy Exam, Hours Attended, Study time for exams, Intelligence Score, Maths Exam[a]	.	Enter

[a]. All requested variables entered.
[b]. Dependent Variable: Science Exam

SPSS essential

- The **Variables Entered/Removed** table shows that the **Enter** method of regression has been used and which variables have been entered into the regression equation.
- As we can see, all our variables have been entered as predictor variables for our dependent variable 'Science Exam'.

The next table in the output is the **Model Summary**. As we have only selected one block of the **Enter** method, only one model has been produced.

Model Summary

Model	R	R Square	Adjusted R Square	Std. Error of the Estimate
1	.959[a]	.921	.821	5.26

[a]. Predictors: (Constant), Literacy Exam, Hours Attended, Study time for exams, Intelligence Score, Maths Exam

Advanced   *Essential*   *Advanced*

SPSS essential

- The **R Square** value in the **Model Summary** table shows the amount of variance in the dependent variable that can be explained by the independent variables.
- In our example the independent variables together account for 92.1 per cent of the variance in the 'Science Exam' scores.

SPSS advanced

- The **R** value (0.959^a) indicates the multiple correlation coefficient between all the entered independent variables and the dependent variable.
- The **Adjusted R Square** adjusts for a bias in R^2 as the number of variables increases. With only a few predictor variables, the adjusted R^2 should be similar to the R^2 value. We would usually take the R^2 value but we advise you to take the adjusted R^2 value when you have a lot of variables.
- The **Std. Error of the Estimate** is a measure of the variability of the multiple correlation.

An **ANOVA** table is then produced, which tests the significance of the regression model.

Test statistic

ANOVA[b]

Model		Sum of Squares	df	Mean Square	F	Sig.
1	Regression	1281.511	5	256.302	9.279	.025[a]
	Residual	110.489	4	27.622		
	Total	1392.000	9			

[a]. Predictors: (Constant), Literacy Exam, Hours Attended, Study time for exams, Intelligence Score, Maths Exam

[b]. Dependent Variable: Science Exam

p value

SPSS essential

- We can see from our table that **Sig.** (p value) $= 0.025$. As $p < 0.05$ our predictors are significantly better than would be expected by chance. The regression line predicted by the independent variables explains a significant amount of the variance in the dependent variable. It would normally be reported in a similar fashion to other ANOVAs:

$$F(5,4) = 9.279; \ p < 0.05$$

SPSS advanced

- Dividing the **Sum of squares** by the degrees of freedom (**df**) gives us the **Mean Square** or variance. We can see that the **Regression** explains significantly more variance than the error or **Residual**.
- We calculate R^2 by dividing the **Regression Sum of Squares** by the **Total Sum of Squares**.

$$\frac{1281.511}{1392.000} = 0.921 = (R^2)$$

The next part of the output, the **Coefficients** table, shows which variables are individually significant predictors of our dependent variable. The significant predictor values are shaded.

Coefficients[a]

Model		Unstandardized Coefficients		Standardized Coefficients		
		B	Std. Error	Beta	t	Sig.
1	(Constant)	−5.849	24.491		−.239	.823
	Study time for exams	.424	.181	.410	2.345	.079
	Intelligence Score	.304	.198	.250	1.531	.201
	Maths Exam	.884	.222	.672	3.975	.016
	Hours Attended	−.552	.282	−.319	−1.961	.121
	Literacy Exam	−3.59E-02	.164	−.035	−.218	.838

[a]. Dependent Variable: Science Exam

SPSS essential

- The **Unstandardized Coefficients** B column, gives us the coefficients of the independent variables in the regression equation including all the predictor variables.

$$\text{Science Exam score} = -5.849 + 0.424 \text{ Study time} + 0.304 \text{ Intelligence}$$
$$+ 0.884 \text{ Maths Exam} - 0.552 \text{ Hours Attended}$$
$$- 0.0359 \text{ Literacy Exam}$$

- Remember, the **Enter** method has included all the variables in the regression equation even though only one of them is a significant predictor.
- The **Standardized Beta Coefficient** column shows the contribution that an individual variable makes to the model. The beta weight is the average amount the dependent variable increases when the independent variable increases by one standard deviation (all other independent variables are held constant). As these are standardised we can compare them. Note that the largest influence on the Science Exam is from the Maths Exam (0.672) and the next is Study time (0.410).
- t tests are performed to test the two-tailed hypothesis that the beta value is significantly higher or lower than zero. This also enables us to see which predictors are significant.
- From our example we can see that the Maths Exam score is significant ($p < 0.05$), therefore, with the **Enter** method, the maths exam score is the only significant predictor (shown shaded in the coefficients table). The next largest t value is for Study time, but here $p > 0.05$.

SPSS advanced

- The **Unstandardized Coefficients Std. Error** column provides us with an estimate of the variability of the coefficient.

Stepwise method

In contrast to the **Enter** method, the **Stepwise** method adds predictor variables to the regression that best correlate with the dependent variable, and subtracts predictor variables that least correlate. In this way we generate a regression equation using only the predictor variables that make a significant contribution to the prediction.

The output tables are very similar to those produced by the Enter method but they may have more rows, depending on how many models the regression has produced.

- Go to the **Analyze** drop-down menu and select **Regression**, then **Linear**.
- Select the variable to be predicted and send it to the **Dependent** variable box. We choose Science Exam as the dependent variable.
- Highlight all the other variables and send them to the **Independent(s)** box.
- From the **Method** drop-down menu select **Stepwise**.
- Click on the **Statistics** button.
- SPSS selects **Estimates** and **Model fit** as default.
- For a basic output we suggest ticking the **Descriptives** box as well.
- Click on **Continue** and then **OK**.

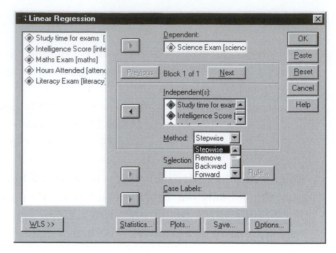

SPSS output

SPSS produces a **Descriptives** table and **Correlation** matrix in a similar way to the Enter method. The tables specific to the Stepwise method are discussed below.

Variables Entered/Removed[a]

Model	Variables Entered	Variables Removed	Method
1	Maths Exam	.	Stepwise (Criteria: Probability-of-F-to-enter <=.050, Probability-of-F-to-remove >=.100).
2	Study time for exams	.	Stepwise (Criteria: Probability-of-F-to-enter <=.050, Probability-of-F-to-remove >=.100).

[a]. Dependent Variable: Science Exam

SPSS essential

- The **Variables Entered/Removed** table shows that the Stepwise method of regression has been used.
- Notice that SPSS has entered into the regression equation the two variables ('Maths Exam' and 'Study time for exams') that are significantly correlated with Science Exam, as seen in the earlier correlation matrix.

By observing the **Model Summary** table below, using the Stepwise method, SPSS has produced two models. Model 1 includes the maths exam results, whereas Model 2 includes the maths exam scores and the study time for exams.

Model Summary

Model	R	R Square	Adjusted R Square	Std. Error of the Estimate
1	.740[a]	.548	.491	8.87
2	.909[b]	.825	.776	5.89

a. Predictors: (Constant), Maths Exam
b. Predictors: (Constant), Maths Exam, Study time for exams

Advanced   *Essential*   *Advanced*

SPSS essential

- The **R Square** value in the **Model Summary** table shows the amount of variance in the dependent variable that can be explained by the independent variables.
- In our example above:
  Model 1   The independent variable 'Maths Exam' accounts for 54.8 per cent of the variance in the scores of the science exam.
  Model 2   The independent variables 'Maths Exam' and 'Study time for exams' together account for 82.5 per cent of the variance in the scores of the science exam.

SPSS advanced

- The **R** value (0.740) in Model 1 is the multiple correlation coefficient between the predictor variables and the dependent variable. As 'Maths Exam' is the only independent variable in this model we can see that the R value is the same value as the Pearson's correlation coefficient in our pairwise correlation matrix.

- In Model 2 the independent variables 'Maths Exam' and 'Study time for exams' are entered, generating a multiple correlation coefficient, $R = 0.909$.
- The **Adjusted R Square** adjusts for a bias in R^2. With only a few predictor variables, the adjusted R^2 should be similar to the R^2 value. We would usually take the R^2 value but we advise you to take the adjusted R^2 value when you have a lot of variables.
- The **Std. Error of the Estimate** is a measure of the variability of the multiple correlation.

Using the Stepwise method SPSS produces an **ANOVA** for each model.

Test statistic

ANOVA[c]

Model		Sum of Squares	df	Mean Square	F	Sig.
1	Regression	762.454	1	762.454	9.689	.014[a]
	Residual	629.546	8	78.693		
	Total	1392.000	9			
2	Regression	1149.064	2	574.532	16.555	.002[b]
	Residual	242.936	7	34.705		
	Total	1392.000	9			

[a]. Predictors: (Constant), Maths Exam
[b]. Predictors: (Constant), Maths Exam, Study time for exams
[c]. Dependent Variable: Science Exam

p value

SPSS essential

- The ANOVA tests the significance of each regression model to see if the regression predicted by the independent variables explains a significant amount of the variance in the dependent variable.
- As with any ANOVA the essential items of information needed are the *df*, the *F* value and the probability value. Both the regression models explain a significant amount of the variation in the dependent variable.

Model 1: $F(1,8) = 9.689$; $p < 0.05$
Model 2: $F(2,7) = 16.555$; $p < 0.01$

SPSS advanced

- Dividing the **Sums of Squares** by the degrees of freedom (**df**) gives us the **Mean Square** or variance. We can see that the **Regression** explains significantly more variance than the error or **Residual**.
- We calculate R^2 by dividing the **Regression Sum of Squares** by the **Total Sum of Squares**. The values for model 1 have been used as an example.

$$\frac{762.454}{1392.000} = 0.548 = (R^2)$$

As with the Enter method, SPSS produces a **Coefficients** table. By applying the Stepwise method only the variables selected for the final model are included.

Coefficients^a

Model		Unstandardized Coefficients		Standardized Coefficients		
		B	Std. Error	Beta	t	Sig.
1	(Constant)	2.151	17.526		.123	.905
	Maths Exam	.974	.313	.740	3.113	.014
2	(Constant)	−2.615	11.726		−.223	.830
	Maths Exam	.761	.217	.579	3.504	.010
	Study time for exams	.569	.171	.551	3.338	.012

^{a}. Dependent Variable: Science Exam

SPSS essential

- The **Unstandardized Coefficients** B column gives us the coefficients of the independent variables in the regression equation for each model.

  Model 1: Science Exam score = 2.151 + 0.974 Maths Exam
  Model 2: Science Exam score = −2.615 + 0.761 Maths Exam + 0.569 Study time

- The **Standardized Beta Coefficient** column informs us of the contribution that an individual variable makes to the model. The beta weight is the average amount the dependent variable increases when the independent variable increases by one standard deviation (all other independent variables are held constant). As these are standardised we can compare them.

- t tests are performed to test the two-tailed hypothesis that the beta value is significantly higher or lower than zero. This also enables us to see which predictors are significant.
- By observing the **Sig.** values in our example we can see that for Model 1 the Maths Exam scores are significant ($p < 0.05$). However, with Model 2 both Maths Exam scores ($p < 0.05$) and Study time for exams ($p < 0.05$) are found to be significant predictors (shaded values in the coefficients table).
- We advise on this occasion that you use Model 2 because it accounts for more of the variance.

SPSS advanced

- The **Unstandardized Coefficients Std. Error** column provides an estimate of the variability of the coefficient.

When variables are excluded from the model their beta values, t values and significance values are shown in the **Excluded Variables** table.

Excluded Variables[c]

Model		Beta In	t	Sig.	Partial Correlation	Collinearity Statistics
						Tolerance
1	Study time for exams	.551[a]	3.338	.012	.784	.914
	Intelligence Score	.309[a]	1.311	.231	.444	.930
	Hours Attended	−.309[a]	−1.261	.248	−.430	.876
	Literacy Exam	−.227[a]	−.937	.380	−.334	.978
2	Intelligence Score	.150[b]	.848	.429	.327	.835
	Hours Attended	−.233[b]	−1.476	.190	−.516	.858
	Literacy Exam	−.005[b]	−.024	.982	−.010	.806

[a]. Predictors in the Model: (Constant), Maths Exam
[b]. Predictors in the Model: (Constant), Maths Exam, Study time for exams
[c]. Dependent Variable: Science Exam

SPSS advanced

- The **Beta In** value gives an estimate of the beta weight if it was included in the model at this time.

- The results of t tests for each independent variable are detailed with their probability values.
- From Model 1 we can see that the t value for Study time for exams is significant ($p < 0.05$). However as we have used the Stepwise method this variable has been excluded from the model.
- As Study time has been included in Model 2 it has been removed from this table.
- As the variable 'Maths Exam' scores is present in both models it is not mentioned in the **Excluded Variables** table.
- The **Partial Correlation** value indicates the contribution that the excluded predictor would make if we decided to include it in our model.
- **Collinearity Statistics Tolerance** values check for any collinearity in our data. As a general rule of thumb, a tolerance value below 0.1 indicates a serious problem.

FAQ

I want to use the Enter method to test if three independent variables are significant predictors and then again with another two independent variables added. Do I have to go through the multiple regression procedure twice?

No, you don't have to do the procedure twice, you can enter your independent variables in blocks by entering the first three variables and then selecting Next and entering the final two independent variables. Your output will display both models with the first three independent variables, and then all five independent variables. To observe the difference in the amount of variance explained, it's a good idea to tick the R Square changed in the Options command.

I have a number of independent variables and a dichotomous dependent variable. Can I still do a multiple regression?

It is possible but it may be more appropriate to conduct a logistic regression, which is a form of regression that is used when the dependent variable is dichotomous.

Details on how to calculate multiple regression and multiple correlation by hand can be found in Chapter 21 of Hinton (2004).

Chapter 17

Introduction to factor analysis

FACTOR ANALYSIS is an umbrella term for a set of statistical procedures that examines the correlations between variables in large sets of data to see if a small set of underlying variables or factors can explain the variation in the original set of variables. Thus, factor analysis can be viewed as a way of summarising or reducing data, often collected in a questionnaire, to a few underlying dimensions.

A factor analysis examines the associations between variables, based on the correlations between them, to see if there are underlying factors. For example, a researcher has collected a large amount of data about the experiences of people in work. There might be questions such as: How much do you enjoy your job? How long does it take to get to work? How many hours a week do you work? How often do you take work home? The researcher may have collected this dataset for two reasons. Other research may show that there are specific factors such as work stress or personality that underlie these questions, and the researcher is looking to see if these factors underlie her data as well. In this case the factor analysis is referred to as a *confirmatory factor analysis*, as the researcher is seeking to confirm (through the factor analysis) the proposed theory.

Alternatively, the researcher does not have any prior beliefs about which, or how many, underlying factors can be found to explain the data. In this case we call it an *exploratory factor analysis*. Whereas in the past it would have been extremely difficult to undertake this analysis, the advent of computer packages such as SPSS means that we can quickly and easily perform an exploratory factor analysis on a collection of results. In this chapter we shall be concentrating on exploratory factor analysis.

There are a number of different methods of performing a factor analysis. We will be examining the most popular, *principal components analysis*, which analyses the total variance and attempts to explain the maximum amount of variance by the minimum number of underlying factors. As it produces more and more factors to explain all the variance some factors explain a lot more variance than do others. So a key decision for anyone undertaking an exploratory factor analysis is how many factors to choose.

✓ Like many statistical analyses factor analysis has its own terminology. Just remember that factors and components are both terms for the underlying variables that can explain the variability in the original data.

The decision we must make is 'how many factors are important?' There are three sources of information to help us make this decision.

- We could simply look at the variance explained by each factor. The output helpfully lists the factors in order of how much variance each one can explain. It is common to choose a cut-off point (usually 5 per cent of the variance) and say that if a factor cannot explain as much as this it is not worth including as an important underlying factor.

- The factor analysis procedure calculates an *eigenvalue* for each factor. An eigenvalue of 1 means that the factor can explain as much variability in the data as a single original variable. Therefore the most commonly used rule for deciding if a factor is important is to only take factors with an eigenvalue of 1 or greater.

- A third approach is to examine the *scree plot* of the factors and eigenvalues. The first factor is likely to have a large eigenvalue and each new factor's eigenvalue is much smaller than the last. However, there comes a point when the eigenvalues of the factors tend to become quite similar – the difference in eigenvalues between factors gets very small. The scree plot charts this effect and we can find the point on the graph where the eigenvalues stop changing very much. The term 'scree' comes from the debris collecting at the bottom of a cliff. When small stones and other debris slide down a cliff they collect at the point at the bottom of the slope where it flattens out enough for the stones to collect rather than keep rolling. We look at our graph of the eigenvalues (analogous to the cliff) and find the point where the slope flattens out (and the debris would collect if it was a real slope). We simply regard the factors up to this point as important factors and those after the point as not important.

Notice there is no hard-and-fast rule to decide which factors are important, so we normally look at the variance explained, the eigenvalue size and the scree plot to try to best judge the relevant factors to take. (Remember also that the statistics can only do so much – we might wish to undertake further research to see if the factors we have identified are supported by subsequent data analysis.)

Now that we have the factors we perform a *rotation* to get the clearest and simplest way of associating the original variables to the factors. Just as we might rotate a picture on a wall so that it lines up horizontally and vertically (but still remains the same picture) we perform a rotation on the factors so that they 'line up' with the variables in the simplest way. By doing this we have a clearer picture of which variables contribute to (correlate) or 'load' onto each factor. As a rule of thumb it is often taken that a variable makes a significant contribution to a factor if the loading is 0.3 or greater. (All variables will load on all factors but we can find a rotation that provides us with the clearest pattern that shows which variables load most on which factors).

Now we have identified the factors and also found the variables that contribute to each of them, the statistical analysis is complete. For the researcher, however, deciding what these underlying factors actually mean theoretically is an important issue. What essential quality does each factor identify? Can each factor be given a name? If all the questions on workload, time at work and health, in the 'people at work' example, are linked by an underlying factor then the researcher might choose to label that factor something like 'work stress'.

Factor analysis relies on linear correlations between variables and therefore the same assumptions are required as with parametric data and linear relationships. So we require interval data from a continuous scale, drawn from normally distributed populations. As we are proposing linearity in the relationship between variables, we also require homoscedasticity; that is, an even spread of data along the scale of the variables.

We also need to examine the data for *multicollinearity* (which we do not want). When two or more variables are co-linear (they follow the same linear pattern) we have multicollinearity. You might think this is what we are looking for – variables that are highly correlated – but we do not want variables that measure the same thing. Correlating people's height and weight might produce interesting data but measuring people's height twice by two different tape measures simply shows collinearity. As also mentioned in Chapter 16 where this is a problem for multiple correlation as well, if we find multicollinearity we may choose to exclude or combine variables to reduce this outcome. In the factor analysis we are able to calculate the Kaiser–Meyer–Olkin measure of sampling adequacy (KMO test) which is related to this. The KMO test is a helpful measure of whether the data is suitable for a factor analysis. As a rule of thumb, if the KMO test comes out at 0.5 or higher, we can then continue with the factor analysis as our data is suitable for it.

There is one more test we can undertake before performing the factor analysis and that is the Bartlett test of sphericity. We have seen the importance of checking sphericity in a repeated measures ANOVA (Chapter 9). We are checking it here for a different reason. We want the Bartlett test to be significant as this indicates that it is worth continuing with the factor analysis as there are relationships to investigate. There is no point in undertaking a factor analysis when we don't think there is anything of interest to find.

Finally, there is the question of how many original variables we need for a factor analysis and how many data points per variable. While the simple answer is the more the better, a rough guide is that a minimum of 100 participants should really be used. However, there should always be more participants than there are variables (with a minimum ratio of 2:1 participants to variables). Therefore, if we have a scale consisting of 60 items that we wish to analyse using factor analysis, we would need a minimum of 120 participants. Our data here does not meet this specification, with only 20 participants and 7 variables. This is because the data is for illustration only and is small enough to allow you to work though the example on your own computer.

Scenario

A psychologist was interested in finding out if there were any underlying factors within simple mental processing tasks. It was hoped that, if factors emerged, they could be linked to student performance on university assessments. However, as this is an exploratory factor analysis only the simple tasks were analysed at this stage. A battery of seven mental tests were chosen. The first three variables examined the correct answers for tests in addition, multiplication and logical sequencing. Also, results for the number of correct moves made in a maze puzzle as well as the number of seconds to complete the task were noted. Finally, participants had to take part in two reaction time tasks. In the first one they had to press a single key when a coloured circle appeared on the computer screen (simple reaction times) and in the second one participants had to choose the right colour key to press when the coloured circle appeared (choice reaction times). These times were measured in milliseconds. Twenty undergraduate students took part in the study. The data were entered into SPSS and were analysed using factor analysis.

We are going to use the principal components method of analysis and select factors that have eigenvalues over 1 as our criteria for how many factors to select.

Data entry

Enter the data as shown below. See Chapter 2 for the full data entry procedure.

	simple	choice	mazemove	addition	multiply	mazeseco	logic
1	884.39	926.96	7.00	17.00	16.00	12.00	11.00
2	1015.50	1050.18	15.00	17.00	14.00	15.00	6.00
3	756.94	866.39	10.00	18.00	11.00	15.00	8.00
4	700.79	1004.55	7.00	19.00	18.00	10.00	11.00
5	981.05	821.63	9.00	16.00	13.00	10.00	9.00
6	867.00	813.29	11.00	20.00	16.00	16.00	11.00
7	1283.53	1246.00	7.00	18.00	16.00	9.00	13.00
8	808.32	878.75	17.00	17.00	13.00	41.00	11.00
9	777.33	726.67	21.00	15.00	12.00	36.00	9.00
10	631.30	585.83	7.00	18.00	17.00	7.00	14.00
11	555.11	613.65	7.00	18.00	13.00	12.00	12.00
12	613.58	651.57	7.00	17.00	16.00	7.00	12.00
13	586.63	615.24	7.00	18.00	10.00	17.00	8.00
14	888.35	670.55	16.00	16.00	16.00	25.00	9.00
15	721.80	836.87	7.00	17.00	19.00	7.00	11.00
16	968.10	1221.64	7.00	13.00	11.00	7.00	8.00
17	935.00	1189.39	20.00	12.00	5.00	45.00	5.00
18	969.16	1050.43	14.00	20.00	19.00	25.00	12.00
19	734.74	797.62	7.00	17.00	16.00	11.00	6.00
20	814.28	768.68	7.00	18.00	19.00	14.00	9.00

Test procedure

- All inferential statistics are found under the **Analyze** drop-down menu.
- Select **Data Reduction** and then **Factor**.

- Highlight all the variables and send them across to the **Variables** box.
- Click on the **Descriptives** button.

✓ When the **Descriptives** box appears you will notice that SPSS offers the **Initial solution** as default. We have selected some additional options to give you a fairly full account of the results in the output.

- Put a tick in the **Univariate descriptives** box to generate the means and standard deviations for each variable.
- Within the **Correlation Matrix** section put a tick in the **Coefficients**, **Significance levels**, **Determinant** and **KMO and Bartlett's test of sphericity** boxes.
- Click on **Continue** and then select the **Extraction** button.

- The **Method** we would like to use is the **Principal components** method, which SPSS selects as default.
- Put a tick in the **Scree plot** box.
- As we stated in the introduction it is a good idea to leave the **Eigenvalues over:** value at 1.
- Click on **Continue** and then select the **Rotation** button.

345

✓ SPSS gives the option to specify the number of factors. However, we have chosen the eigenvalue criterion for factor selection in our example.

- Select the **Varimax** rotation method.
- Click on **Continue**.

Factor Analysis: Rotation

Method
- ○ None
- ● Varimax
- ○ Direct Oblimin
  - Delta: 0
- ○ Quartimax
- ○ Equamax
- ○ Promax
  - Kappa: 4

Display
- ☑ Rotated solution
- ☐ Loading plot(s)

Maximum Iterations for Convergence: 25

[Continue] [Cancel] [Help]

SPSS essential

- The **Method** we have selected is the **Varimax** rotation method. This rotates the factors in such a way that when the final factors are produced they are not correlated (i.e. orthogonal) with each other. This method may not always offer the best factor definition but is one of the simplest to interpret.

SPSS advanced

- The **Display** option that is set as default means that the **Rotated solution** will be displayed in our output. As we are interested in seeing these results, we suggest that you leave this ticked.
- The **Maximum Iterations for Convergence** refers to how many times your data is rotated to arrive at the factors that are produced.

✓ If you were undertaking a confirmatory factor analysis you might choose a specific number of factors and an oblique rotation such as **Promax**.

Factor Analysis: Options ✕

Missing Values
- ⦿ Exclude cases listwise
- ○ Exclude cases pairwise
- ○ Replace with mean

Coefficient Display Format
- ☐ Sorted by size
- ☑ Suppress absolute values less than: .4

[Continue] [Cancel] [Help]

- Next select the **Options** button to produce the **Factor Analysis: Options** window.
- All variables load onto all factors, but we only want to display the highest loadings. We generally take 0.3 or 0.4 as a cut-off point for deciding which variables to show loading onto each factor. As our example dataset is small we have decided to select a cut-off point of 0.4.

- Under **Coefficient Display Format** click in the check box of **Suppress absolute values less than:** and type in .4.
- Finally click on **Continue** and then **OK**.

SPSS output

The first table that SPSS produces is the **Descriptive Statistics**.

Descriptive Statistics

	Mean	Std. Deviation	Analysis N
Simple reaction times	824.6450	175.7623	20
Choice reaction times	866.7945	204.5345	20
Maze task moves correct	10.5000	4.8286	20
Addition task correct answers	17.0500	1.9861	20
Multiplication task correct answers	14.5000	3.5615	20
Maze task time in seconds	17.5000	11.5050	20
Logic task correct answers	9.7500	2.4468	20

SPSS essential

- The label for each of our variables is shown in the first column of the **Descriptive Statistics** table with the **Mean** and **Standard Deviation** for each variable. This provides us with an initial summary of each of the variables.

The **Correlation Matrix** shows the pairwise correlations. The significant correlations (at $p < 0.05$) are shaded. This can give us an indication of the relationships between variables.

Correlation Matrix[a]

		Simple reaction times	Choice reaction times	Maze task moves correct	Addition task correct answers	Multiplication task correct answers	Maze task time in seconds	Logic task correct answers
Correlation	Simple reaction times	1.000	.778	.248	−.190	−.027	.118	−.123
	Choice reaction times	.778	1.000	.162	−.304	−.188	.133	−.234
	Maze task moves correct	.248	.162	1.000	−.392	−.428	.904	−.368
	Addition task correct answers	−.190	−.304	−.392	1.000	.673	−.369	.566
	Multiplication task correct answers	−.027	−.188	−.428	.673	1.000	−.505	.589
	Maze task time in seconds	.118	.133	.904	−.369	−.505	1.000	−.332
	Logic task correct answers	−.123	−.234	−.368	.566	.589	−.332	1.000
Sig. (1-tailed)	Simple reaction times		.000	.146	.212	.456	.310	.303
	Choice reaction times	.000		.248	.096	.214	.288	.160
	Maze task moves correct	.146	.248		.044	.030	.000	.055
	Addition task correct answers	.212	.096	.044		.001	.055	.005
	Multiplication task correct answers	.456	.214	.030	.001		.012	.003
	Maze task time in seconds	.310	.288	.000	.055	.012		.076
	Logic task correct answers	.303	.160	.055	.005	.003	.076	

[a]. Determinant = 1.113E-02

SPSS essential

- The **Determinant** of the R-matrix should be greater than 0.000001. If it is lower this suggests multicollinearity. Our value is 1.113E-02 (this means 0.01113) and is therefore greater than 0.000001.
- We advise that you inspect your correlation matrix to see if there are any variables that correlate highly (for example $r > 0.8$). If this is the case an option is to eliminate one of these variables from your investigation.
- For example, by observing the correlation matrix above we can see that Maze task time in seconds and Maze task moves correct are highly correlated ($p < 0.001$).

Before conducting a factor analysis it is essential that we check our sampling adequacy and sphericity to see if it is worth proceeding with our analysis.

KMO and Bartlett's Test

Kaiser-Meyer-Olkin Measure of Sampling Adequacy.		.602
Bartlett's Test of Sphericity	Approx. Chi-Square	71.221
	df	21
	Sig.	.000

} *Essential*

SPSS essential

- The **Kaiser-Meyer-Olkin Measure of Sampling Adequacy** (**KMO**) is calculated using correlations and partial correlations to test whether the variables in our sample are adequate to correlate. That is, it calculates whether variables are so highly correlated that we cannot distinguish between them (multicollinearity). A general rule of thumb is that a KMO value should be greater than 0.5 for a satisfactory factor analysis to proceed. The higher the value the better. By observing the above results we can see that our KMO is 0.602, therefore we can proceed with our factor analysis. A value nearer to zero suggests that the partial correlations are high in relation to the actual correlations.
- **Bartlett's Test of Sphericity** lets us know if there is a relationship between the variables. If no relationship is found then there is no point in proceeding with the factor analysis. We may simply have too few participants for us to find the effects we are looking for and therefore insufficient power for a factor analysis. A p value < 0.05 indicates that it makes sense to continue with the factor analysis. Since we have found $p < 0.001$ we can conclude that there are relationships between our variables.

In factor analysis we are looking for variability in one variable common to other variables, as this indicates that they are linked by an underlying factor. At first SPSS assumes (in a principal component analysis) that 100 per cent of the variance of each variable is common variance, so gives each variable a *communality* of 1.000. However, when it has extracted the factors it works out how much of the variability of each variable really can be explained by the extracted factors, and gives an updated value of communality.

Communalities

	Initial	Extraction
Simple reaction times	1.000	.910
Choice reaction times	1.000	.890
Maze task moves correct	1.000	.951
Addition task correct answers	1.000	.761
Multiplication task correct answers	1.000	.790
Maze task time in seconds	1.000	.954
Logic task correct answers	1.000	.699

} *Advanced*

Extraction Method: Principal Component Analysis.

SPSS advanced

- By observing our example we can see that all the variance of 'Simple reaction times' is initially given a communality value of 1.000, but after extracting the factors we find it has a communality of 0.910. This indicates that 91 per cent of its variability is explainable by the factors.

Using our criterion of selecting eigenvalues over 1, we can see from the highlighted numbers in the **Total Variance Explained** table that three components (or factors) have been produced that have eigenvalues greater than this amount.

Total Variance Explained

Component	Initial Eigenvalues			Extraction Sums of Squared Loadings			Rotation Sums of Squared Loadings		
	Total	% of Variance	Cumulative %	Total	% of Variance	Cumulative %	Total	% of Variance	Cumulative %
1	3.259	46.554	46.554	3.259	46.554	46.554	2.232	31.879	31.879
2	1.604	22.907	69.461	1.604	22.907	69.461	1.923	27.466	59.345
3	1.094	15.625	85.086	1.094	15.625	85.086	1.802	25.741	85.086
4	.456	6.514	91.600						
5	.323	4.610	96.210						
6	.199	2.839	99.048						
7	6.661E-02	.951	100.000						

Extraction Method: Principal Component Analysis.

Advanced

SPSS essential

- The **Initial Eigenvalues Total** column shows the eigenvalues we are interested in. Only three factors have eigenvalues greater than 1.

- The **% of Variance** column shows how much variance each individual factor can explain. Had we had chosen to select all factors that accounted for more than 5 per cent of variance, we would have had four factors rather than three. If this was the case we would produce another factor analysis but this time select that we want four factors rather than eigenvalues over 1.
- The **Cumulative %** column shows the amount of variance accounted for by each consecutive factor added together.
- From our example we can see that factor 1 has an eigenvalue of 3.259, which accounts for 46.554 per cent of the variance. Our criterion for factor selection is eigenvalues greater than 1, so we therefore have three factors which can explain a cumulative 85.086 per cent of the variance in the data.

SPSS advanced

- You can see that the **Extraction Sums of Squared Loadings** values are exactly the same as the **Initial Eigenvalues**, however only the three factors that have been extracted are shown.
- The rotation method changes the eigenvalues and variances explained by each factor but keeps the total variance the same. The extracted factors are shown in the **Rotation Sums of Squared Loadings** column.

The **Scree Plot** is then shown. The factors are the X-axis and the eigenvalues are the Y-axis. The factor with the highest eigenvalue is the first component and the second component has the second highest eigenvalue. Remember that by observing where the line starts to level out is a criterion for selecting how many factors to extract.

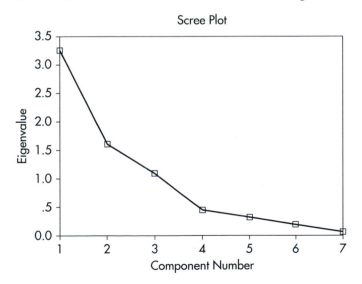

Scree Plot

SPSS *essential*

- The scree plot depicts the amount of variance explained by each factor and can aid judgement regarding factor extraction.
- From our example we can see that our plot is starting to level out at the fourth factor.

✓ The scree plot indicates that four factors could be chosen. We might wish to re-run the factor analysis specifying four factors.

The **Component Matrix** details the factor loadings onto our three factors before they have been rotated.

Component Matrix[a]

	Component		
	1	2	3
Simple reaction times	.402	.851	
Choice reaction times	.479	.810	
Maze task moves correct	.778		.556
Addition task correct answers	−.765		.415
Multiplication task correct answers	−.774		
Maze task time in seconds	.762		.537
Logic task correct answers	−.704		.432

Extraction Method: Principal Component Analysis.
  [a]. 3 components extracted.

SPSS *advanced*

- This table gives us the initial picture of the loadings of the variables onto the factors, but it can be made clearer by rotation. For example, we can see that all variables appear to load onto factor 1 to a reasonable extent. However, rotation will simplify the picture and show which variables really are important to factor 1.

As we have selected the **Principal Component Analysis** with a **Varimax** rotation, the **Rotated Component Matrix** gives us a clearer picture than the **Component Matrix** of our factor loadings onto the three factors.

Rotated Component Matrix^{a}

	Component		
	1	2	3
Simple reaction times			.946
Choice reaction times			.921
Maze task moves correct		.938	
Addition task correct answers	.837		
Multiplication task correct answers	.836		
Maze task time in seconds		.942	
Logic task correct answers	.819		

Extraction Method: Principal Component Analysis.
Rotation Method: Varimax with Kaiser Normalization.
  ^{a}. Rotation converged in 5 iterations.

SPSS essential

- We now have a much clearer picture of our three factors. Rotation has shown that different variables load onto different factors. We can now look at the variables loading onto each factor and choose suitable names for factors.
- Factor 1 seems to be related to variables that assess mathematical or logical ability.
- Factor 2 is related to variables that deal with problem solving abilities.
- The variables included in factor 3 seem to be testing reaction time abilities.

The final table produced by SPSS is the **Component Transformation Matrix**.

Component Transformation Matrix

Component	1	2	3
1	−.717	.604	.348
2	.219	−.279	.935
3	.662	.747	.068

Extraction Method: Principal Component Analysis.
Rotation Method: Varimax with Kaiser Normalization.

SPSS advanced

- The **Component Transformation Matrix** shows the correlations used in transforming the **Component Matrix** to the **Rotated Component Matrix**. This table has little importance in the interpretation of our findings.

FAQ

My Rotated Component Matrix has factor loadings for every variable in every factor so that I can't see clearly which variables load highly onto which factors.

Rotated Component Matrix[a]

	Component		
	1	2	3
Simple reaction times	−2.08E-03	.101	.947
Choice reaction times	−.205	1.022E-02	.921
Mask task moves correct	−.201	.960	7.880E-02
Addition task correct answers	.824	−.201	−.179
Multiplication task correct answers	.831	−.314	1.470E-02
Maze task time in seconds	−.257	.946	4.666E-02
Logic task correct answers	.839	−8.33E-02	−9.50E-02

Extraction Method: Principal Component Analysis.
Rotation Method: Varimax with Kaiser Normalization.
[a]. Rotation converged in 5 iterations.

*When completing the factor analysis procedure you have the option not to show all the factor loadings in the rotated component matrix. Under the **Options** and **Coefficient Display Format** select **Suppress absolute values less than** and type in .4. This will ensure that only variables that have high loadings onto each factor are shown in the rotated component matrix, making it easier to interpret. However, remember that this value is subjective, some books/lecturers may decide that a value of 0.3 is sufficient.*

Chapter 18

Using SPSS to analyse questionnaires: Reliability

S PSS IS EXCELLENT FOR analysing questionnaires. We can use crosstabs to show the relationship between different questions. So if you asked people to give their gender in one question and religious beliefs in a second question, you could crosstabulate the two questions, which would show how many men and how many women follow each religion. A test, such as a chi-square, can also be performed to compare the patterns of these data.

Many of the tests discussed earlier can be used to analyse the results of questionnaires, and different questionnaires will lead to the use of different tests such as the *t* tests, or ANOVA. The procedures outlined in the relevant chapters can be employed either on individual question results or on the overall scores on the questionnaire, as appropriate.

In Chapter 17 we considered the technique of factor analysis, which is often employed on questionnaire data. Having asked a lot of questions about a particular topic it is of interest to search for underlying factors associated with clusters of questions.

Yet none of these different analyses will be very meaningful unless our questionnaire is *reliable*. Reliability is the ability of the questionnaire to consistently measure the topic under study at different times and across different populations. Imagine having a tape measure that measured a person as 1 metre 60 centimetres on one day and 1 metre 70 centimetres on another day. This is a very unreliable tape measure. There are a number of different ways of assessing reliability. We shall describe the procedure for Cronbach's Alpha which is the most popular method of testing reliability.

Reliability analysis: Cronbach's Alpha

When we undertake a questionnaire we are often using it to measure a particular construct, such as anxiety, health or happiness. In the questionnaire we will ask a range of questions concerning this construct, so for 'happiness' we might ask questions such as: *To what extent do you enjoy your work? How much do you like being with your family?* So if Susan is a genuinely happy person and the questionnaire measures this accurately then it is a valid measure of the construct. It should be able to measure other people appropriately as well, correctly giving their level of happiness. The questionnaire should not only be valid but also reliable. We should expect that if we gave the questionnaire to Susan again then it would show the same result.

Reliability can be assessed in a number of different ways. We can split our questionnaire into two and see if the first half of the questions come up with the same result as the second half (split-half reliability). We can examine each question in turn and see how diagnostic a question it is. Do all the happy people (who get high scores on the questionnaire) answer this particular question in the same way and do all the sad people (who get low scores on the questionnaire) answer the question the same way? If not then it may not be a particularly good question and so we might choose to take it out.

Cronbach's Alpha is the most popular method of examining reliability. The calculation of Cronbach's Alpha is based on the number of *items* (i.e. the number of questions on a questionnaire) and the average inter-item correlation. If we assume that the questions are measuring a true score (for example a person's true level of happiness) then each individual question will measure the true score plus a certain amount of random error. A high correlation between the different items will indicate they are measuring the same thing as there will be only small values for the error. A low correlation will indicate that there is a lot of error and the items are not reliably measuring the same thing.

Cronbach's Alpha ranges from 0 for a completely unreliable test (although technically it can dip below 0) to 1 for a completely reliable test. What value of Cronbach's Alpha do we need for a questionnaire or a measure to be reliable? There is some debate around this, with some statisticians suggesting 0.7 or higher whereas others recommend 0.8. It will depend to a certain extent on the number of items in the test and the number of participants, but 0.75 is a sensible compromise value to take as the benchmark (if you are concerned about your own data you may need to follow this up in the statistical textbooks as it is not a decision that SPSS can make for you).

Cronbach's Alpha relies on the same assumptions that we have considered in our chapters on linear correlation and multiple correlation as it employs a correlational analysis. It is also employing a model in that it is assumed that the observed scores are the true score plus error, and so, as explained in Chapter 9, for this model to be appropriate the errors must be random (and hence unbiased). If the assumptions are not met then the value of Cronbach's Alpha may be either an underestimation or an overestimation of the correct value.

Scenario

A team of researchers have constructed a questionnaire to examine consumer behaviour, and want to test its reliability with their sample of participants. Forty-five people completed the 15-item questionnaire, which comprised individual question responses measured on a 6-point likert scale, with 1 being disagree and 6 being agree.

Note: you can use the **Compute** command once your questionnaire data has been entered, to generate total scores which can be used for further analysis (see Chapter 5).

Data entry

In order to complete a reliability analysis in SPSS data must be entered as shown below.

	q1	q2	q3	q4	q5	q6	q7	q8
1	3	5	1	2	1	1	2	1
2	5	3	3	5	4	3	4	4
3	4	2	1	3	2	1	3	2
4	5	3	2	2	2	1	2	5
5	5	2	2	2	1	1	2	2
6	5	4	2	3	3	1	4	3
7	5	3	4	3	1	1	3	3
8	5	3	2	4	2	3	3	2

As can be seen in this example, each participant's score is entered for every question. Questions form the columns (i.e. variables), and participant scores are entered into the rows. In our example we have 15 questions and 45 participants completing the questionnaire, and hence our dataset comprises 15 columns and 45 rows (for illustration purposes we have only shown eight questions and eight participants' scores here).

Test procedure

To conduct a reliability analysis the procedure below should be followed. Please note, however, that this chapter is designed as an introduction to questionnaire analysis and reliability analysis by Cronbach's Alpha, and hence only the analyses based on Cronbach's Alpha are detailed below.

- As with all statistical commands in SPSS, reliability analysis is found under the **Analyze** drop-down menu.
- Choose **Scale** and **Reliability Analysis**.

• Send each question across to the **Items** box.
• The default model for reliability analysis, **Alpha**, will be explained here. For analysis using other models select the drop-down options using the **Model** command in the bottom left-hand corner of the box.

SPSS advanced

• Alternative models of reliability analysis can be found under the arrow drop-down menu next to **Model**. However, we recommend the use of Cronbach's Alpha because of its flexibility in application to both dichotomous/binary responses, and data measured on a larger scale. Cronbach's Alpha will give us a reliability calculation based on the whole of the questionnaire.
• One further type of reliability, which you may want to assess, is **Split Half** reliability. Here the questions are divided into two groups. If the scale is reliable we would expect the two halves to be positively correlated. If this is not found to be the case then we can infer that our participants are responding differently in the two parts of the questionnaire.
• Note that the default option for split-half reliability in SPSS is to group the two halves by the first questions and then by the end questions.

• Click on **Statistics**.
• The common options selected for analysis using Cronbach's Alpha are as follows.
• Under the **Descriptives for** option, choose **Item**, **Scale**, and **Scale if item deleted**.
• Under the **Summaries** options, select **Means** and **Variances**.
• Click on **Continue**, then **OK**.

SPSS output

The following tables will be produced by SPSS when the above procedure has been followed.

R E L I A B I L I T Y A N A L Y S I S – S C A L E (A L P H A)

		Mean	Std Dev	Cases
1.	Q1	4.2222	1.2227	45.0
2.	Q2	3.4667	1.3246	45.0
3.	Q3	2.4222	1.2701	45.0
4.	Q4	3.0444	1.3810	45.0
5.	Q5	2.3556	1.1313	45.0
6.	Q6	2.0000	1.3652	45.0
7.	Q7	3.2000	1.1794	45.0
8.	Q8	2.6000	1.3038	45.0
9.	Q9	3.1111	1.3521	45.0
10.	Q10	2.3333	1.1677	45.0
11.	Q11	2.6889	1.2937	45.0
12.	Q12	2.6667	1.3314	45.0
13.	Q13	2.7778	1.1259	45.0
14.	Q14	2.4889	1.2545	45.0
15.	Q15	3.2444	1.1512	45.0

N of Cases = 45.0

SPSS essential

- The first part of the output gives a summary of responses by the participants to individual questions, and provides information regarding the **Mean** and **Std Dev** (standard deviations) for responses to each question, and a report stating how many participants completed the question.
- From our example we can see that all 45 of our participants answered all our questions. We can also see which questions elicited a wide variety of responses, as shown by the larger standard deviations.
- In the example above, responses were measured on a scale from 1 to 6. Higher mean scores therefore indicate questions where participants were at the agreement end of the rating scale.

The next set of results gives a descriptive summary for the whole questionnaire.

Statistics for Scale	Mean	Variance	Std Dev	N of Variables
	42.6222	116.3768	10.7878	15

Item Means	Mean	Minimum	Maximum	Range	Max/Min	Variance
	2.8415	2.0000	4.2222	2.2222	2.1111	.3086

Item Variances	Mean	Minimum	Maximum	Range	Max/Min	Variance
	1.5873	1.2677	1.9071	.6394	1.5044	.0488

SPSS essential

- **N of Variables** is the number of items in our questionnaire. In our example there were 15 questions.
- The **Statistics for Scale** row gives the descriptive statistics for the scale as a whole. In our example, when the total scores of the questionnaire are examined, participants scored a mean of 42.6222, with a variance of 116.3768, and a standard deviation of 10.7878. The small standard deviation thus indicates that there are not wide variations in the scores of our participants for the overall total score on the questionnaire.

SPSS advanced

- The **Item Means** row details descriptive statistics for a response on individual questions. As we can see from the above example, the mean score on items is 2.8415. A mid-score such as this would be expected from averaging scores on a range of items employing a 1–6 Likert scale.
- The **Minimum** and **Maximum** values are the two most extreme scores selected by participants. In our case these are 2 and 4.2222, indicating that no respondents selected responses from the most extreme ends of the scale.
- The **Item Variances** row shows the variance in scores when looking at individual items.

The next table produced by SPSS enables each question's reliability to be examined, and the effect on the overall questionnaire if an individual question was removed.

RELIABILITY ANALYSIS – SCALE (ALPHA)

Item-total Statistics

	Scale Mean if Item Deleted	Scale Variance If Item Deleted	Corrected Item-Total Correlation	Squared Multiple Correlation	Alpha If Item Deleted
Q1	38.4000	113.5182	.0523	.5212	.8652
Q2	39.1556	107.3162	.2662	.4498	.8556
Q3	40.2000	103.7545	.4255	.4750	.8465
Q4	39.5778	99.7949	.5319	.7132	.8406
Q5	40.2667	100.6545	.6362	.7147	.8359
Q6	40.6222	101.1495	.4867	.5353	.8433
Q7	39.4222	97.2949	.7604	.6906	.8288
Q8	40.0222	102.0677	.4786	.5219	.8436
Q9	39.5111	99.0737	.5749	.6145	.8380
Q10	40.2889	102.8010	.5157	.5575	.8418
Q11	39.9333	98.8818	.6149	.7392	.8358
Q12	39.9556	94.9980	.7554	.6656	.8271
Q13	39.8444	103.0434	.5278	.6217	.8413
Q14	40.1333	100.7091	.5598	.6492	.8392
Q15	39.3778	111.6495	.1398	.3334	.8601
	Advanced	*Essential*	*Advanced*	*Essential*	

SPSS essential

- The SPSS output shows the findings of the analysis for each item on the questionnaire.
- In our example the questions that offer potential concern are shaded in gray.
- The **Corrected Item-Total Correlation** column shows the relationship between the responses on individual questions and the overall total score on the questionnaire. We would expect a reliable question to have a positive relationship with the overall total, ideally being above 0.3. An item displaying a weak positive or a negative relationship

to the total indicates a question that may be poor on reliability and is thus affecting the findings from the whole scale. In the example above, we can see that question 1 is the weakest item, because its correlation with the overall total is only 0.0523.

- The effects that individual questions can have on the overall reliability of the questionnaire are highlighted by the inverse relationship between the **Corrected Item-Total Correlation** and the **Alpha If Item Deleted** columns. The importance of the weak relationship between question 1 and the overall total score on the question-naire is reflected in the increase in the alpha score for the questionnaire if this item is omitted. An examination of the table further down the output gives us an overall alpha value of 0.8522. While this figure is high, the removal of question 1 from the final questionnaire would see this figure rise to 0.8652 (as can be seen from the table).

SPSS advanced

- The **Scale Mean If Item Deleted** column shows the effects on the overall mean of the scale if an individual question is deleted. In the example above, if question 1 was omitted from the final version of the questionnaire, the overall mean of the scale would fall from 42.6222 to 38.4000. Similar effects can be seen from examining the **Scale Variance If Item Deleted** column.
- The **Squared Multiple Correlation** column gives us a value for the amount of variability on this item that can be predicted by the items in the rest of the questionnaire.

In order to determine the overall Alpha value for our questionnaire, and hence judge the measured reliability of our construct measurement, we need to examine the final table below.

Reliability Coefficients	15 items
Alpha = 0.8522	Standardized item alpha = 0.8520

SPSS essential

- The reliability coefficient for all 15 items is displayed as a simple **Alpha**, and a **Standardized alpha**. The values are usually approximately the same and either can be reported. People usually choose the Standardized alpha.
- An Alpha score above 0.75 is generally taken to indicate a scale of high reliability, 0.5 to 0.75 is generally accepted as indicating a moderately reliable scale, while a figure below this generally indicates a scale of low reliability.

SPSS *advanced*

• The Standardized alpha is usually chosen. Indeed, while it is preferable if our scales are similar (for example all questions are measured on a 10-point scale), it may not be really any better than the raw Alpha in other circumstances.

FAQ

Sometimes when I conduct a reliability analysis, the Alpha and Standardized alpha values are missing from the screen – how do I obtain these values?

This may be the case if the questionnaire contains many items. In these instances click on the output box once to select the text, then place the cursor on the middle square of the enlarging bar at the bottom of the box, and drag down until the box is big enough to display the desired information.

Alternatively, print your output screen, and the complete analysis should be visible.

I have got my alpha figure but how do I know whether this indicates a reliable scale or not?

There is much debate among researchers as to where the appropriate cut-off points are for reliability. A good guide is:

• *0.90 and above shows excellent reliability*
• *0.70 to 0.90 shows high reliability*
• *0.50 to 0.70 shows moderate reliability*
• *0.50 and below shows low reliability.*

I have measured the reliability of my questionnaire using Cronbach's Alpha, how can I assess the validity of my questionnaire?

To assess test validity you could ask participants to complete a previously validated questionnaire, which purports to measure the same thing, in addition to the newly created questionnaire. The scores from the two questionnaires need to be positively correlated in order for the new test to be considered valid.

I have assessed the reliability of my questionnaire but would now like to analyse it to look for relationships and differences within my respondents – how could I do this?

There are numerous options available to you.

- *Use the Compute command to generate total scores, or sub-scale scores (Chapter 5).*
- *Look for differences between groups of participants filling in the questionnaire by using tests of difference (t tests, Chapter 7; nonparametric two sample tests, Chapter 8; ANOVA, Chapter 10; nonparametric ANOVA, Chapter 13).*
- *Look for associations between responses to individual questions (chi-square, Chapter 14).*
- *Look for relationships between scales using correlations (Chapter 15).*
- *Examine whether one score reliably predicts other scores using regression (Chapters 15 and 16).*

Glossary

ANOVA An acronym for the **AN**alysis **O**f **VA**riance. By analysing the variance in the data due to different sources (e.g. an independent variable or error) we can decide if our experimental manipulation is influencing the scores in the data.

Asymp. Sig. (asymptotic significance) An estimate of the probability of a nonparametric test statistic employed by computer statistical analysis programs. This is often used when the exact probability cannot be worked out quickly.

beta weight The average amount by which the dependent variable increases when the independent variable increases by one standard deviation (all other independent variables are held constant).

between subjects Also known as independent measures. In this design, the samples we select for each condition of the independent variable are *independent*, as a member of one sample is not a member of another sample.

case A row in the Data Editor file: the data collected from a single participant.

Chart Editor The feature in SPSS that allows the editing of charts and graphs.

comparisons The results of a statistical test with more than two conditions will often show a significant result but not where the difference lies. We need to undertake a comparison of conditions to see which ones are causing the effect. If we compare them two at a time this is known as pairwise comparison and if we perform unplanned comparisons after discovering the significant finding these are referred to as post hoc comparisons.

component   The term used in the principal components method of factor analysis for a potential underlying factor.

condition   A researcher chooses levels or categories of the independent variable(s) to observe the effect on the dependent variable(s). These are referred to as conditions, levels, treatments or groups. For example, 'morning' and 'afternoon' might be chosen as the conditions for the independent variable of time of day.

confidence interval   In statistics we use samples to estimate population values, such as the mean or the difference in means. The confidence interval provides a range of values within which we predict lies the population value (to a certain level of confidence). The 95 per cent confidence interval of the mean worked out from a sample indicates that the population mean would fall between the upper and lower limits 95 per cent of the time.

contrasts   With a number of conditions in a study we may plan a set of comparisons such as contrasting each condition with a control condition. These planned comparisons are referred to as contrasts. We can plan complex contrasts, for example the effects of conditions 1 and 2 against condition 3.

correlation   The degree to which the scores on two (or more) variables co-relate. That is, the extent to which a variation in the scores on one variable results in a corresponding variation in the scores on a second variable. Usually the relationship we are looking for is linear. A multiple correlation examines the relationship between a combination of predictor variables with a dependent variable.

critical value   We reject the null hypothesis after a statistical test if the probability of the calculated value of the test statistic (under the null hypothesis) is lower than the significance level (e.g. 0.05). Computer programs print out the probability of the calculated value (e.g. 0.023765) and we can examine this to see if it is higher or lower than the significance level. Textbooks print tables of the critical values of the test statistic, which are the values of the statistic at a particular probability. For example, if the calculated value of a statistic (i.e. a t test) is 4.20 and the critical value is 2.31 (at the 0.05 level of significance) then clearly the probability of the test statistic is less than 0.05.

crosstabulation   Frequency data can be represented in a table with the rows as the conditions of one variable and the columns as the conditions of a second variable. This is a crosstabulation. We can include more variables by adding 'layers' to the crosstabulation in SPSS.

Data Editor   The feature in SPSS where data is entered. Saving the information from the data editor will produce an SPSS .sav file. There are two windows within the Data Editor: Data View and Variable View.

Data View   The data view window within the Data Editor presents a spreadsheet style format for entering all the data points.

degrees of freedom   When calculating a statistic we use information from the data (such as the mean or total) in the calculation. The degrees of freedom is the number of scores we need to know before we can work out the rest using the information we already have. It is the number of scores that are free to vary in the analysis.

dependent variable   The variable measured by the researcher and predicted to be influenced by (that is, depend on) the independent variable.

descriptive statistics   Usually we wish to describe our data before conducting further analysis or comparisons. Descriptive statistics such as the mean and standard deviation enable us to summarise a dataset.

discriminant function   A discriminant function is one derived from a set of independent (or predictor) variables that can be used to discriminate between the conditions of a dependent variable.

distribution   The range of possible scores on a variable and their frequency of occurrence. In statistical terms we refer to a distribution as a 'probability density function'. We use the mathematical formulae for known distributions to work out the probability of finding a score as high as or as low as a particular score.

effect size   The size of the difference between the means of two populations, in terms of standard deviation units.

eigenvalue   In a factor analysis an eigenvalue provides a measure of the amount of variance that can be explained by a proposed factor. If a factor has an eigenvalue of 1 then it can explain as much variance as one of the original independent variables.

equality of variance   see homogeneity of variance.

Exact. Sig. (2-tailed)   The exact probability of a nonparametric test statistic. This may take an extremely long time for a computer statistical analysis program to work out so an estimate (see Asymp. Sig. (asymptotic significance)) is often presented as well.

factor   Another name for 'variable', used commonly in the analysis of variance to refer to an independent variable. In factor analysis we analyse the variation in the data to see if it can be explained by fewer factors (i.e. 'new' variables) than the original number of independent variables.

general linear model   The underlying mathematical model employed in parametric statistics. When there are only two variables, X and Y, the relationship between them is linear when they satisfy the formula $Y = a + bX$ (where a and b are constants). The general linear model is a general form of this equation allowing as many X and Y variables as we wish in our analysis.

grouping variable   In analysing data in SPSS we can employ an independent measures independent variable as a grouping variable. This separates our participants into groups (such as introverts versus extraverts). It is important when inputting data into a statistical analysis program that we include the grouping variable as a column, with each group defined (i.e. introvert as '1' and extravert as '2'). We can then analyse the scores on other variables in terms of these groups, such as comparing the introverts with the extraverts on, say, a monitoring task.

homogeneity of variance   Underlying parametric tests is the assumption that the populations from which the samples are drawn have the same variance. We can examine the variances of the samples in our data to see whether this assumption is appropriate with our data or not.

homoscedasticity   The scores in a scatterplot are evenly distributed along and about a regression line. This is an assumption made in linear correlation. (This is the correlation and regression equivalent of the homogeneity of variance assumption.)

hypothesis   A predicted relationship between variables. For example: 'As sleep loss increases so the number of errors on a specific monitoring task will increase'.

illustrative statistics   Statistics that illustrate rather than analyse a set of data, such as the total number of errors made on a reading task. Often we illustrate a dataset by means of a graph or a table.

independent measures   A term used to indicate that there are different subjects (participants) in each condition of an independent variable: also known as 'between subjects'.

independent variable   A variable chosen by the researcher for testing, predicted to influence the dependent variable.

inferential statistics   Statistics that allow us to make inferences about the data – for example whether samples are drawn from different populations or whether two variables correlate.

interaction   When there are two or more factors in an analysis of variance then we can examine the interactions between the factors. An interaction indicates that the effect of one factor is not the same at each condition of another factor. For example, if we find that more cold drinks are sold in summer and more hot drinks sold in winter then we have an interaction of 'drink temperature' and 'time of year'.

intercept   A linear regression finds the best fit linear relationship between two variables. This is a straight line based on the formula $Y = a + bX$, where b is the slope of the line and a is the intercept, or point where the line crosses the Y-axis. (In the SPSS output for an ANOVA the term 'intercept' is used to refer to the overall mean value and its difference from zero.)

item   When we employ a test with a number of variables (such as questions in a questionnaire) we refer to these variables as 'items', particularly in reliability analysis where we are interested in the correlation between items in the test.

levels of data   Not all data is produced by using numbers in the same way. Sometimes we use numbers to name or allocate participants to categories (i.e. labeling a person as a liberal, and allocating them the number 1, or a conservative, and allocating them the number 2). In this case the data is termed 'nominal'. Sometimes we employ numbers to rank order participants, in which case the data is termed 'ordinal'. Finally, when the data is produced on a measuring scale with equal intervals the data is termed 'interval' (or 'ratio' if the scale includes an absolute zero value). Parametric statistics require interval data for their analyses.

Likert scale   A measuring scale where participants are asked to indicate their level of agreement or disagreement to a particular statement on, typically, a 5- or 7-point scale (from strongly agree to strongly disagree).

linear correlation   The extent to which variables correlate in a linear manner. For two variables this is how close their scatterplot is to a straight line.

linear regression   A regression that is assumed to follow a linear model. For two variables this is a straight line of best fit, which minimizes the 'error'.

main effect   The effect of a factor (independent variable) on the dependent variable in an analysis of variance measured without regard to the other factors in the analysis. In an ANOVA with more than one independent variable we can examine the effects of each factor individually (termed the main effect) and the factors in combination (the interactions).

MANOVA   A Multivariate ANalysis Of VAriance. An analysis of variance technique where there can be more than one dependent variable in the analysis.

mean   A measure of the 'average' score in a set of data. The mean is found by adding up all the scores and dividing by the number of scores.

mean square   A term used in the analysis of variance to refer to the variance in the data due to a particular source of variation.

median   If we order a set of data from lowest to highest the median is the point that divides the scores into two, with half the scores below and half above the median.

mixed design   A mixed design is one that includes both independent measures factors and repeated measures factors. For example, a group of men and a group of women are tested in the morning and the afternoon. In this test 'gender' is an independent measures variable (also known as 'between subjects') and time of day is a repeated measures factor (also known as 'within subjects'), so we have a mixed design.

mode   The score which has occurred the highest number of times in a set of data.

multiple correlation   The correlation of one variable with a combination of other variables.

multivariate   Literally this means 'many variables' but is most commonly used to refer to a test with more than one dependent variable (as in the MANOVA).

nonparametric test   Statistical tests that do not use, or make assumptions about, the characteristics (parameters) of populations.

normal distribution   A bell-shaped frequency distribution that appears to underlie many human variables. The normal distribution can be worked out mathematically using the population mean and standard deviation.

null hypothesis   A prediction that there is no relationship between the independent and dependent variables.

one-tailed test   A prediction that two samples come from different populations, specifying the direction of the difference: that is, which of the two populations will have the larger mean value.

outlier   An extreme value in a scatterplot – in that it lies outside the main cluster of scores. When calculating a linear correlation or regression an outlier will have a disproportionate influence on the statistical calculations.

Output Navigator   An SPSS navigation and editing system in an outline view in the left-hand column of the output window. This enables the user to hide or show output or to move items within the output screen.

***p* value**   The probability of a test statistic (assuming the null hypothesis to be true). If this value is very small (e.g. 0.02763) then we reject the null hypothesis. We claim a significant effect if the *p* value is smaller than a conventional significance level (such as 0.05).

parameter   A characteristic of a population, such as the population mean.

parametric tests   Statistical tests that use the characteristics (parameters) of populations or estimates of them (when assumptions are also made about the populations under study).

partial correlation   The correlation of two variables after having removed the effects of a third variable from both.

participant   A person taking part as a 'subject' in a study. The term 'participant' is preferred to 'subject' as it acknowledges the person's agency: i.e. that they have consented to take part in the study.

population   A complete set of items or events. In statistics this usually refers to the complete set of subjects or scores we are interested in, from which we have drawn a sample.

post hoc tests   When we have more than two conditions of an independent variable, a statistical test (such as an ANOVA) may show a significant result but not the source of the effect. We can perform post hoc tests (literally post hoc means 'after this') to see which conditions are showing significant differences. Post hoc tests should correct for the additional risk of Type I errors when performing multiple tests on the same data.

power of a test   The probability that, when there is a genuine effect to be found, the test will find it (that is, correctly reject a false null hypothesis). As an illustration, one test might be like a stopwatch that gives the same time for two runners in a race but a more powerful test is like a sensitive electronic timer that more accurately shows the times to differ by a fiftieth of a second.

probability   The chance of a specific event occurring from a set of possible events, expressed as a proportion. For example, if there were 4 women and 6 men in a room the probability of meeting a woman first on entering the room is 4/10 or 0.4 as there are 4 women out of 10 people in the room. A probability of 0 indicates an event will never occur and a probability of 1 that it will always occur. In a room of only 10 men there is a probability of 0 (0/10) of meeting a woman first and a probability of 1 (10/10) of meeting a man.

rank   When a set of data is ordered from lowest to highest the rank of a score is its position in this order.

regression   The prediction of scores on one variable by their scores on a second variable. The larger the correlation between the variables, the more accurate the prediction. We can undertake a multiple regression where the scores on one variable are predicted from the scores on a number of predictor variables.

reliability   A reliable test is one that that will produce the same result when repeated (in the same circumstances). We can investigate the reliability of the items in a test (such as the questions in a questionnaire) by examining the relationship between each item and the overall score on the test.

repeated measures   A term used to indicate that the same subjects (participants) are providing data for all the conditions of an independent variable: also known as 'within subjects'.

residual A linear regression provides a prediction of the scores on one variable by their scores on a second. The residual is the difference between actual score and a predicted score on the first variable. (A linear regression predicts that the data follow a linear model. The residuals indicate the extent to which the data do not fit the model.)

significance level The risk (probability) of erroneously claiming a relationship between an independent and a dependent variable when there is not one. Statistical tests are undertaken so that this probability is chosen to be small, usually set at 0.05 indicating that this will occur no more than 5 times in 100.

simple main effects A significant interaction in a two factor analysis of variance indicates that the effect of one variable is different at the various conditions of the other variable. Calculating simple main effects tell us what these different effects are. A simple main effect is the effect of one variable at a single condition of the other variable.

sphericity An assumption we make about the data in a repeated measures design. Not only must we assume homogeneity of variance but homogeneity of covariance – that is, homogeneity of variance of the differences between samples. Essentially we must assume the effect of an independent variable to be consistent across both conditions and subjects in these designs for the analysis to be appropriate.

standard deviation A measure of the standard ('average') difference (deviation) of a score from the mean in a set of scores. It is the square root of the variance. (There is a different calculation for standard deviation when the set of scores are a population as opposed to a sample.)

standard error of the estimate A measure of the 'average' distance (standard error) of a score from the regression line.

standard error of the mean The standard deviation of the distribution of sample means. It is a measure of the standard ('average') difference of a sample mean from the mean of all sample means of samples of the same size from the same population.

standard score The position of a score within a distribution of scores. It provides a measure of how many standard deviation units a specific score falls above or below the mean. It is also referred to as a z score.

statistic Specifically, a characteristic of a sample, such as the sample mean. More generally, statistic and statistics are used to describe techniques for summarising and analysing numerical data.

subject The term used for the source of data in a sample. If people are the subjects of the study it is viewed as more respectful to refer to them as participants, which acknowledges their role as helpful contributors to the investigation.

sums of squares The sum of the squared deviations of scores from their mean value.

test statistic The calculated value of the statistical test that has been undertaken.

two-tailed test A prediction that two samples come from different populations, but not stating which population has the higher mean value.

Type I error The error of rejecting the null hypothesis when it is true. The risk of this occurring is set by the significance level.

Type II error   The error of accepting the null hypothesis when it is false.

univariate   A term used to refer to a statistical test where there is only one dependent variable. ANOVA is a univariate analysis as there can be more than one independent variable but only one dependent variable.

value labels   Assigning value labels within the variable view screen in SPSS ensures that the output is labelled appropriately when grouping variables are used. For example 1 = males, 2 = females.

Variable View   The screen within the SPSS Data Editor where the characteristics of variables are assigned.

variance   A measure of how much a set of scores vary from their mean value. Variance is the square of the standard deviation.

weighting/loading   The contribution made to a composite value (such as a regression equation or a factor in a factor analysis) by a variable. We use the calculated size of the weighting to assess the importance of the variable to the factor in a factor analysis.

within subjects   Also known as repeated measures. We select the same subjects (participants) for each condition of an independent variable for a within-subjects design.

z **score**   see standard score.

Index

What do you want to do?	Number of variables/ conditions	Design	Parametric/ nonparametric	Recommended statistical test	Statistical procedure		Chapter
Look for differences between conditions	One variable: two conditions	Independent	Parametric	Independent samples t test	Analyse	Compare means	Independent samples t test	7
		Repeated measures	Parametric	Related t test	Analyse	Compare means	Paired samples t test	7
		Independent	Nonparametric	Mann–Whitney U	Analyse	Nonparametric tests	Two independent samples	8
		Repeated measures	Nonparametric	Wilcoxon	Analyse	Nonparametric tests	Two related samples	8
	One variable: more than two conditions	Independent measures	Parametric	One factor independent measures ANOVA	Analyse	General linear model	Univariate	10
		Repeated measures	Parametric	One factor repeated measures ANOVA	Analyse	General linear model	Repeated measures	10
		Independent measures	Nonparametric	Kruskal–Wallis	Analyse	Nonparametric tests	K independent samples	13
		Repeated measures	Nonparametric	Friedman	Analyse	Nonparametric tests	K related samples	13
	Two variables	Independent measures on both variables	Parametric	Two factor independent ANOVA	Analyse	General linear model	Univariate	11
		One independent and one repeated measures factor	Parametric	Two factor repeated measures ANOVA	Analyse	General linear model	Repeated measures	11

What do you want to do?	Number of variables/conditions	Design	Parametric/nonparametric	Recommended statistical test	Statistical procedure			Chapter
		Repeated measures on both variables	Parametric	Two factor mixed design ANOVA	Analyse	General linear model	Repeated measures	11
	More than one dependent variable	Independent measures	Parametric	Independent MANOVA	Analyse	General linear model	Multivariate	12
		Repeated measures	Parametric	Repeated MANOVA	Analyse	General linear model	Repeated measures	12
Compare frequency counts (in categories)		Association	Nonparametric	Chi-square	Analyse	Descriptives	Crosstabs	14
Correlate variables	Two variables	Correlational	Parametric	Pearson	Analyse	Correlate	Bivariate	15
		Correlational	Nonparametric	Spearman	Analyse	Correlate	Bivariate	15
		Correlational	Nonparametric	Kendall tau-b	Analyse	Correlate	Bivariate	15
	More than two variables	Correlational	Parametric	Multiple regression	Analyse	Regression	Linear	16
Reduce data	Many variables	Correlational	Parametric	Factor analysis	Analyse	Data reduction	Factor	17
	Many variables	Correlational	Parametric	Reliability analysis	Analyse	Scale	Reliability analysis	18